## Peace Corps Index

Number of volunteers [illegible]

Number of people who have served [illegible] in 1961: 135,000

Applications received by the Peace Corps in 1964: 45,654

Applications received in 1984: 13,917

Applications received in 1992: 17,438

Percentage of male enrollment today: 46

Percentage of male enrollment during the Vietnam War: 70

Percentage of current volunteers who belong to a minority: 12

Percentage of current volunteers who are over fifty years old: 10

Approximate percentage of all volunteers who did not complete the standard two-year hitch: 40

Total number of volunteers who have died in service: 216

Number of volunteers who have tested positive for HIV since 1985: 29

Cost per year of maintaining a volunteer in the field: $30,000

Number of countries in which volunteers are now serving: 94

Number of languages and dialects the Peace Corps teaches trainees: 200

Number of job descriptions filled by volunteers: 60

Number of U.S. senators who served in the Peace Corps: 2 [Paul Tsongas, D-Mass. (Ethiopia, 1962–64); Christopher Dodd, D-Conn. (Dominican Republic, 1966–68)]

Number of Cabinet members who served in the Peace Corps: 1 [Donna Shalala (Iran, 1962–64), Secretary, Health and Human Services]

SOURCES: All statistical information was provided by the Peace Corps press office and other departments within the agency.

About the Author

KAREN SCHWARZ is a freelance writer whose articles have appeared in such national publications as the *Wall Street Journal, Manhattan, Inc., Rolling Stone,* and the *Chicago Tribune.* She lives in Alexandria, Virginia.

# What You Can Do for Your Country

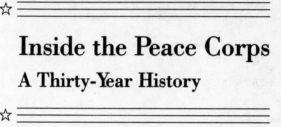

## Inside the Peace Corps
### A Thirty-Year History

**Karen Schwarz**

ANCHOR BOOKS
DOUBLEDAY
New York London Toronto Sydney Auckland

AN ANCHOR BOOK
PUBLISHED BY DOUBLEDAY
a division of Bantam Doubleday Dell Publishing Group, Inc.
1540 Broadway, New York, New York 10036

ANCHOR BOOKS, DOUBLEDAY, and the portrayal of an anchor are trademarks of
Doubleday, a division of Bantam Doubleday Dell Publishing Group, Inc.

*What You Can Do for Your Country* was originally published in hardcover
by William Morrow and Company, Inc. in 1991. The Anchor Books edition
is published by arrangement with William Morrow and Company, Inc.

Library of Congress Cataloging-in-Publication Data

Schwarz, Karen.
What you can do for your country: inside the Peace Corps—
a thirty-year history/Karen Schwarz.—1st Anchor Books ed.
   p.   cm.
Includes bibliographical references and index.
1. Peace Corps (U.S.)—History. I. Title.
HC60.5.S39   1993
361.6—dc20   93-12147
CIP

ISBN 0-385-46898-9
Copyright © 1991 by Karen Schwarz
Epilogue Copyright © 1993 by Karen Schwarz
Peace Corps Index © 1993 by Karen Schwarz

*This book is dedicated to my parents,
Barbara and Joseph M. Schwarz;
my sister, Maggie; and Jeffrey Peisch*

# Preface

☆===

This book is an annotated oral history. Each chapter opens with an introductory essay that provides the historical context for the testimonies that follow. These essays also elucidate the Peace Corps' complexities, which are not explicitly stated in the oral histories.

To locate returned volunteers, I pursued several routes. The most successful were the 1986, 1987, and 1988 annual conferences of the National Council of Returned Peace Corps Volunteers, held in Washington, D.C., Madison, Wisconsin, and Boulder, Colorado, respectively. Interview subjects were also contacted through a 1986 symposium at Columbia University sponsored by the Returned Peace Corps Volunteers of Greater New York. Local alumni groups, such as those in Los Angeles, Chicago, Washington, D.C., and Atlanta, were particularly helpful as were country-of-service groups, such as Friends of Ethiopia, Friends of Togo, Friends of Afghanistan, Friends of the Marshall Islands, and Friends of Nigeria. In addition, many interviewees were referred by other interviewees. Volunteers were also located through newspaper and magazine articles and the 1981 Peace Corps Directory of Former Volunteers and Staff, published by the Peace Corps Institute.

The interviews included in this book were chosen to illuminate different points of view on various issues central to the book's thesis. The selection of interviews should in no way be interpreted as a scientifically accurate sampling. In many instances, the recollections of Peace Corps staff and directors have also been included to present a more balanced and comprehensive account. Some returned volunteers supplied me with

7

letters and journals. These materials have been incorporated and identified as such to give greater clarity than memory provides.

Research on the Peace Corps was conducted at the Peace Corps' Library in Washington, D.C.; the John F. Kennedy Memorial Library in Boston; the Lyndon Baines Johnson Library in Austin, Texas; and the National Archives–Nixon Presidential Materials in Alexandria, Virginia. Previously classified documents in the Johnson and Nixon libraries were released upon the author's mandatory review, as were Peace Corps documents under the Freedom of Information Act. I also visited Peace Corps operations in Mali and St. Lucia.

Except where otherwise noted, all quoted material was obtained by me in interviews conducted between 1986 and 1990. Unless attributed to other sources, all statistical information was derived from Peace Corps documents or supplied to me by Peace Corps officials who were kind enough to respond to specific requests.

# Acknowledgments

I am grateful to all those returned Peace Corps volunteers and Peace Corps staff who shared their memories and opinions with me, and who helped me understand the Peace Corps experience, the organization's inner workings and the many challenges of trying to make a difference.

Students of the Peace Corps will find themselves referring again and again to six excellent books: *The Bold Experiment: JFK's Peace Corps* by Gerard T. Rice, *Come As You Are: The Peace Corps Story* by Coates Redmon, *A Moment in History: The First Ten Years of the Peace Corps* by Brent Ashabranner, *The Making of an Un-American* by Paul Cowan, *Of Kennedys and Kings: Making Sense of the Sixties* by Harris Wofford, and *Keeping Kennedy's Promise* by Kevin Lowther and C. Payne Lucas. Presenting a wide range of perspectives, these works helped me understand the organization's many facets, as well as its complex history. *The Bold Experiment*, in particular, meticulously documents the Corps' founding and its operations in the early 1960s.

The National Council of Returned Peace Corps Volunteers' fine publication, *World View*, has been an indispensable tool in following the Peace Corps in recent years. Its editor, Jeff Drumtra, was a valuable contact. I'm also grateful to the National Council for helping me locate individual volunteers.

At the Peace Corps headquarters in Washington, D.C., Dana Bama in Media Relations was consistently helpful, extremely efficient and always pleasant. Peace Corps librarian Marian Francois was also a great help, going above and beyond the call of duty on many occasions.

Many former volunteers and staff searched their files, attics, and basements for memos, letters, petitions, news clippings, and other documents. I owe many thanks to the following individuals for their digging and their willingness to share this material: Guy Baehr, Sam Brown, Robert Burkhardt, David Drake, Scout Duke, Tom Elam, Roger Flather, Jim Greene, Linda Hatch, Kirby Jones, Kenny Karem, Roger Landrum, Betsy Lebenson, John Pincetich, Caroline Ramsey, Lisa Swenarski, Dan Taubman, Hazel Vespa, Flo and David Wagner, Sue White, Warren Wiggins, and Lowell Wiley. I would also like to thank the many former volunteers who sent in photos for inclusion in this book, and I regret that the names of many of those who took these pictures escape memory.

I am especially grateful for the assistance of Alice Hageman and Elaine Fuller, who helped me piece together the story of the Committee of Returned Volunteers, and shared with me their collections of CRV newsletters, position papers, and other publications. I would also like to thank the many contributors to those publications, particularly, the CRV's collection of essays, *Volunteer?* Jonathan M. Weisgall provided documents valuable to my research on Micronesia.

I am indebted to the following former volunteers, staff members, and alumni groups who offered their assistance in a number of capacities: Marian Abernathy, Colette Bruegal, Richard Celeste, John Chromy, Murray Cox, John Coyne, John Evans, Dennis Grubb, Steve Hellinger, Christine Just, Mary E. King, David Levine, and Reginald Petty.

I owe a special debt to Jo Manning, who dug up the most obscure publications and, in the eleventh hour, helped me complete the Notes for this book. I am also deeply appreciative for the assistance of Maarja Krusten and Joan Howard at the National Archives-Nixon Presidential Materials in Alexandria, Virginia; and of Tinky Weisblat, my researcher at the Lyndon Baines Johnson Library in Austin, Texas.

The following individuals were wonderful hosts and I am grateful for their hospitality: Scott Bowles, Norman Bramble, Laura George, Todd and Hope Jenkins, James Kitfield, Susan and Michael Rappaport, and Hilary Whittaker.

For helping me conquer my fear of my computer, I would like to thank Dick Lutz and Brian Kolins. For helping me conquer other kinds of fears, I would like to thank Linda Brown. For their help in tracking down the origins of the term *third world*, I am grateful to David and Genevieve Peisch.

I am thankful for the talents and time of Robert Sabat, who gave me merciless and invaluable criticism and saved me from taking myself too seriously. I am grateful for our many laughs. Assistant editor Pam Altschul's many constructive comments greatly improved the manuscript. The meticulous work of copy editor David Falk made a significant contribution to the overall quality of this book. My mother, Barbara Schwarz, made any number of good suggestions. She is my greatest supporter.

At General Media, Inc., I am thankful to Bob Guccione and David Myerson for their support of this project. Peter Bloch has been a good friend throughout. His encouragement and his continual interest in the project helped me through many difficult moments.

I am indebted to my agent, Robin Straus, and my editor, Adrian Zackheim, for taking their chances on a novice.

Finally, Jeffrey Peisch. This project taught me what it means to love one's work; Jeffrey taught me what it means to love another person. His devotion and his concern for the success of this book were the fuel that got me to the finish line.

# Contents

# Introduction

This book was written by a sympathetic outsider. In 1982, two years out of college but still in an "entry-level" job where I spent endless days at the photocopy machine and filing cabinets, I decided it was time to redirect my energies toward something of greater consequence. Peace Corps volunteers, I had long been aware, dedicated themselves for two years to living and working with people in very poor countries. Nothing, it seemed to me, could be more worthwhile than that. When I told a friend that I was thinking of signing up, he reminded me that volunteers' work was arduous—they dug wells and latrines, and lived in mud huts infested with large insects. I realized I would not last two weeks, let alone two years, and instead volunteered to man a booth at Alexander's department store where I solicited memberships for the Public Broadcasting Service.

Then, in 1985, I happened to read an article in *The New York Times* that reawakened my interest, and made me look at the Peace Corps from another perspective. Some returned volunteers, it seemed, were upset about what they viewed as the organization's inappropriate compliance with the Reagan administration's foreign policy agenda. Volunteers had been dispatched to Grenada shortly after the United States' 1983 invasion of the island nation, and massive numbers of volunteers were being sent to our country's allies in Central America. The Peace Corps, the returnees thought, was tailoring its humanitarian mission to political interests. The *Times* article also mentioned that the Corps was planning a twenty-fifth-anniversary celebration. These two noteworthy items prompted me to look further into the organization as the subject of a possible magazine story.

Early on, I discovered how far my original idealized perception of the organization was from reality. I learned, for example, that many volunteers neither toughed it out in bug-ridden huts nor toiled at backbreaking work; they enjoyed fairly comfortable homes and performed jobs ranging from teaching high school to raising poultry to cataloging plant species. I also discovered that of the 130,000 people who have served in the Peace Corps to date, almost 40 percent did not complete the standard two-year hitch. In fact, in the mid and late 1960s, generally considered the Peace Corps' heyday, the number of volunteers who did not complete their first year reached an all-time high of 57 percent. These statistics suggested to me that the Corps was a lot more complex, and a lot less perfect, than I had always thought it to be.

Indeed, I learned that not all who joined were devoted idealists, and that the agency has sent legions of highly motivated volunteers into meaningless assignments. Moreover, the most popular conception of the Peace Corps—that it was President Kennedy's idea, and that it attracts only idealistic college kids who perform essential work—grossly romanticizes an organization that, charged with ambiguous objectives, struggles to live up to its hallowed reputation. During three and a half years of research— my article, meanwhile, had turned into a book—I was struck again and again by the disparity between what I had once assumed about the Peace Corps and what countless former volunteers were telling me.

The Peace Corps, I ultimately realized, is a kind of modern-day myth that projects an idealized portrait of the American character. "The Peace Corps is our dream for ourselves," waxed *Look* magazine in 1966, "and we want the world to see us as we see the volunteers—crew-cuts and ponytails, soda-fountain types, hardy and smart and noble."[1] Over its thirty-year life span, despite the self-absorption of the "Me Generation" and the disillusionment of the Vietnam War, the qualities attributed to the Peace Corps—altruism, Yankee ingenuity, and egalitarianism—have endured, cloaking the organization in a protective mystique. It is the point of this book to explore the reality behind this mystique as it is revealed through the experiences of the volunteers.

The origins of the Peace Corps' mystique can be traced to the agency's genesis. The idea for a government-sponsored overseas volunteer program had its forerunners among the numerous private and ecumenical organizations that sponsored work-study trips to developing countries. In the postwar years, various student groups, labor unions, and educational associations proposed the idea of a publicly supported overseas service program.[2] But the idea did not accumulate significant strength until it entered the political arena. In 1957 Congressman Henry Reuss (D-Wisc.), traveled to Cambodia to inspect American foreign aid projects. The "crowning jewel" of the United States assistance program, Reuss wrote, was "a superb American-built highway stretching from the capital, Phnom Penh, to the sea." Cambodia's rulers were no doubt pleased with the United States' gift, but, Reuss noted, the engineering feat had little impact on the lives of the country's people. "The super-highway's largest meaning for most Cambodian peasants," he observed, "lies in the use of its shoulder as a trail for their water buffalo." What most impressed Reuss was a chance encounter with some United Nations workers who were helping villagers set up their first elementary schools. "This was a brave new world, and the Cambodians loved it."[3]

After his trip, the congressman came to the opinion that the United States government's foreign assistance efforts—mostly colossal shipments of military hardware and massive engineering projects—should be augmented by programs like the UN's in Cambodia. Foreign aid, he believed, could be much more effective "if we relied more heavily on a group of some thousands of young Americans willing to help with an irrigation project, digging a village well, or setting up a rural school." But Reuss viewed this idea as far more than an adjunct to America's foreign aid apparatus. The Point Four Youth Corps, as he called it—naming it for the Point Four technical assistance agency founded by President Truman in 1949—would deepen the participants' understanding "of the problems facing other peoples and nations, and thereby help them better understand American policies and purposes abroad." Endowing his idea with another, still loftier aspiration, Reuss envisioned it as "a means to demonstrate vividly the genuine and generous interest that Americans have in the well-being of developing nations and their people."[4]

Then Senator Hubert Humphrey (D-Minn.) advocated the formation of an overseas volunteer agency, and in his 1960 campaign for the Democratic nomination for President, he pledged to start one. Fusing high moral purpose with cold war concerns, he called the proposed program the "Peace Corps." A few months later, when presidential candidate Senator John F. Kennedy adopted the idea, he injected a dose of urgency that gripped the public. "On the other side of the globe," Kennedy said just a week before the election, "teachers, doctors, technicians, and experts desperately needed in a dozen fields by underdeveloped nations are pouring forth from Moscow to advance the cause of world communism. . . . I am convinced that our young men and women, dedicated to freedom, are fully capable of overcoming the efforts of Mr. Khrushchev's missionaries who are dedicated to undermining that freedom."[5]

Besides exploiting cold war anxiety, Kennedy's evocation of the Peace Corps—freedom-loving, hardworking Americans sharing their skills with the world's poor—repudiated the widely held notion that the nation's stature around the world was slipping. A series of recent international humiliations had, in fact, caused a crisis in confidence. In 1957, the Soviet Union had launched the Sputnik, beating the United States into space with the deployment of the first earth satellite; not long after that, crowds in South America had greeted Vice President Richard Nixon with a shower of rocks; and in 1959 Fidel Castro expropriated all American-owned enterprises in Cuba. Causing the country's self-esteem to sink to new lows were a spate of compelling books—among them, *The National Purpose* by Walter Lippmann, *The Affluent Society* by John Kenneth Galbraith, and *The Lonely Crowd* by David Riesman—that described American society as self-indulgent and complacent, lolling about upon a bed of prosperity. *The Ugly American*, a best-selling novel by Eugene Burdick and William Lederer, described the bumbling incompetence of American diplomats while communism furthered its reach into a fictional Asian country, and summed up for readers the United States' waning eminence. The Peace Corps, as the candidate presented it, would counteract the Ugly American image because its volunteers would reflect a nation "full of young people eager to serve," who would live in the communities where they worked, speak the local language, and respect the culture and traditions of their hosts.[6]

Then, in his inaugural address, President Kennedy, like Hubert Humphrey, elevated the Peace Corps from a weapon in the United States' cold war arsenal, to a worldwide humanitarian mission in which he asked average Americans to take part: "To those people in the huts and villages of half the globe struggling to break the bonds of mass misery, we pledge our best efforts to help them help themselves, for whatever period is required—not because the Communists may be doing it, not because we seek their votes, but because it is right." The fight against communism, Kennedy said, was just one concern in "a struggle against the common enemies of man: tyranny, poverty, disease and war itself. . . . Will you join in that historic effort? . . . And so, my fellow Americans: Ask not what your country can do for you—ask what you can do for your country."[7]

Sargent Shriver, who was married to the President's sister Eunice, and who shared the vision put forth in Kennedy's inaugural address, was appointed the first Peace Corps director. As he wrote to the President early in 1961: "It is important that the Peace Corps be advanced not as an arm of the Cold War but as a contribution to the world community." The new program, Shriver continued, "is not a diplomatic or propaganda venture but a genuine experiment in international partnership."[8] In countless speeches and articles, Shriver promoted the grand experiment, reminding Americans that volunteers "have been able to cross barriers of language and culture, religious faith and social structure, to touch the deep chords of common hope and principle, which belong to all men."[9]

The Peace Corps Act of 1961 embraced the ideas of Reuss, Humphrey, Kennedy, and Shriver. The new agency, the act declared, would "promote world peace and friendship" through the execution of its three goals: "to help the peoples of interested countries meet their needs for trained manpower, and to help promote a better understanding of the American people on the part of the peoples served and a better understanding of other peoples on the part of the American people."[10]

The act also described how these high-minded goals were to be pursued under the auspices of the executive branch of the federal government. The director of the Peace Corps would be selected by the President and "the Secretary of State shall be responsible for the continuous supervision and general direction [of the Peace Corps such that] . . . the foreign policy of the United States is best served thereby." The act also called for "the coordination of Peace Corps activities with other activities of the United States government in each country, under the leadership of the chief of the United States diplomatic mission."[11]

Despite its obvious ties to politics, for three decades, it has been an article of faith that the Peace Corps is essentially apolitical. To support this conviction, volunteers point to the fact that they are under no obligation to agree with or defend the policies of the United States government. They add that most volunteers work in remote locations under the supervision of host country ministries, and contact with Peace Corps officials, let alone embassy personnel, is minimal.

It is tempting to believe that Peace Corps volunteers, living in isolated villages and working at the "grass roots," are completely disconnected from politics. Such a level of intimacy between peoples, the Corps maintains, can eventually lead to world peace. By skirting the harsh realities of politics, economics, and self-serving leadership that perpetuate tension and human suffering, this optimistic outlook on achieving peace is as intoxicating as it is inspiring. A song written by a former volunteer and performed at a commemoration of the twenty-fifth anniversary of President Kennedy's assassination captures this sentiment:

> *Some people say*
> *Love doesn't work,*

*If we believe them*
*Then there never will be peace on earth*
*We can have it*
*If only we believe . . .*
*We're not that different, you and me.**

The faith that the organization is apolitical continues to thrive. The Peace Corps community expressed great dismay over Bush-appointed Corps director Paul Coverdell's habit of calling the organization the "United States Peace Corps," and the appearance of the new name on the front of the building where the Corps has its headquarters. "I do not believe we should hide the name of the country that has sponsored the wonderful things we have done around the world," Coverdell explained to *The Washington Post.*[12] Sargent Shriver called the alteration of the name "a serious mistake." Senator Alan Cranston (D-Calif.) said the new name would destroy the Peace Corps' "magic symbolism."[13] "Of course people know we're a government agency," says Jon Keeton, the Peace Corps' director of international research and development. "However, the United States prefix is contrary to an image. It makes it sound more political."

But from the outset, the organization's noble goals have been tethered to diplomatic relations and the political process. Whether the Peace Corps can execute its idealistic mission under the aegis of the United States government has been questioned over the years from a wide range of perspectives. In a 1968 position paper, the Committee of Returned Volunteers—an organization of Peace Corps alumni and veterans of other overseas programs—wrote: "The ultimate purpose of volunteer service is as an expression of cooperation between people to deal with the problems common to all men, and not a relationship of representatives of one society to another."[14]

By and large, the Peace Corps dispatches volunteers to those countries with which the United States government has friendly relations. A program in a given country is usually initiated by the American ambassador assigned there or by his host country counterparts. Staying within the channels of United States diplomacy, the largest Peace Corps programs are usually in those countries that are the United States' closest allies in the developing world. But, says Mary King, who was deputy director of Action in the Carter Administration, "If you're only working in countries that are your friends, where programming volunteers is easier, then you cannot claim to be a humanitarian organization. You are ob-

---

*Copyright © 1988, Adryan Russ, "Writer's Dream."

viously just an extension of U.S. foreign policy. The only way you can show you are a humanitarian organization is to work in those countries that are not partisan to the United States."* Joseph Blatchford, who was appointed Peace Corps director by President Nixon, believes that "the health of a program dedicated to fostering human understanding should not be vulnerable to political forces. The Peace Corps has been kicked out of countries when new governments that were hostile to the United States came to power, and some governments will not invite the Peace Corps as a matter of pride."

Because Peace Corps programs are predicated on amicable United States–host country relations, the volunteers' performance is often subordinate to larger diplomatic goals. "The host government officials with whom we work don't force the issue," says Jon Keeton. "The volunteers aren't doing any damage, and they know it's part of their country's relationship with the United States. So why worry about it?" Adds Dr. Carolyn Payton, who was a selection officer and country director in the 1960s and director of the agency from 1977 to 1978, "Some countries love us. But some couldn't care less. It was an easy way to win brownie points." A foreign government's decision to invite the Peace Corps "is part of the give and take of bilateral relations," adds Mary King.

On some occasions, the Peace Corps has even gone so far as to proffer its services to further specific foreign policy needs. Shriver himself, who was adamant and high-minded about distancing the organization from such practices, wiped the dew from his eyes at times and saw how the Peace Corps could help Washington win friends away from Moscow. After discussing the Corps with Guinea's socialist president, Sekou Toure, Shriver wrote Kennedy: "Here we have an opportunity to move a country from an apparently clear Bloc orientation to a position of neutrality or even one of orientation to the West."[15] On another occasion, he informed the President that "the leading Commie in Colombia" had just returned to South America with 280 Colombian students he had escorted to Moscow for a three-month study trip. "To make a real dent in the Colombian situation," Shriver thought the Peace Corps should send 500 volunteers and eventually supply volunteers to at least half of Colombia's twelve thousand small towns.[16]†

When the Peace Corps responded to a specific foreign policy situation

---

*Action is the federal agency created in 1971 to consolidate various government volunteer programs. The Peace Corps was a division of Action from 1971 to 1983.

†Thanks to Gerard T. Rice, author of *The Bold Experiment: JFK's Peace Corps*, for locating these documents.

and sent exceedingly large groups into certain countries, volunteers have sometimes found themselves in poorly planned assignments. In the mid-1980s, when the Reagan administration focused special attention on the spread of Marxism in Central America, the number of volunteers sent to Belize, Honduras, Guatemala, and Costa Rica increased dramatically. "I had the impression that my work didn't matter," says Marian Abernathy, who served in Honduras from 1986 to 1988. "My program manager never asked me how my work was going. It was like being at camp. I had thought we were there to get something done." In Belize, volunteers kept themselves occupied working at the Peace Corps office, repairing staff vehicles, and doing miscellaneous carpentry jobs.[17] Bluntly summing up the problem, a Belizean government official complained, "There are too many Peace Corps volunteers in proportion to our needs."[18]

Even without a foreign policy situation prompting the dispatch of large contingents to a given country, the Peace Corps has been criticized in reports by Congress, the General Accounting Office, and by its own internal evaluators, for sending more volunteers overseas than it could adequately manage. Volunteers and mid-level staff have, through the years, expressed the concern that the agency's leadership was more interested in achieving impressive statistics for domestic consumption than in the quality of the work performed.

Even though the political process compromises some of the ideals of the Peace Corps, it also fuels a vigorous ongoing debate about how the organization can best foster development. While the vast majority of volunteers have been recent college graduates assigned to jobs in education, agriculture, or health, each administration interprets anew the Peace Corps' mandate and institutes corresponding initiatives that modify this basic profile.

In the early years, for example, when Peace Corps officials needed some quick successes, they established a predisposition toward young volunteers and education assignments because large numbers could be moved into teaching slots with relatively little prior planning. These assignments, it was thought, matched the talents of the recent liberal arts college graduate, or "B.A. generalist"—the Peace Corps' most plentiful type of applicant. During the Nixon and Ford administrations, the Corps placed greater value on older Americans who could provide host countries with the specific skills and expertise they had requested. From 1969 to 1977, recruiters aggressively sought out plumbers, electricians, businessmen, and corporate executives, and invited them to bring their families. Many of these volunteers spent their two years in capital cities, working as advisers to government ministries and living quite comfortably.

When Jimmy Carter was elected President, the Peace Corps changed its course yet again. Newly appointed officials believed that highly skilled volunteers reinforced the donor-recipient syndrome and disregarded the Corps' goal of cultural reciprocity. B.A. generalists were welcomed once again, and assigned to jobs that conformed to a new theory of development assistance then gaining currency. Dubbed "Basic Human Needs," it prescribed that volunteers' work address survival necessities such as adequate food supply and access to potable water. English teaching, for years the Peace Corps' bread-and-butter activity, began to be phased out.

While continuing many of the programs developed during the Carter administration, in the 1980s, the Peace Corps adopted President Reagan's belief that the answer to third world poverty lay in small-business development. Placing volunteers in "microenterprise" assignments became an agency priority.

When President Bush visited newly independent Hungary in 1989, he announced a modest package of assistance that included a contingent of Peace Corps volunteers who would teach English. Soon after, programs were planned for Poland, Czechoslovakia, Romania, and Bulgaria. The prospect of entering Eastern Europe renewed a perennial argument over the Peace Corps' relationship to foreign policy, and whether the Corps should teach English to relatively self-sufficient peoples or devote itself to those countries in dire need.

Reflecting George Bush's campaign themes, the Peace Corps is now stressing education and the environment. Volunteers are being trained by the Environmental Protection Agency in how to show poor farmers the proper way to handle toxic fertilizers and pesticides. Paralleling Bush's desire to be "the education President," the Peace Corps began the "World Wise" program, in which volunteers exchange letters with elementary-school students in the United States. Also following the lead of the White House, Corps director Paul Coverdell has encouraged returned volunteers to lend a hand in literacy campaigns and the war on drugs.

The thesis for this book crystallized on a September weekend in 1986, at the Peace Corps' twenty-fifth-anniversary celebration in Washington, D.C. In a gigantic white tent on the Mall, Sargent Shriver reminded a crowd of six thousand returned volunteers that "we are a corps, a band of brothers and sisters, united in the conviction that if we work hard enough to eradicate our fears and increase the reach of our love, we truly can avoid war—and achieve peace within ourselves, within our nation, and around the world." [19] While listening to these uplifting words, I glanced around at people's name tags, which also displayed the country and date of service: Afghanistan, 1965–67; Tonga, 1971–73; North Borneo, 1961–63, and so on. I wanted to know what it was like in those places and what Shriver's speech had meant to those volunteers.

From hundreds of interviews with former volunteers and staff, I learned that catchphrases and clichés about idealism actually belittle the Peace Corps and distort its history. I learned too that volunteers are not a homogeneous group of wholesome idealists. Many signed up because they wanted "to find themselves," or because it would enhance their résumé, or because it would keep them out of Vietnam. They have not all been youthful either. Though the vast majority of volunteers have been people in their twenties, in recent years, the percentage of "seniors," those over fifty, has been steadily climbing.

Volunteers themselves are often surprised that the Corps is not a homogenized group of young liberals. "I had an image of the Peace Corps from the sixties," says Janet Coffey (Honduras, 1986–87), "that volunteers would have these intelligent, philosophical discussions late into the night. But many had no interest in serious issues. And a lot were hardcore Reaganites and born-again Christians."

Once overseas, volunteers came to grips with how difficult it was to make even the smallest measure of progress. For many, learning the language and acclimating to their surroundings were their most significant accomplishments. Some volunteers found reserves of inner strength that enabled them to tolerate the frustration and to keep going, and some simply lost interest. "There were volunteers who went from their classrooms to the British expatriate's club and didn't intersect with Nigeria at all," says Tom McGrew, who served there in the mid-1960s.

While many volunteers criticize the Peace Corps for its poor planning, its susceptibility to politics, and its insufficient attention to providing meaningful assistance, they all recite what could be taken for the Peace Corps mantra: "It was the most profound experience of my life. I got more out of it than I was able to give." Some contend that the exposure of so many Americans to peoples of other countries, and vice versa, is by itself an extraordinary achievement. Others say that the Peace Corps should mark its accomplishments according to the actual assistance it renders, and trust that the cross-cultural exchange will then follow naturally.

Ultimately, it is the ambiguity of the Peace Corps' purpose that deepens its mystique, and it is the volunteers' experiences that ultimately illuminate that mystique.

# Part One

## The Kennedy Years, 1961-63

# Chapter 1

# Modern Miracles

On the night of November 6, 1960, three days before the presidential election, a caravan of six cars left the campus of the University of Michigan at Ann Arbor, and headed for the airport in Toledo, Ohio, sixty miles away. Presidential candidate John F. Kennedy would be landing there in his plane, the *Caroline*, for a campaign stop and Michigan Democratic party workers had arranged for Kennedy to meet briefly with two University of Michigan graduate students, Alan and Judy Guskin. Kennedy was running late. The Guskins, the campaign staff, and reporters from the student newspaper sat in the airport all night and watched the sun rise on an empty runway.

Finally, early in the morning, the little plane appeared in the sky and the group from Ann Arbor rushed outside. When the senator approached, Alan Guskin asked him point-blank, "Are you really serious about the Peace Corps?"

Three weeks earlier, Kennedy had come to spend the night on the Ann Arbor campus before making a campaign swing through southern Michigan. No appearance was planned. But a crowd of ten thousand students had waited on the green outside the Student Union, and on the front steps a microphone stood at the ready. "I think he was surprised to see that many people out there," Judy Guskin recalls. "He started off by saying, 'I've come here to go to sleep, but I guess I should say something.' " Then Kennedy asked the crowd:

"How many of you are willing to spend ten years in Africa or Latin America or Asia working for the United States and working for freedom?

27

How many of you who are going to be doctors are willing to spend your days in Ghana; technicians or engineers, how many of you are willing to work in the foreign service and spend your lives traveling around the world? On your willingness to contribute part of your life to this country will depend the answer whether we as a free society can compete. I think Americans are willing to contribute, but the effort must be far greater than we have made in the past."[1]

Kennedy was warmly received but his remarks, Alan Guskin recalls, "didn't have much impact" at the time. Indeed, the phrases "working for freedom" and "whether we as a society can compete," sounded the familiar notes of cold war rhetoric, and the Michigan students were ready for something new. "We wanted to have a sense of usefulness in the world," says Guskin, "The message during the fifties was, 'Don't sign anything. Keep quiet, and get your Ph.D.' But the civil rights movement was changing things. We had picketed Kresge's and Woolworth's because they wouldn't serve blacks at their lunch counters. All these countries were being created and the only international conception we had was about the cold war. It seemed pretty hopeless."

But Kennedy's impromptu speech gained considerable resonance a few days later when Chester Bowles, the candidate's foreign policy adviser, visited the campus and spoke to a capacity crowd in the Ann Arbor Union ballroom. "Someone asked him a question about Kennedy's speech," Alan Guskin recalls, "and Bowles started telling us about his son, Sam, and Sam's wife Nancy, who were in Nigeria teaching school through the African-American Institute. These were two people who were out there doing something. We realized that Kennedy was telling us that we had something to offer. The world was changing and we were needed. We could make a difference. After Bowles's speech, Judy and I went to the local greasy spoon for dinner and started writing a letter to the school newspaper on some napkins."

The letter read, in part:

Chester Bowles and Senator Kennedy . . . both emphasized that disarmament and peace lie to a very great extent in our hands and requested our participation throughout the world as necessary for the realization of these goals. . . . We both hereby state that we would devote a number of years to work in countries where our help is needed. . . . We express our faith that those of us who have been fortunate enough to receive an education will want to apply their knowledge through direct participation in the underdeveloped communities of the world.[2]

After the letter appeared, the Guskins' phone rang constantly. With a few of their friends, they founded a group called Americans Committed to World Responsibility, and hundreds of students came to their meetings. A petition was drawn up urging Senator Kennedy, if elected, to start an overseas work program. Meanwhile, students on other campuses learned of Kennedy's Ann Arbor speech and their letters poured into Democratic party headquarters in Washington. The Guskins told the local Kennedy campaign coordinator that they wanted to tell the candidate, in person, that they expected him to follow up on the youth service idea he and Bowles had advocated. The senator's campaign itinerary included another trip to Michigan, and they were told they could meet him at the Toledo airport.

That morning Judy Guskin showed Kennedy a list of eight hundred signatures. "He took them in his hands," Judy Guskin recalls, "and started looking through the names. He was very interested."

"When I asked him about the Peace Corps," Alan says, "he said, without a hitch, 'Until Tuesday [Election Day] we'll worry about this nation. After Tuesday, the world.' " Kennedy left the airport for his Toledo appearance and the Guskins went to the airport coffee shop with campaign aides Dick Goodwin and Ted Sorensen. "Sorensen joked, 'Is this the first platoon of the Peace Corps?' " recalls Judy. "But I had the sense this wasn't just a lark. Something was going to happen." The Guskins were among the first volunteers to go to Thailand in 1962.

After Kennedy's narrow victory, the Peace Corps captured America's heart almost overnight. Thousands of would-be volunteers wrote to the White House for information on how to sign up, labor unions and religious and educational organizations voiced their support, and a Gallup poll showed that 71 percent of those interviewed favored the Peace Corps.

Despite his endorsement of the idea before the election, Kennedy and his aides now had their doubts. The new President, after all, had been elected by the narrowest margin in the history of American presidential politics, and a hastily organized program could lead to diplomatic fumbles for which he would take the blame. Furthermore, some leading opinion makers made no secret of their skepticism. *The Wall Street Journal,* for example, commented: "Who but the very young themselves can really believe that an Africa aflame with violence will have its fires quenched because some Harvard boy or Vassar girl lives in a mud hut and speaks Swahili?"[3] The White House, therefore, proceeded cautiously, stating two weeks before the inauguration that "because of the experimental nature of the program . . . it should certainly be started on a small scale."[4]

Kennedy then asked his brother-in-law, Sargent Shriver—who during the campaign had been an adviser on civil rights issues and had scouted talent for the new Cabinet—to figure out what to do next. Shriver reported back a month later and his recommendations were the exact opposite of what Kennedy's aides had advised. The Peace Corps, he said, should be of significant size and launched immediately, "so that the opportunity to recruit the most qualified people from this year's graduating classes will not be lost. Nor should we lose the opportunity to use this summer for training on university campuses . . . the Peace Corps could have several hundred persons in training this summer for placement next fall."[5] There were two other considerations unrelated to the academic calendar, for an immediate start-up of dramatic proportions. First, "if the president was going to have a program of his own creation that was significant," says Shriver, "it couldn't be a tiny little thing." The second reason was brought to light by foreign aid officials Warren Wiggins and William Josephson, who saw the Peace Corps as the realization of Kennedy's "New Frontier" campaign theme. In their report on the Peace Corps, aptly titled "A Towering Task," which made a deep impression on Shriver, Wiggins and Josephson pointed out that if the organization began timidly, "an anticipated bold 'new frontier' may fall into disrespect rather rapidly . . . it may prove to be the case that it should be at the 30,000, the 50,000 or possibly even at the 100,000 [volunteer] level."[6]

Thus, it was concluded, if the new agency was to have any chance of success, it had to be undertaken on a large scale, despite the risk of damage to President Kennedy's prestige should it fail. In light of the above factors, Kennedy's next move was that of a master politician. Capitalizing on the popularity of the idea among the general public, the President signed an executive order establishing the Peace Corps on March 1, 1961. But to appease skeptics, the order called for a "pilot" program.

The President's ambivalence showed up again when Shriver, who was appointed the Peace Corps' director, insisted that its success required that it have the freedom and visibility of an autonomous agency, contrary to Kennedy's original intention of installing it as a division of his soon to be established Agency for International Development. The President acquiesced to Shriver's request, but he left it entirely in the new director's hands to convince Congress to enact the law that would establish the Corps as a new agency. It was Shriver, not Kennedy, who was responsible for carrying the Peace Corps beyond the pilot stage.

Shriver had six months before Congress would either vote the Peace Corps into oblivion or midwife its official birth. The proposed agency had its supporters on Capitol Hill, but many legislators had serious beefs: Few relished the prospect of shelling out their constituents' tax dollars on a foreign aid scheme; Kennedy's end run around Congress with the executive order was rather offensive; and finally, many members of Congress had their doubts about the value of the program itself. Mike Mansfield, Democratic Senate majority leader at the time, said, "I felt that it might be a failure and have adverse repercussions on the administration."[7] Congressman Frances Bolton (R-Ohio) found the idea "terrifying,"[8] and Congressman John Rhodes (R-Ariz.) criticized it as an easy mark for Communist infiltrators.[9]

Despite President Kennedy's lukewarm enthusiasm for the Peace Corps, Shriver and his aides forged ahead with a multipronged strategy to get the proposed Peace Corps Act through Congress. The President's own brother-in-law would lobby personally; the Peace Corps selection staff would accept among the first volunteers at least one applicant from each of the fifty states and notify his or her congressional representatives of that fact; and, most important, the volunteers would be at work, around the world, as quickly as possible so that when the Peace Corps bill reached Congress in September 1961, doubting legislators would find it difficult to vote down a program headed by a Kennedy relative, attracting their own constituents, and already off and running.

In just a few weeks' time, an application procedure was thrown together and, during their spring vacation, thousands of college students took a standard aptitude test in post office basements around the country. By July 1961, fifty-two trainees were at the University of California at Berkeley preparing for their two-year assignments in the newly independent West African nation of Ghana. They attended lectures on the customs and history of the country and studied Twi, the predominant language. After eight weeks at Berkeley, the first group of Peace Corps volunteers, referred to in the agency as Ghana I, went to Washington, where President Kennedy, now enthusiastic, shook hands with each of them in the Oval Office. Later that day they boarded a four-engine Pan Am prop jet for the eighteen-hour flight to Africa.

Shriver had made the same flight earlier that spring when he careened around the globe asking key heads of state in the developing world to take part in the new program his brother-in-law had started. He emphasized that volunteers would be trained to perform the tasks that their hosts requested, and that they would learn the language of the country. President Kwame Nkrumah of Ghana had said he could use teachers, plumbers, and electricians. Shriver told him he could send the teachers. However, only sixteen of the fifty-two volunteers bound for Ghana had ever taught professionally and very few could muster more than a few words of Twi. Nevertheless, when a welcoming party of Ghanaian officials greeted them on the runway in Accra and played a recording of their national anthem, the fifty-two "teachers," sweating through their rumpled cotton dresses and summer suits, sang along as best they could.

Shriver's aggressive strategy worked. On September 22, 1961, as the Ghana I volunteers were heading out from Accra to their assignments, and 494 other trainees were sitting in lectures and grappling with Tagalog, Swahili, Hausa, Hindi, and Spanish, Congress passed the Peace Corps Act by a wide margin.

In the first eighteen months the volunteers were a mixed lot. Many actually did approximate the imaginings of Peace Corps boosters in Congress and the press as "idealistic, patriotic, freedom-loving, adventuresome youths."[10] According to *The Washington Post:* "The young men in the group bound for Ghana had a crisp Ivy-League look, while the women wore gay summer dresses. Almost every volunteer had a camera."[11] But many others, needless to say, were slightly more prosaic. According to Peace Corps evaluators at the time, these other volunteers "were never the brightest nor the best educated; they were less rather than more interested in politics."[12] Harris Wofford, who opened the Peace Corps' program in Ethiopia, recalls that of the first volunteers there, numbering some three hundred, "many came from colleges I'd never heard of." Before recruiting efforts targeted the large universities, and before the Peace Corps' advertising agency, Young and Rubicam, and the media typecast the volunteer as a twenty-two-year-old white middle-class liberal arts major, almost one out of three volunteers was at least five years, and sometimes thirty years, past college commencement.

"When the Peace Corps started," says John Coyne (Ethiopia, 1962– 64) "there was a sort of backlog of Americans who wanted some adventure in their lives, and who would join something that might be called the Peace Corps. One woman in our group was about thirty-five," he recalls. "She had taught on a military base in the Philippines and decided to go overseas again." Madge Shipp, a black schoolteacher from Detroit, was fifty-five when she went to St. Lucia, and John C. and Miriam Kennedy (no relation to the President) were in their mid-fifties when they left their farm in Ohio to go to the Philippines. "All our lives we've wanted to do something like this," John Kennedy, a Quaker, told *Time* magazine. "We've talked about doing something personal for peace. This is our chance."[13]

. Any contribution toward peace in 1961 had to be within the context of the cold war. To a great extent, the Peace Corps' early operations were shaped by America's concern over Communist expansion in the third world. Congress, for example, insisted that volunteers take loyalty oaths and that the Peace Corps provide them with instruction in the "philosophy, strategy, tactics, and menace" of communism.[14] "This is a vital part of the intellectual equipment you will take overseas," stated the *Peace Corps Handbook*. "You must be prepared for communist attempts to provoke you, subvert you, or deflect you from the work you have been sent to do."[15] The ways in which the Peace Corps readied the volunteers for their confrontation with communism varied among the numerous universities at which training was conducted. Roger Landrum (Nigeria, 1961–63), whose group was trained at Michigan State University, recalls a lecture by a State Department expert on "The International Communist Menace." Following the lecture, Landrum says, "he called us all up one at a time and made us debate with him about the Soviet role in Africa. He advocated communist revolution there and we had to take the opposite position. It was very intimidating."

With a communist agitator lurking behind every hut and tree, the Peace Corps took great care in deciding who went where. "We sent the marginal volunteers to the Philippines," says one Peace Corps official, "because it was thought to be a safe country. The cream of the crop went to Ghana because Nkrumah was a left-leaning leader and we thought that would make it a tough assignment."

The cold war was the least of the volunteers' concerns. The closest they actually got to it were the occasional articles in left-wing newspapers that described them as Yankee imperialists, and accusations by radio broadcasts—from China, Russia, or Cuba—that they were really CIA agents. The "tough assignment," many volunteers found, was figuring out what it was the Peace Corps had sent them overseas to do.

"Only the most careful planning and negotiation can ensure [the Peace Corps'] success," President Kennedy had said in a message to Congress upon signing the executive order.[16] But the urgency of getting the program on its feet left Shriver's aides and field representatives little time to develop the jobs in which volunteers could perform "the modern miracles" Kennedy had referred to in one of his campaign speeches.

"Our men were under tremendous pressure to make deals," says Charlie Peters, the Peace Corps' director of evaluation from 1961 to 1968. "They were heroes if they came back with a program in their pocket. So the tendency was not to check out the jobs too carefully. Pakistan was the worst. In the first group of fifty-nine volunteers, only fifteen had real jobs."

Even in the Philippines, where it was thought amicable Philippines-United States relations would facilitate a large infusion of English teachers, many volunteers found themselves in half-baked assignments working as "teacher's aides."* In making arrangements with Filipino education officials, the Peace Corps neglected to consider the high unemployment rate among Filipino teachers at the time. The volunteers were already on their way when the Peace Corps office in Manila was informed that the Americans would not be teaching their own classes; they would be "teacher's aides" instead. "The education official I met with said, 'Maybe they'll run a science project, or help the teacher,' " recounts Larry Fuchs, the first country director in the Philippines. "We weren't sure just what the relationship would be in the schools. . . . It was a hope-for-the-best sort of thing," says a staffer who planned the program. One volunteer described it as the "never-mind-about-the-job-go-out-and-be-a-hero school of programming." [17]

In Latin America, most volunteers found themselves in a similarly ambiguous job called community development, or CD. It was the task of the CD volunteer to coax peasants into organizing self-help projects that would gradually build their confidence and lead them to assert greater control over their lives. Recent liberal arts graduates, who made up the largest segment of the applicant pool, were ideally suited for CD because Peace Corps officials felt that it required no specific technical skills. As the children of an up-by-the-bootstraps democratic society, these volunteers would set an example of Yankee ingenuity and stick-to-itiveness. By 1963, almost fifteen hundred volunteers were assigned to CD in nineteen Latin American counties; and worldwide, community development accounted for 25 percent of the volunteers. But the romantic conception of CD was at odds with the expectations of social service bureaus in Latin America, which viewed the CD worker as an organizer who possesses the specific technical knowledge needed for community projects. "They said they were community development workers," said a Peruvian official, "but they didn't know how to do anything."[18] One CD volunteer recalls, "They had a name for me. It was *vago*. . . . They weren't being mean or anything, but I didn't have a job or even a government title, so that's just what I was— a vagabond."[19]

Situations like those in the Philippines and Latin America were common. The Peace Corps' independent evaluators reported a preponderance of volunteers all over the world languishing in poorly defined jobs. The quality of the programs was suffering, they said, because the Corps was sending out more people than could be adequately placed. Peace Corps headquarters, they maintained, was more concerned about expansion than

---

*By the end of 1961 there were 182 volunteers in the Philippines. A year later there were 572.

the volunteers' actual contribution. Sargent Shriver counters that he and other officials had no way of calculating the right number of volunteers to send to a country. "It wasn't as if there was a great body of experts in the State Department who knew how many we should send or what we should do up-country in Malaya," he says. According to Warren Wiggins, who became deputy director of the Peace Corps, he and Shriver were indeed "driven to make it as large as possible quickly" for fairly specific reasons. "I knew there would be a lot of problems getting the Peace Corps started: There weren't any jobs waiting for the volunteers. Third world leaders weren't making speeches asking the United States to send them our young folk. And most of the people applying weren't skilled. To get around these problems, we needed to make it important, and it couldn't be important unless it was big."

The teacher's aides boondoggle in the Philippines notwithstanding, education programs were some of the more successful ventures of the Peace Corps' early years. For the first three years, such programs accounted for 62 percent of all volunteers. By assigning volunteers to teach in schools, the Corps satisfied a pressing need of host countries as well as its own need to expand rapidly. The heads of state in the newly independent nations of Africa and Asia were anxious to replace foreign professionals, businesspeople, and civil servants with nationals, but first, their citizens had to be educated and the school systems left behind by colonial governments were grossly inadequate.

English instruction especially was a task well suited to the Peace Corps, for a few reasons. According to Warren Wiggins, teaching offered the fewest opportunities for major embarrassments. "We were scared shitless that they might screw up. Bill Josephson and I had a pact," Wiggins says, referring to his agreement with his "Towering Task" coauthor Bill Josephson, who became the Peace Corps general counsel. "We'd never have volunteers try anything more difficult than teaching English. Anyone can do that if they're a native speaker."

Additionally, by placing volunteers in available teaching positions—a practice later called slot-filling—the Peace Corps was able to establish itself quickly as an organization of some consequence. "In some countries," says Wiggins, "volunteers were teaching one out of four high school students. With those figures, you don't have to doubt if you're successful."

The education program satisfied the Peace Corps' institutional needs, but the teachers themselves were not necessarily fulfilling the Corps' less tangible objectives of cross-cultural exchange. Instead of living among the native population, volunteers adopted the life-style of contract teachers, who lived and worked on the school grounds, venturing into towns and villages only occasionally. Volunteers assigned to schools that did not board faculty, typically roomed together in houses built especially for them by education ministries. Few, if any, dwelled in the mud huts of Peace Corps legend, and most had a servant—usually one of their students whose school fees were paid by the volunteer—who prepared their meals and tended to the housecleaning and laundry.

Teaching assignments, however, did not guarantee volunteers an easy two years. "We had real jobs," says John Coyne (Ethiopia, 1962–64), "but our students were used to rote learning: When we tried to get them to think instead of memorize, they got very angry. They didn't think we were real teachers. Some of them hated us, and we were devastated. We had extended ourselves and then got slapped in the face." Volunteers' frustrations were exacerbated by overcrowded schools. Coyne taught seven fifty-five-minute classes a day with thirty-five to forty students in each class. "A lot of us couldn't wait to go home," he recalls.

The first volunteers learned to lower their expectations drastically. Saving the world, even in tiny increments, was indeed a towering as well as a humbling task. Rather than working miracles, they likely more often showed that some Americans were likable and trustworthy. A few, maybe, improved the quality of people's lives in small, unrecorded, almost unprovable ways.

Back in the United States, the Peace Corps' skillful public relations office had the country believing that volunteers were indeed working modern miracles, proving, said *U.S. News and World Report*, that "the U.S. is determined to build a peaceful world."[20] In each of its first few years, Congress voted dramatic funding increases and Sargent Shriver made the cover of *Time* in 1963.

What follows are volunteers' accounts of their experiences in the Peace Corps in its formative years.

## Michael Tudor (Nigeria, 1961–63)

I went into the Peace Corps first and foremost because I adored President Kennedy. I was in love with him. I was a nineteen-year-old medical student and he was my hero. Eisenhower never made me feel like a citizen, like this was my country. But Kennedy made me feel that way. I felt tremendously proud to be an American and I wanted to share that with others.

## Roger Landrum (Nigeria, 1961–63)

I didn't go to a lot of speeches in college but I went to hear Kennedy because someone told me he was probably going to run for President. This was in 1959. I remember him quoting the line from the Robert Frost poem that went, "miles to go before I sleep," and then dashing off the stage. It was like a meteor going through the room. I followed his campaign and when he announced the Peace Corps idea, I wrote him a letter saying, "If you will do it, I will volunteer."

I grew up in rural Michigan and I'd never been overseas before. I was at my mother's house when the telegram came inviting me to train for Nigeria. I remember my hands were shaking as I opened it. I had never heard of Nigeria but I definitely felt I was participating in history. This was a new era of American participation in the world. Peace Corps volunteers were the front-line people making fresh contact with a whole bunch of newly independent nations. There was a sense of exhilaration about maybe carrying forth democracy and establishing new relations with Asia, Africa, and South America.

## Parker Borg (Philippines, 1961–63)

I was studying international relations in college and the Peace Corps was an opportunity to live overseas. I was much more interested in learning than in making a breakthrough in the third world. There was a lot of psychological testing in training. I had to go back for several interviews with the staff psychiatrists because my level of idealism wasn't as high as they would have liked.

## Michael Moore (Togo, 1962–64)

I was a plain vanilla middle-class American kid who had the good fortune to go to Yale. I belonged to a fraternity and was into the Ivy League scene. There was nothing in my background that would have led me to join the Peace Corps. I think it was solely the circumstances of America in 1961 after Kennedy's election.

I remember reading about the Freedom Riders in jail in Jackson, Mississippi. Until then, I wasn't aware of the nature or extent of poverty or discrimination in America. Then, the chaplain at Yale began making it clear to all of us that "Hey, guys, there's a whole lot more to the world than what's going on here." When Kennedy said that Americans should do something for their country, I was captivated.

In my senior year at Yale, I applied to the Peace Corps, the African American Institute, and the American Friends Service Committee. I was also admitted to the Yale Drama School. A week before graduation I got a telegram from the Peace Corps asking if I would like to serve in Togo. I sent a telegram back right away saying I'd go. Then I went to the library to look up Togo. I had no idea where it was. A lot of people from my class at Yale went into the Peace Corps. But a lot more went to graduate school or law school. We were the crazies. We were going to waste two years of our lives when we could be out making money.

### Thaine Allison (Borneo, 1962–64)

When I was a kid, my parents took me to the YMCA to hear some missionaries speak about their experiences working and living in China. Their stories were fascinating. That's where I first started thinking that I might like to live in another country someday. When I went to college, I got involved with the Methodist Church youth movement and the option came up to work overseas as a missionary. But I didn't want to proselytize.

When the Peace Corps was announced, it just felt like the right thing to do after graduation. I had just gotten married and my wife wanted to get out of Iowa, where she'd lived all her life. At Chico State there were five graduates that year from the brand-new school of agriculture. Three of us went into the Peace Corps. The department chair was a bit upset that we were turning down real jobs.

When we found out we were going to Borneo, my dad said, "You guys quit running around. You sound like the wild man from Borneo."

### Sylvia Feinman (Togo, 1962–64)

My father gave me a very hard time about joining the Peace Corps. He was an immigrant and like many fathers of that time, he believed that a young woman graduated from college and became a teacher. He told me, "I didn't come here from Russia to work hard so my children could have it better, and then have my daughter go to Africa and get lice." But he couldn't win. I was going anyway.

### Dennis Grubb (Colombia, 1961–63)

After two months of training, at Rutgers, we went home to pack our things. We were told to meet back in Washington at Peace Corps headquarters a week later. At nine A.M. we were all there and we climbed onto a bus and drove over to the White House. We sat in Lyndon Johnson's office and met Hubert Humphrey and Barry Goldwater. Johnson said, "I think this is the greatest idea I ever heard of." Humphrey told us that the Peace Corps was something he'd dreamed about, and Barry Goldwater said that we were "the core of America." Then we went on a tour of the White House. We were listening to the guide when Shriver comes in and says, "Guys, this is the President." Kennedy said something like "Look, all I can say is it's now a reality. You're going over there, and good luck." That was it. Then he walked around and shook everybody's hand. "My name is John Kennedy," he said. "What's your name?" It made me feel like I was a part of history.

### John Coyne (Ethiopia, 1962–64)

We flew out of New York on TWA. We landed in Athens, laid over, then flew down overnight and landed in Addis Ababa about dawn. I remember smelling eucalyptus and seeing the overwhelming poverty as soon as our bus got out of the airport. We were all just silent. That first day one woman said she wanted to go home and she did.

The Ethiopians stared at us all the time. I would step outside my door and people would come up and just stare at me. They would stop their cars to watch us. Eventually it drove you crazy. You'd start staring back at them and then they'd get pissed off.

Volunteers were getting ripped off all the time. In Africa they steal anything and everything, because whatever you have is so much more than they have. I lived on a street whose name meant "Don't Holler for Help." We hired a guard to watch our house while we were gone.

Then there were the ants. After it rained, there would be ants on everything—the walls, the food, the pots and pans. I couldn't deal with it. I used to just leave the house and when I came back they'd be gone. They moved right through. But we got so used to these things. I heard about a volunteer who baked a chocolate cake for a dinner she was having. The ants hit the cake and she just layered them in.

### Tom Livingston (Ghana, 1961–63)

In 1961, many of the nonaligned countries saw the Peace Corps as another aspect of American imperialism. A couple of the Ghanaian newspapers were very circumspect in their coverage of our arrival. The implication was "You better behave yourself. We're watching you." Even

President Nkrumah's party was very opposed to having the Peace Corps. But Nkrumah was trying to expand the education system in Ghana. He'd just built about twenty new secondary schools and didn't have enough teachers.

Despite the political line, the Ghanaians were very warm and welcoming. We were the first white people they had seen ride the mammy wagons, which were these flatbed trucks with wooden benches and a canopy over the top. Some British people I knew in Accra told me we were scandalizing the Europeans in Ghana because we would ride those things. But it was a revelation to the Ghanaians and they loved it. They thought we were real characters and they used to say, "Marry my daughter! Marry my daughter!"

## Sylvia Feinman

My first year I lived in an apartment in the capital with two other volunteers and taught in a high school. Then, for my second year, I moved to a village seventy miles from the city. I had a cement house with a tin roof and windows with shutters, no glass or screens. It was fairly advanced for the village at the time. It had a flush toilet and a shower. I also had a spigot in the kitchen but there was no sink, so I collected the water in pots.

The village had never had a white person live there before the volunteer who preceded me. So I was a curiosity at first, but we were honored guests. Every once in a while someone would leave a papaya in front of my door.

The Togolese were very welcoming. They used to watch out for us. One man in my village, Mr. Anthony, was my self-appointed father. One day, I bought a chicken at the market, not realizing that they just pick up this live chicken, tie its legs together, and hand it to you. When I brought it back to the village, Mr. Anthony just looked at it and asked, "Would Mademoiselle like someone to take care of that?" I said, "Yes," and it was delivered to me an hour later in quarters. Mr. Anthony gave me a lecture one day because I had left the village without telling him where I was going. "What if the Peace Corps director had come and asked me, 'Where is Sylvia?' " he said. "I wouldn't be able to tell him where you were. How dare you do that." I remember thinking, "I traveled four thousand miles away from my parents to have Mr. Anthony down the road."

## Tom Scanlon (Chile, 1961–63)

(The following is from an unpublished manuscript by Tom Scanlon.)

Every morning it was an effort to come out and face this strange world, and the best part of each day was when it came to an end and the fight with the cold and the language was over. Then I could crawl into my sleeping bag . . . and lose myself in sleep.

One long Sunday afternoon I attended a dance . . . and had to rock and roll with every girl under forty in the place and answer questions about Brenda Lee for six hours—all in a language I acquired recently and then pronounced miserably and while a bunch of microbes played havoc in my lower intestines. But it was worth it when one of the men asked me for my autograph.

We worked in one community that was so poor they ate only one meal a day, and all it might be was a piece of onion and hot water. They didn't even have names for the three different meals, or for the days of the week. There were pockets of poverty where they made clothes out of flour bags. Sometimes, a guy would show up with his sick wife draped across the back of his horse. Sometimes she was dead already, but if she was still alive we'd try to get her to the hospital in our jeep. In a settlement of about one hundred families where one Peace Corpsman was, six babies died within two days. We heard about this in training. We were glad to be able to help. These were experiences you never have in the United States.

## Tom Livingston

When my headmaster took me to the house I was to live in, he introduced me to this woman named Comfort. "This is your cook," he said. "I can't have a cook," I told him. "I think it would be wrong for me to have a cook. I can make my food myself." He said, "All the teachers have a cook and you're going to be too busy. How are you going to get up and boil the water or prepare the fire? School begins at ten minutes to seven." He was right. The modalities of life would have kept me busy. I wouldn't have had time to prepare a lesson.

There was no such thing as a laundromat there, so I also had a washerman wash my clothes by hand. Since there was no electricity, he heated the iron in a fire. I was never so beautifully dressed in my life. I had ironed and starched shirts and trousers every day. And every day, when I came home from school, Comfort would serve tea.

A reporter and photographer from *Time* magazine came to visit and asked, "Can we get a picture of you pulling water from the well?" I told them I didn't know how to because my cook drew the water. They said, "Come on, let's get the picture." I said, "I refuse. There may be other volunteers who have to draw their own water but I'm not one of them." *Time* wanted to show us roughing it in darkest Africa. But we weren't going into darkest Africa at all. It was highly civilized.

## Roger Landrum

The president of Nigeria, Nnamdi Azikiwe, told Sargent Shriver that he wanted to establish a four-year American-style university. There was only one other university in Nigeria at the time. He told Shriver he was having trouble recruiting faculty and asked him for a big contingent of teachers. The Peace Corps made up a third of the teaching staff at this new university.

They put us in these one-room cells in the student dorms. There were no screens on the windows, so whenever I turned on the light swarms of bugs came in. These three-inch rhinoceros beetles would fly in and when they hit the wall it sounded like a bomb exploding. The mattress was made of packed straw, so after a time your body position was sunk into the straw and you couldn't move.

We were a little intimated living among all these Africans and it was hard to cope. The students were from the villages and they'd wake up when the sun rose. There would be this tremendous hubbub of noise as they headed down to the showers. They'd be chattering away at the top of their lungs and singing and turning on their radios. We never got enough sleep. One of the volunteers in our group was this very crusty veterinarian and one morning he came out of his room and yelled, "You black bastards, shut off those radios."

Africans have no sense of private property. They would go into your room when you weren't there and shuffle through your things. That was culturally appropriate behavior. Some of the volunteers threatened to quit. But the rest of us were wedded to the Peace Corps ideals and we were going to stick it out no matter how miserable it got.

## Robert Burkhardt (Iran, 1962–64)

I taught beginning English to boys between the ages of sixteen and twenty-five. I'd have fifty kids in a class and the assigned text was *Gulliver's*

*Travels.* It was very hard to maintain continuity because whenever the weather was good the principal would say, "Mr. Burkhardt, it's good weather. They must work the crops. When it rains they go to class. But now, they must go to the crops," and he'd yank them out of class. But what was I to do? He was the boss.

In every class I gave, there would be an agent from the Savak [Iranian secret police] sitting among the students. At first, I was very insulted by this. Hadn't they heard of the First Amendment? The other teachers would say to me, "You don't understand." In one class the students asked me what I thought of "Red China" joining the United Nations. I said that I thought China should be part of the UN—after all, it's a country. They all burst into applause and, of course, the Savak guy is busy writing down all these subversive thoughts. Then, I gave them the okay sign [a circle with the thumb and forefinger] which in Iran, unbeknownst to me, means, "I'm a homosexual. Would you like to get it on with me?" I had no idea what was going on.

I worked with a Presbyterian minister there and we started a school for young women who wanted to learn English so they could get better jobs with the oil companies. These women were just like vacuum cleaners about English. You couldn't give them enough. I created this character named Shereen Kucheek, which means "sweet young thing" in Farsi. She was an Iranian girl who goes to America to study at Vassar College. I would make up these stories about her travels around the United States.

Being in the Peace Corps, I felt a part of this incredible pattern going on—in the Philippines, Colombia, Kenya, Iran, Tunisia, and Guatemala—and I was just one little digit in the great wheel of history. It was a great sensation.

I think some volunteers felt that our job was to raise up the heathen. I didn't see it that way. It was a struggle to teach English. At a conference of volunteers, a lot of people voiced complaints about the food, the different customs, and having to speak Farsi all the time with these people who don't understand us. After about forty minutes of this, the principal of my school stood up and said, "I welcome you to my country. I'm glad that you come to work with us and help us. But we don't *need* you Americans. We tolerate you. You think you're so goddamned superior but our culture is four thousand years old and yours is two hundred years old." He was great, but a whole bunch of volunteers didn't understand him at all.

## Thaine Allison

My wife was assigned to teach English at a village school and I was an agricultural extension agent. I was told what the British colonial government was trying to do for agricultural development in my area and instructed to just go do it. "If you screw up," the Peace Corps said, "we'll see what we can do about it. Write us once a month and let us know how you're coming along." We were four hours by boat from the nearest volunteer.

I worked with Chinese and Muslim farmers. About a third of them were doing fairly well in that they had enough to eat: a lot of rice, some fresh fish, and sometimes dog or monkey. The rest grew just enough food to survive. I learned to speak Malay in training but it didn't help when I visited the Chinese farmers. They would say, "You Yankee Red dog, you come to talk to me and you don't even know my language." I took lessons in Mandarin Chinese from a school principal in the area and then went back to the Chinese farmers. They said, "You Yankee Red dog, since our language is obviously too difficult for you, why don't you just speak in English to us?"

I tried to tell the poorer farmers about ways to irrigate their crops, about the benefit of planting paddy rice instead of hill rice, and helped start some vegetable gardens. But much of the time, I never felt like I really knew what was happening. It seemed like it was more important that I show up in the villages for ceremonial purposes, rather than for anything I was able to do. These were people who wore loincloths and were barely able to grasp the notion that I had come from far away to help them, and there I was—asking them to plant their rows straight.

I took my wife with me to one village where they had never seen a white woman before. The women gathered around her and wanted to talk to her and touch her. I asked some of them to watch after her while I went to look at some crops and she had fifty women and kids following after her. She couldn't have gotten lost if she tried. In many of the villages, they'd never seen anyone with hairy arms before so they all liked to pet my arms.

Why my wife and I didn't have children was totally baffling to them. When we first got there, we used the excuse that we had just gotten married. But after we'd been there awhile and my wife obviously wasn't pregnant, they began asking questions. I knew I had gotten pretty good speaking Malay when I could tease them about Americans being like elephants, which take three years to gestate. When the time came for us to go on vacation, a group of women showed up at our door and gave my wife some money. They said, "We don't know what you have but we want some because we don't want any more babies."

☆

On the day President Kennedy was assassinated, almost seven thousand volunteers were posted in forty-four countries. His ringing words of sympathy for the poor and for the aspirations of young countries resounded in the most remote corners of the world. Volunteers discovered newspaper pictures of the President fixed to the walls of huts next to those of Jesus Christ. Host country nationals drew a distinct connection between the Peace Corps and Kennedy. Volunteers in parts of Africa were called wakina Kennedy ("one who walks with Kennedy") and los hijos de Kennedy ("children of Kennedy") in Latin America.

### Robert Burkhardt

The Iranians all knew for a fact that Lyndon Johnson had assassinated Kennedy. It happened in Texas, Johnson's home state. Who had the most to gain? He became President of the United States. I kept saying to them, "No. You don't understand." And they would just say back, "No. *You* don't understand."

### Elaine Fuller (Colombia, 1963–65)

Our neighbor came to our house very excited about something. We could understand "Dallas," "Kennedy," and "his head." This made no sense to us but we pretended we understood. He finally brought us his radio. Although our Spanish wasn't good enough to understand the news, we finally got it that he was dead. We were stunned and decided to hitchhike down to the city. The people in the town thought since Kennedy was dead, all the Peace Corps volunteers had to go. They said, "Please don't leave. Stay with us." We didn't know how to say in Spanish that we were just going to find out what had happened.

### Donna Shalala (Iran, 1962–64)

I remember staying up all night listening to the funeral on the radio. I also recall a beggar walking up to me in the street and I said, "No, I don't have any money." He said, "I don't want money. I just want to tell you how sorry I am that your young President died."

I remember how difficult it was to sleep and I remember turning cold, which is one of the first signs of shock. Kennedy was the first President we had voted for. He represented a break with the past and we had bought all that. His assassination forced us to grow up.

## John Coyne

When I went to school the morning after I heard it on the radio, none of the students would talk to me. They wouldn't say anything. So I called them over to my desk and as soon as they gathered around, they all had questions like, "Is John-John, the son, going to become President?"

## Michael Tudor

The memorial service at the school where I taught was an extraordinary experience. Six hundred students wailed with sorrow. I had written to President Kennedy telling him how much the Nigerians admired him and how grateful they were for his Peace Corps. I got a letter back and I read it to the students. It said something like: "I'm so pleased that the Nigerians like me so much but their love, in no small part, is due to people like yourself who have put your lives on the line to represent me over there. So I don't deserve the credit, you do."

# Part Two

## The Johnson Years, 1963-69

# Introduction

In the fall of 1967, Peace Corps staff member Kirby Jones (Dominican Republic, 1963–65) made a recruiting trip to the University of California at Berkeley. The display he set up in front of Sproul Hall competed for students' attention with those of any number of other organizations. "It was a beehive of activity," he recalls. "From A to Z, you had a table for everybody. I got into a debate with Jerry Rubin. It was the same week Stokely Carmichael spoke at the Greek Theater and Robert Kennedy was speaking there that Saturday."

"There is an electric climate here at Berkeley and one of which I am proud to be a part this week," Jones told a crowd of students. "Carrying picket signs and taking LSD trips may be activity, but it is minus involvement. Much of it is phony, amateurish and superficial. Participation these days means more than . . . carrying signs or wordy protests. It means VISTA,* civil rights, and Peace Corps: sharing the lives of the poor and the outcasts."[1]

By the mid-1960s, it was not uncommon for recruiters to encounter students who viewed the Peace Corps as hopelessly irrelevant in the face of urban riots, the civil rights struggle, and America's deepening involvement in the Vietnam war. Even though the Corps' enrollment was growing rapidly, reaching a peak of 15,556 volunteers in 1966, the organization was losing its cachet. "When we joined the Peace Corps in 1962, we thought we were the revolutionaries," remembers John Coyne (Ethiopia, 1962–

---

*Referred to as the domestic Peace Corps, VISTA (Volunteers in Service to America) was established in 1964 as part of President Johnson's War on Poverty.

64). "When I came home, it was incredible to me that students at Berkeley had closed down the university."

The Peace Corps tried to adapt to the new landscape. Standard-issue fraternity brothers, of whom the Corps had thousands, were perfectly acceptable applicants in 1962. But just a few years later, they seemed rather bland compared with those who had taught in Mississippi freedom schools or organized rent strikes in Chicago. These types, however, were hard to recruit. "When we go on the porch and whistle," a training officer said in 1965, "we're hoping that a few alley cats will enter the door along with the tame tabbies who've been showing up."[2]

Anne Karin Glass (Brazil, 1966–69) was one such "alley cat" applicant. "I was expelled during my junior year at Skidmore because I wrote articles in the college paper criticizing the school's policies. The Peace Corps thought people like me could either really accomplish something or be real troublemakers. I learned that they classified me 'high risk/high gain.' Our regional director in Brazil watched over me like a hawk. He was scared to death I might get pregnant."

To attract applicants of similar mettle, Deputy Director Warren Wiggins sought advice from Carl Oglesby and Paul Booth, officers of the pioneering activist organization Students for a Democratic Society. "We want highly motivated people," Wiggins said at the time, "people who would like to see the world a little different than it is now. We have found that we're not communicating too well with this sort of student."[3] The Peace Corps also courted activist leader Tom Hayden. Shortly after Hayden's return from North Vietnam in early 1966—where he had toured the country at the invitation of the government—he met with Peace Corps official Frank Mankiewicz, who offered him a position in the Corps' Latin American division. "I said no," recalls Hayden. "By that time, I thought it was a sort of fanciful idea to send twenty-two-year-olds into the storm center of Latin American revolution and get some Indians to make bricks."

While Peace Corps officials used all manner of polling and focus groups to figure out how to keep the interest of their college constituency, the agency's new director, Jack Vaughn, set himself to the task of "making the Peace Corps as good as Sarge said it was."[4] (Shriver was asked by President Johnson to do for his War on Poverty what he'd done for Kennedy's Peace Corps; he left the Corps in March 1966). While Shriver was hailed for having built a thriving organization out of a mere campaign promise, Jack Vaughn went to work on some of the serious problems sown in those early, frantic years. Vaughn came to grips with the imbalance between the number of volunteers sent into the field and that of substantive assignments available.

"I was tired of volunteers telling me that they had been 'parachuted' into the country," says Vaughn, "that nobody at their site even knew they were coming. I didn't think that was fair to the volunteer or the host country." To reconcile the number of volunteers with the Peace Corps' ability to make well-defined assignments, Vaughn undertook a dramatic redistribution. Contingents in several countries were slashed by 25 to 50 percent, and several new programs in South Korea, Western Samoa, Botswana, Burkina Faso (then Upper Volta), Tonga, Libya, and the Gambia were established. A few rapidly expanding programs, such as those in Micronesia, India, Ghana, and Colombia, also absorbed the Peace Corps' climbing enrollment.

Volunteer training was of particular concern to Vaughn. Since 1961, the Corps had contracted with various universities but their training programs, Vaughn said at the time, were simply not up to the task: "[Volunteers] arrived overseas with an inadequate knowledge of the host country language, an incomplete appreciation of the host country culture, and an insufficient amount of technical skill."[5] Vaughn doubled the number of hours devoted to language instruction and gradually relocated training from American campuses to the countries where the volunteers would be serving. Staffing was also an issue for the new director. "Very few staff members could relate well to young adults," Vaughn recalls. "They tended to adopt the model of the high school football coach or the homeroom teacher. We hired the outstanding volunteers as they finished their service and they saved our necks. They knew good training, good programming, and good communication."

Vaughn's concern for quality, though, was in some instances negated by the Peace Corps' increasing responsiveness to American foreign policy. Vaughn's predecessor, Sargent Shriver, had been adamant about distancing the Corps from policy interests. "The White House asked us to take an interest in the Congo and Nicaragua," Shriver recalls, "but we wouldn't go to either of those countries. There was a lot of fandangoing in the Congo, and I didn't want it to appear as though the Peace Corps was helping a conspicuous dictator like Nicaragua's Somoza."*

By the mid-sixties, with ten thousand volunteers doing America proud, the organization was becoming a program of consequence. Peace Corps volunteers had proved their effectiveness as ambassadors of goodwill all over the world, and the Johnson administration, therefore, felt that they

---

*The "fandangoing" in the Congo was the CIA-assisted overthrow of Premier Patrice Lumumba in 1961. The Peace Corps opened a program in Nicaragua and the Congo in 1968 and 1970 respectively.

were ideally suited to serve as informal emissaries in the State Department's program to "win hearts and minds" in Vietnam. Following State Department instructions, two Peace Corps officials, Warren Wiggins and Ross Pritchard, visited Vietnam in January 1966 to "probe areas where the Peace Corps might make a lasting contribution, stressing secondary education, skills training and community development."[6] "McGeorge Bundy [national security adviser] and Walt Rostow [special assistant to President Johnson] believed that the Peace Corps should be a part of the total national effort in Vietnam and anything we could do to help should be done," says Pritchard.

Vaughn opposed the idea of a Peace Corps program in Vietnam because "it was just inappropriate to send volunteers to a country at war." But he sent Wiggins and Pritchard on the exploratory trip so that "if it ever came to a really serious request, we wanted to be able to say with very good solid base fact, 'It won't work.' " Pritchard believed that "volunteers could definitely have done some good there. But I realized we couldn't see a way to keep the Peace Corps on course with the CIA or other U.S. presence."

The Vietnam idea was not pursued further. The Peace Corps *did* become embroiled in White House policy toward India. President Johnson was enraged when the Indian government in 1965 spent millions on its war against Pakistan while the Indian people suffered a near famine caused by a drought that same year. To force India to settle the dispute, President Johnson suspended all United States aid. This included a group of 170 volunteers who were just weeks away from their departure. It was clear that the President was using the Peace Corps as "an instrument of political pressure," U.S. Ambassador to India Chester Bowles wrote to Johnson's special assistant and former Peace Corps public affairs chief Bill Moyers. This action, Bowles warned, could seriously damage the Peace Corps' credibility. "We have been telling the Indians that the United States food program and the Peace Corps are wholly unrelated to politics and that they represent a humanitarian effort by the American people," he wrote to Moyers. "If Indian officials and opinion makers once became convinced that the United States Government plans to turn the Peace Corps as well as the Food for Peace program* on and off as a political lever, I am convinced that within a foreseeable period of time the Peace Corps will no longer be welcome in India."[7]

But to Johnson, quid pro quo was part and parcel of foreign aid. As

---

*Food for Peace was founded in 1962 as an emergency relief agency within the White House. It is now a part of the State Department.

he told Kennedy aide Ralph Dungan in 1961, "You put out the [foreign aid] dollars to buy the votes. . . . You line up these countries to be on our side."[8] Peace Corps officials were mortified. "We couldn't admit to the volunteers that the President was perverting the Peace Corps for foreign policy considerations," says Warren Wiggins. "So we put together additional training and they had no idea what was going on." The volunteers were delayed by less than a month.

A year later, though, when President Johnson revised his policy toward India, Vaughn suddenly found it entirely fitting for the Peace Corps to participate. The drought in India had devastated the country's grain harvest and Johnson decided to substantially increase food and agricultural assistance. Vaughn suggested to the White House that this new effort include a massive infusion of volunteers. The administration approved the idea, and Jack Vaughn stated that the total number of volunteers in India could reach three thousand in the coming year.[9] Such an ambitious undertaking was, according to Brent Ashabranner, country director in India at the time, "courting disaster" and "the results were entirely predictable."

In Ashabranner's book *A Moment in History: The First Ten Years of the Peace Corps*, he explains what happened: "A campaign to recruit substantial numbers of volunteers with farm backgrounds failed completely. The new groups [totaling 700, bringing the India contingent to almost 1,300] were made up almost entirely of B.A. generalists, and their training was for the most part inferior because of the haste and size of the operation."[10] What they would actually do was also haphazardly planned. "Programming was throwing darts at a map," remembers Norman Bramble, another staff person in India. "It was a disaster." Said one volunteer, "It seems to us that the Peace Corps has not fulfilled the responsibility it had to us, of finding us a job for two years. It has played a big game with us, gotten us to India, given us a 'site,' put us on a list, and is not taking responsibility for the consequences of that action."[11] An Indian agricultural official commented to Ashabranner about a volunteer assigned to his supervision, "He knew nothing of agriculture and I realized immediately that the Peace Corps is not a program of technical assistance but rather one of cultural exchange. I am not opposed to cultural exchange, but we should not receive it under the false label of agricultural help. Our problem is too serious for that."[12]

Though many volunteers left India before the end of their two years, Vaughn has no regrets. "When you start big, you're going to have some congestion, and all sorts of glitches. But that doesn't bother me. It was a wonderful thing to do. I visited all over India then and I was very pleased with what I saw."

# Chapter 2

# *Realism Versus Idealism: Views from the Field*

"Volunteers are more knowledgeable, more inquisitive, more activist," Jack Vaughn observed in the mid-1960s. "But they are not necessarily happier. In the early days the happiness was, I think, a blissful ignorance about what was necessary to get from point X to point Y."[1]

By the mid-1960s, an increasing number of volunteers began to feel that the goals to which the Peace Corps had committed itself were hopelessly unrealistic. Those assigned to community development were probably the most skeptical. Their job was to propel a barrio or rural village toward a common objective, such as building a footbridge, paving a road, or clearing a playing field. Once the group recognized its capabilities, it would then attempt more ambitious projects. According to the theory of CD, the participants would gradually gain a sense of power in determining the course of their lives, and the community would "self-develop." Community development was "essentially revolutionary," wrote Frank Mankiewicz, regional director for Latin America in the early 1960s. "The ultimate aim . . . is nothing less than a complete change, reversal—or a revolution if you wish—in the social and economic patterns of the countries to which we are accredited."[2]

"That would be great if it were true," says Patrick Mertens (Colombia, 1966–69). "That was the whole notion that was presented to people who wanted to join the Peace Corps, that they could really make a difference." The dream of fomenting "revolution" was characteristic of the Peace Corps' early spirited rhetoric. In Latin America, where the Peace Corps concentrated its community development efforts, volunteers learned quickly that a rigid class system kept peasants virtually paralyzed on the bottom rung. And few volunteers could grasp an assignment that depended more on patience and social skills than specific tasks. It was the rare CD volunteer who could motivate a community to any significant, lasting degree. From 1962 to 1968, about 25 percent of all volunteers were assigned to community development. In 1968, the Peace Corps began phasing it out and by 1972, community development accounted for only 4.2 percent of the volunteers.

## Patrick Mertens (Colombia, 1966–69)

The Peace Corps' line on community development actually continued the *patrón* system. In my community, I was the gringo who could lend a little bit of credence to the demands of the people for some government funding for projects like building halls, parks, and meeting places. We went to the house of a senator one Saturday morning and he came to the door in his smoking jacket and said, "We'll take a look at your petition and try to help you. Good-bye."

After my first year in Colombia, I woke up. The Peace Corps was not designed to accomplish anything in the host countries. After going through this personal disillusionment, I decided, "I'm going to get serious here." I took a course at the agrarian institute where I learned about different kinds of crops and planting methods. Then I sent letters off to foundations that made interest-free loans for small-scale development projects. I didn't tell the Peace Corps anything. I just did it.

☆

[In a letter home, dated November 26, 1968, Mertens described a visit to the remote mountain hamlet of Altamira, where the farmers had agreed to try Mertens's new planting techniques in a community plot next to the school. Visiting Altamira was a seven-hour journey: three hours by train and four hours by horseback. His guide for the latter part of the trip, up through the mountain trail, was Luis Angel, the young son of Manuel Antonio, president of the Altamira *minga*, or community council. Luis Angel was one of eleven children, six of whom had died. Mertens's letter reads:]

I asked Luis Angel if he was hungry. "No, señor." Had he had lunch? "No, señor." This little kid about three feet high had ridden horseback four hours [to meet Mertens's train] and was telling me he wasn't hungry. . . . I noticed that Luis Angel was chewing *coca.* . . . This is a popular thing among these people because it dulls the hunger center in the brain. . . .

The potato plants were about a foot in height. They had been in the ground five weeks. The plants that the people had planted ten weeks ago with their own seed, without fertilizer, without fungicides, without insecticides were only half as high. I asked Manuel Antonio what the people thought of it. "They think it's beautiful, don Patricio."

When I arrived back at the house of Manuel Antonio . . . Luis Angel asked me to sit down in the cookroom where I had not been permitted to enter before. I looked around. The walls were all black from years of smoke pouring up from the hearth. . . . There was one candle in the room. There was no ceiling, just a high thatched roof which you could see the end of in the dim light. I asked Manuel Antonio if he would plant the potatoes [on his own land] in the next planting season. No, he would not. I asked why. This is the answer he gave: His land was not the same land as that of the school. He didn't think that the seeds from this current planting would work. Besides he had plantains in his plot right now, and that would take two years to harvest.

I asked what the profit on these plantains would be after two years if he just considered an area the size of the one where we planted the potatoes. Forty pesos. Two and a half dollars. If he were to harvest four potato plantings—we figured it out with the highest possible price for seed and lowest market prices for sold potatoes—his profit would be twenty-one hundred pesos. One hundred twenty dollars. But he keeps saying that he doesn't know how well it would do. . . . I tell him there's no reason for it not to work out, if he does what I teach him. . . . "What's the matter? Don't you want to be rich?" And he said, "Well, mi don Patricio, when one has been poor all his life . . ."

The next morning we made the long journey down again. This time Luis Angel carried a box with him with a doll in it. There were some flowers and the words EL NIÑO—"the child." He was going to ask people in Suarez for alms so that the people of Altamira could hire a priest to come and celebrate Christmas Eve mass. As soon as we arrived, I noticed his features change. He was no longer the intimate, cheerful friend I had known in Altamira. He became the slack-jawed, glassy-eyed Indian. Begging. No displays of humor. Complete submissiveness before the white community.

## *Marisue Zillig (Panama, 1965–67)*

I was assigned to Barriada San José, a town which was only three or four years old. People were coming into David, the nearby city, from the country and they couldn't find homes, so the government of Panama divided an old World War II airstrip near David into plots. There were five thousand people living on this open stretch of mud and clay. People used corrugated cardboard and tin, bamboo poles, or whatever they could afford to build their houses. There was some electricity but no running water.

I had big ideas about community development. I arranged all these meetings but no one ever showed up because they didn't see any economic value to them. The CD volunteer before me taught English classes, which I thought was just an easy way out. But on the other hand, the people were so grateful for it. I ended up teaching five classes a week myself with fifty to sixty kids in each. I also worked at a school for the severely retarded a few times a week.

I helped organize a big three-day, pre-Lenten festival to raise money to add more classrooms to the regular school in San José, which had only four rooms for six hundred fifty kids. The community had gotten as far as completing the foundation for the new rooms when they ran out of money for materials. We went to the businesses in David and asked them to donate prizes and sell tickets for us. We used the foundation as a dance floor, held raffles, and sold food. Hundreds of people came. The new classrooms got built and there was some money left over to start construction on a new church.

After the first year the warts appeared. Despite our success with the festival, the reality of the situation is that things can't happen overnight. Panama is an oligarchical society. The government is corrupt and made only halfhearted efforts to improve the lives of the poor. A lot of volunteers were cynical about this. But I was young and apolitical. I felt the Panamanians we worked with weren't doing enough for themselves.

I started a homemaking club and showed the mothers how to make an oven with a kerosene stove, a five-gallon lard tin, coat hangers, and bobby pins. We baked meats and I made cakes that didn't require any dairy ingredients. I also tried to teach the mothers about boiling water. Each plot on the airstrip had its own well and they eventually got contaminated. Kids would cough up worms all the time.

A lot of the kids were malnourished and measles would kill them. But the parents just accepted the fact that some children died. When one little boy got very sick with the measles, I took him and his mother to the hospital but they wouldn't admit him or even give us water for him. I got some money from the Peace Corps office and we took him to a doctor who gave us medicine and told us to feed him clear liquids. By the time we got back to the boy's home, the neighbors were arriving for the wake.

They just assumed he wouldn't live through the day. We gave him the medicine, fed him Jell-O, and he survived.

I wasn't terribly busy all the time. Some days I just played with the kids and wrote letters. I used to listen to classical records since they were cheap there and I didn't have a radio. My neighbors got to know the William Tell Overture and Mendelssohn's Fourth Symphony. I used to take some kids with me on the bus to David where we'd go to church, and then get ice cream. Then we'd go to the Peace Corps office where I'd take a shower and they'd play with the toilet, which was quite a novelty to them.

I have no doubt that the Peace Corps was basically a public relations campaign. The Panamanians loved President Kennedy and they thought it was great that the United States sent young Americans to get to know other countries, and through me they came to know an ordinary American. In the whole scheme of things, there's nothing more important than friendship.

## Margot Jones (Ecuador, 1965–67)

We were assigned to replace the early volunteers, the ones Kennedy had told to "go out there and do it!" I thought a lot of them were real fruitcakes. They did their missionary crusader thing, but I don't know that they accomplished more than we did.

I was supposed to take over the work of these two volunteers who built a community center in a barrio in Guayaquil. The center taught cake decorating, pattern making, and English. I didn't think cake decorating was bizarre at first. The community should determine what its needs are, and if cake decorating is meaningful to them, so be it.

The part of the barrio where I lived was built over a swamp. The houses were built on sticks and you had to take a little canoe to get from street to street. The people wanted to get the army to bring dirt to fill it in. They had to go to the army because they had the trucks to deliver it. In order to get the army to bring the dirt, you had to petition them in person.

These sweet little women got all dressed up and we took this long bus trip to army headquarters to see this captain. They sat in the back of the room while I spoke to him. They would mouth messages to me like "Smile" and come over to me and fix my hair. Those women knew what they were doing; they knew they had a patsy on their hands. The captain sent the dirt and, of course, I had to promise to be there when it was delivered. I didn't mind. I just didn't know the rules of the game. No one had explained to me exactly what my role was going to be in Ecuador—which was basically window dressing.

I also worked at an orphanage for a while. It was prestigious to have me there and I was like their pet. One Friday the children were going to the country for the day. The bus they were using was actually a big pickup truck with extensions built over the sides and the back. It could hold about forty people and there were seventy children. They couldn't get another bus so they all squeezed on. They got into an accident. The bus rolled over three times. When I heard what happened, I went to the hospital and tried to help out.

I was holding kids down on tables while doctors picked glass out of their faces without using an anesthetic. The doctor asked me to identify the one little girl, Teresa, who had been killed. It was a municipal hospital so there were few supplies. I asked a volunteer who happened to be nearby to go to the Peace Corps office and get as many medical supplies as possible from the storeroom. A little while later the Peace Corps director came by the hospital with this one little first aid kit and said to me, "Thank God you weren't on the bus. Since they always defer to the gringo, it would look as though you authorized the trip. The Peace Corps could have been sued and it might have been in the papers."

After it was over, I walked out of the hospital and broke down in tears. There was this nagging doubt that I was the Peace Corps volunteer and I was somehow supposed to do good. Nobody told me in training that there would be terrible accidents and that I was going to see human life treated very casually.

I looked at my life in this community center and realized that this was it for two years: Collecting dues for cake decorating classes. The notion that any kind of social change can occur through the efforts of naive, well-intentioned American college kids is totally ludicrous. I came to the conclusion that the volunteers' purpose was to do public relations for Uncle Sam.

☆

Community development volunteers weren't the only ones to feel that their assignments had little impact. Teachers, like Betsy Lebenson, were often assigned to schools attended by the wealthy, and some volunteers were assigned to sites where anti-Americanism ran high and thwarted their efforts.

## Betsy Lebenson (Afghanistan, 1963–65)

The training instructors kept drumming it into us what the Peace Corps was all about. An important point was that the volunteers work with the poor. So I figured I would be teaching Afghan peasants. But in a country that's ninety-five percent illiterate in its own language, who is going to be in school studying English? My students were the princess, the prime minister's daughter, and other children of the elite. They would arrive at school in a chauffeur-driven Mercedes and I would get there on my bicycle.

Some of my students were in their fifth year of English, but they still couldn't say one sentence. The passing grade was thirty-five percent and they all cheated to make that. I tried hard to get them to stop cheating and was then told by the principal to pass everyone. This was the cultural difference that was so impossible to relate to. They didn't think cheating was wrong.

They had no work ethic in Afghanistan. Their ideal was to sit on their rumps and drink tea. The Peace Corps English teachers were supposed to train Afghan counterparts so they too could teach English. But the Afghans figured we were doing their jobs for them so they didn't bother to do anything. They thought the Peace Corps was a real boon.

I felt like a failure because my students weren't learning English and I didn't have any Afghan friends. I tried to make friends with some of the women teachers. But they weren't allowed to associate with me because their families thought I was a bad influence. I couldn't be friends with the male teachers because if I were seen talking to one of them that immediately meant I was sleeping with them.

I think the Corps' goal of providing midlevel manpower was a failure in Afghanistan. The only volunteers who accomplished anything were the vaccinators. All they had to do was give people shots. The other goal of the Peace Corps, to make people more aware of Americans, was basically propaganda couched in idealistic terms. This was very successful in Afghanistan. They loved us. We were the only foreigners who ever bothered to learn their language or show interest in their culture.

## Frank Neubauer (Turkey, 1964–66)

I was assigned to work in an orphanage in Afyon, a town of forty thousand people. I was supposed to do anything I could think of to make the orphanage better. When I arrived, I found the two-, three-, and four-year-olds in the only room in the place that was heated. They were sitting around a table with absolutely nothing to stimulate them. There were no decorations, no toys, no playground. They weren't allowed to do anything but sit.

The board of directors were five older businessmen who didn't have too many notions of what child care was all about. I had to push them for everything. I was a thorn in their side. I was constantly nagging them for things. I started a playroom and decorated the building with posters I got from airlines. I got some potted plants, some rugs, and put up some curtains. I hustled the stuff from wherever I could—from people in the town or Americans in Ankara. I had the girls' technical high school make stuffed animals and I got the boys' high school to make a set of building blocks. I made some wooden airplanes, toy trucks, and houses. I got the Turkish Army to bring sand in for a sandbox.

But in the end, I think I was a great failure. When I returned a year after I left Afyon, the playroom was locked up. They opened it only to show visitors "this wonderful thing that our American guest built for us." Referring to me as a guest made the situation more tolerable for them. If they regard you as a guest, they can more easily accept some of the imposition you make on them.

When I came back from my summer vacation, I learned from the Peace Corps director that the orphanage's board of directors had made some complaints about me to the private organization that runs most of the orphanages in Turkey. The charges were trumped up, clearly an effort to get me out of there. I was quite surprised by it, but on the other hand, I sort of understood.

I transferred to a community development project in a shantytown outside Ankara. I got involved in starting a nursery school in an old coffeehouse and was there for five months. This particular project was getting a lot of flak in the newspapers, which were accusing the volunteers of having ties to the CIA and teaching Christianity. Two months after I left that project, the government threw the volunteers out of that community.

I moved to a teaching position at the university. I taught English to a group of professors and graduate students in the science department. I was merrily teaching English there for several months when the board of regents of the university voted to throw out the Peace Corps teachers. As it happened, my students were very enthusiastic about learning English, so they decided that they would disregard the board of regents and had me stay on in a more or less concealed fashion.

For the most part, the Peace Corps staff in Turkey was very cooperative and helpful but they wanted very badly to see success and perhaps were blind to the failures. So many volunteers were accomplishing very little, but the country director was telling them, "You're doing a wonderful job." Maybe that was their way of encouraging us. I came to the conclusion that what really counted to the Peace Corps in Washington and to Congress was the diplomacy that was being carried out. Turkish officials weren't telling the Peace Corps, "We desperately need English teachers or agricultural specialists." They made deals. The American government told the host countries that if they want such and such from the United States they were going to have to accept volunteers.

When I went into the Peace Corps, I thought the American government really wanted to go over and do something good for other people. "Help people help themselves" was the phrase they used in training. I believed that.

# Chapter 3

☆ ═══

# Micronesia: The Peace Corps Goes to Paradise

In May 1966, the Peace Corps launched a recruiting blitz for "paradise," complete with posters of turquoise lagoons and palm-fringed beaches. Four months later, 316 volunteers arrived on the Pacific islands of Micronesia. They found a tropical idyll strewn with the rusting hulks of World War II planes and tanks—and a population that was disease-ridden, malnourished, uneducated, and desperately poor. The United States was to blame for these conditions and it offered the Peace Corps as restitution. When the volunteers landed in Micronesia that fall, they discovered themselves caught in a paradox. By initiating a program in Micronesia, the Peace Corps placed volunteers in a contentious policy situation. Nevertheless, the Peace Corps insisted that it was an apolitical organization, and therefore, volunteers should distance themselves from the policy issues.

The roots of Micronesia's abhorrent conditions can be traced back to the years immediately following World War II. After the United States drove out the Japanese occupying forces during the war, Washington was presented with a valuable opportunity to extend its security apparatus farther west across the Pacific. The United Nations obliged and named Micronesia a trust territory of the United States. The UN stipulated that the United States could build military bases on the islands and that the United States was responsible for developing the islands' economic, social, and political infrastructure so that within a reasonable amount of time Micronesia would be ready for self-determination. Over the next twenty years bases were built but the islanders were practically ignored.

In the mid-1960s, the United Nations Trusteeship Council issued severe and highly embarrassing criticism of America's negligent stewardship. The UN's reports found their way into the media and a spate of articles entitled "The Forgotten Islands," "Showcase of Neglect," "Our Bungled Trust," "America's Paradise Lost," and the like described conditions.[1] Public education was far below any reasonable standard, for instance, and preventable diseases, such as polio and tuberculosis, were widespread.

When Ross Pritchard, the Peace Corps' regional director for East Asia, read about conditions in Micronesia, he envisioned the organization dispatching to the islands "a new generation of Americans [who] can duplicate the success of the Marshall Plan."[2] Peace Corps director Jack Vaughn took the idea to Stewart Udall, secretary of the interior, whose department was charged with developing the islands, and received full support for a large volunteer contingent to be recruited immediately. The White House approved the plan and it was announced by U.S. Ambassador to the United Nations Arthur J. Goldberg, who stated that the United States fully intended to fulfill its obligation to the people of Micronesia.

According to the Peace Corps Act of 1961, however, the agency was authorized by Congress to serve only under *foreign* governments. The United States and its trust territories were off-limits. But in 1966, the year in which the Peace Corps made plans for Micronesia, the act was amended such that the word "territories" was deleted. That opened up new possibilities, and Vaughn and Udall even considered sending volunteers to Alaska.[3]

In under two years, seven hundred volunteers were sent to Micronesia, most of them to teach. "All you had to do is walk and be semiliterate and we'd make you an English teacher," says Jim Byrne, regional director in Pelau. Many of these volunteers saw their placement in Micronesia as a public relations exercise aimed at diffusing increasingly bitter feelings among Micronesian leaders toward the United States. "I knew the government was using us," says James Clark, (Utrick, 1966–68). "The Peace Corps could mobilize a number of people quickly and inexpensively to cut off the criticism from the UN." Adds Robert Learmonth (Rota, 1966–68), "We did become pretty cynical about the reasons for sending the Peace Corps to Micronesia. There's an irritation that you get when you think you're being manipulated like that."

Pritchard maintains that the Peace Corps didn't go to Micronesia to be a temporary salve, although he acknowledges that "the UN's criticism was blunted by the fact that the Peace Corps was there. It helped to indicate that the United States was interested in helping Micronesia toward self-determination." Adds John Pincetich, Peace Corps country director in Micronesia at the time, "There was no design to soften the Micronesians [with the Peace Corps]. That evolved from their own extrapolation of events." Of the youthful volunteers, Pincetich says, "It is typical of their age to look for quick answers to complex questions."

Volunteers' suspicions that a political undercurrent had steered the Peace Corps to Micronesia were exacerbated by the stark contrast between the enticing recruiting posters and the reality of island conditions. Volunteers on Ujelang in the Marshall Islands district found the people living in shacks made of rusted scraps of tin left over from the war. The rat infestation was so bad, volunteers reported, that the children's feet were scarred from gnawing.

"There was an incredible dirtiness about the place. People defecated on the ground," recalls Nancy Caswell (Truk, 1967–68). "If you weren't careful, you might drink water from a stream that someone had gone to the bathroom in and you'd be sick for months. But my husband and I gave it everything we had. We got books from America and turned a shack into a library. We staged Dickens's *A Christmas Carol* with scenery and a cast of sixty kids. We built a three-room school out of cement and broken-up coral. Every single night we had kids in our house cooking popcorn and playing games. We made them feel like America really does care about them."

Some volunteers addressed themselves to the underlying causes of Micronesia's poverty and wrote angry letters to trust territory officials, their congressmen, and newspapers describing vividly the conditions in the islands. Instead of supporting the United States' claims of good intentions toward Micronesia, the volunteers' letters and other actions provided more publicity for a national embarrassment.

"The volunteers, mostly, were coming off campuses back home that were erupting in the free-speech movement with sit-ins, defiance of authority, and opposition to Lyndon Johnson's war in Vietnam," recalls John Pincetich. "The ceaseless chore faced by the staff [was to] make certain that volunteer indignation, so freely and often expressed, did not blow the program out of the water."

Todd and Hope Jenkins (Kili, 1967–68) did not join the Peace Corps right off of their college campus, but were newly married New Jersey schoolteachers. Nevertheless, they managed to embarrass the White House, the Interior Department, and the Peace Corps. Their story dramatically illustrates how the Corps' mission to serve the poor and disenfranchised may, in some instances, be at odds with other American interests.

The Jenkinses were assigned to teach in the Marshall Islands district, on the island of Kili—the "temporary" home to the people of Bikini, who had been relocated to the uninhabited island of Kili twenty years earlier, when the U.S. Navy had asked to use their atoll as a site for testing hydrogen bombs.* These experiments, Navy officers told them, would help achieve world peace. The Bikini people were proud to make such a contribution and agreed to move. Over the next twelve years, the atoll was bombed twenty-two times.

Life on Kili brought considerable hardship. Unlike the Bikini atoll, a crescent of twenty islands attached by underwater coral formations, Kili is a single island with no calm lagoon providing a rich array of food. Fishing in Kili's open surf is not only unproductive but also extremely dangerous. The people of Bikini used the atoll's several islands for different functions. But on Kili, they were forced to crowd together their homes, livestock, and farming activities. The concentration was further exacerbated by Kili's dense rainfall, which creates mosquito-breeding swamps.

## Hope Jenkins (Kili, 1967–68)

It was explained to us in training that Kili was not your typical island. The Bikini people lived there and we were told that they complained a lot. They didn't know much English but they knew enough to say, "Bikini great, Kili no good."

The people were unhappy and they told us often. But they couldn't have opened their hearts to us more. They thought that Americans were great because we had defeated the Japanese, whom they hated. They were very anxious to learn English and when they would visit us in the evenings they wouldn't let us speak Marshallese. "Speak English, speak English," they'd insist.

Conditions on Kili were desperate. They never had enough food and were shocked to see us filet a fish and throw away the remains. They ate everything. It was partly their culture, but they also couldn't afford to waste anything. They'd scour the beach for periwinkles [snails] and smash them to get the little bit of meat inside. They could buy rice and other staples from the trading ships which came every few months, but sometimes the ships would sail right by because the waves were too rough to make it in. The Kili people couldn't go out fishing for the same reason. The one thing they had plenty of was bananas and when they brought us

---

*Bikini was chosen for its proximity to the U.S. naval base on Kwajalein.

some fish we'd make them a banana cream pie. But they never asked us for any of our food, which we brought with us. [Because of the scarcity of food on many of the islands, volunteers in Micronesia were issued enough staples and canned goods to last several months.]

Despite the fact that they were eager to learn English, we noticed that the school was gradually disappearing. They were taking it apart little by little to use the materials for their houses. We wanted to rebuild it but the people resisted because this would indicate to the American government that they accepted Kili as their home, and they did not want to do anything that would make it look like they were happy.

These were displaced people. The United States government had told them that their land was needed for world peace, and now they expected to be treated fairly. We had heard that they could go back to Bikini when the radiation level was safe, but we felt that they had just been forgotten. So we wrote to our senator asking him to look into this. He referred it to somebody else, which we took as a put-off. We thought about who else we could alert and decided to write the United Nations Trusteeship Council.

[The following is from the Jenkinses' letter, dated February 15, 1968.]

. . . When the United States wanted a Pacific atoll for atomic testing, they chose Bikini. The people living there were "asked" to temporarily relocate. . . . [Kili] has now been their temporary home for twenty years! They don't want to stay on Kili, and they give many convincing arguments. We feel their arguments are worth being listened to, and we want you to be aware of their unnecessary hardships. . . .

Kili is a single island surrounded by treacherous waves. This accounts for very poor fishing and hazardous trading situations much of the year [the chief source of income for the Marshallese comes from selling coconut meat to traders who come by ship]. . . . During these months the people must buy their food from the field trip ships. . . . Generally, these ships come every three or four months. The last ship stayed sixteen hours, but because of the waves it was unable to do any trading.

. . . What advantages does Kili provide? It is described as a "lush" southern island, and there is no question that Kili gets a good deal more rain than Bikini does. . . . However, I don't think the abundant water supply impresses the Kili people as much today for they realize that rain brings swamps and swamps are breeding grounds for mosquitoes. Now they face the problems of infections from the mosquitoes and flies; no one is without sores or scars. . . .

. . . There is now severe overcrowding with the increase in population. Sanitation has become a problem. Animals, garbage, insects, all kinds of wastes, are concentrated in this small area. . . .

For all their trouble, the Kili people received [a total of] $25,000 cash and $325,000 placed in bonds from which they receive interest. This is not a spectacularly large amount, but neither is it a trifle. As we examine the reality, however, we are less and less impressed. The money settlement was not made until 1957, ten years after they were moved! There was no retroactive clause or arrears paid. The interest from the trust fund [is] . . . exactly $12 per person. This amount is paid semiannually. It does not amount to much on an island where the cost of one gallon of kerosene is $1. These people are not satisfied; they want to go home. . . .

. . . The Kili people ask, and we hope you ask, "Why can't the Kili people return to Bikini?" We have a letter in our possession addressed to the Kili magistrate from High Commissioner Norwood [William Norwood, then the highest-ranking United States official in Micronesia]. This letter gives the people hope and confidence because in it the High Commissioner says: "It may be possible to resettle Bikini in the not too distant future. . . . Mr. Rasmussen (of the Atomic Energy Commission) told me that the Atomic Energy Commission scientists have decided that Bikini is now ready for human habitation." It is NOW READY for human habitation. This letter was dated September 1966. When is the near future? . . .

Can your council look into the Kili situation? Please don't give these people lip service. Don't just tell them you know of their problem, but help them solve it. They want to go home. We can see no reason why they should live under these conditions. If Bikini is free of radiation and is fit for human habitation, please call on the United States to return these people to their homes.

☆

The Jenkinses' letter found its way to the offices of *The Washington Post*, which ran a story about the plight of the Bikini people, titled "Islanders Miss Bikini Home."[4] *Time*, too, published an article on the incident— "They Want to Go Back to Bikini."[5] Playing a starring role in those stories were the Peace Corps' own Todd and Hope Jenkins. Congressman Theodore Kupferman, a member of the House committee that oversees the Pacific trust territories, wrote to country director John Pincetich, that "regardless of the complaints in [the Jenkinses'] letter (and as to many of the items, I cannot say that he is wrong), it is very bad for the interests of the United States for him to be communicating this complaint to the Trusteeship Council."[6] Five days later, an Interior Department official wrote to another concerned member of Congress, expressing the department's "extreme concern . . . for the Bikini people" and stating that "we in the Department of the Interior regret most seriously that Mr. Jenkins has chosen to try to help the people of Kili through an appeal to the Trusteeship Council and thereby to the press."[7]

Pincetich wrote to Todd Jenkins explaining that the Peace Corps' "mission is to serve people, within their system. . . . The proper channel for your concern is to, and through the High Commissioner. . . . The direct approach between Peace Corps volunteer and the UN is contrary to our apolitical charter, and might well be counterproductive."[8]

According to Pincetich, the whole episode boiled down to "an issue of judgment rather than political involvement. For instance, had Todd and Hope simply identified themselves as 'American teachers,' which they were, that in no way would have vitiated the thrust of their emotional plea."

Following the publicity over the Jenkinses' letter, Peace Corps regional director Jim Huttar gave a talk at a conference of volunteers cautioning them against using "special privileges" to help the Micronesians. "He cited writing to your congressman as a s.p. [special privilege] because you are a constituent," Hope Jenkins wrote in her notes. "Yet it seems to me . . . writing to your congressman is one of the responsibilities of citizenship which is greatly encouraged and esteemed. . . . Here in Micronesia, don't the same standards apply?"

In fact, Peace Corps officials in Micronesia did not believe their own scolding. "I secretly applauded what the Jenkinses did," says Huttar. Pincetich says today that his letter to the Jenkinses was "bureaucratically ritualistic—making the proper noises and moves to placate others while avoiding damage to our own operation." Another Peace Corps staffer in Micronesia, Dirk Ballendorf, wrote to the Jenkinses:

> As you can imagine, this letter of yours has caused some stir in various government circles. I want to heartily congratulate you on this accomplishment. You have acted, as I see it, as noble, honest defenders of helpless underdogs. To be cliché-ish, you have acted in accordance with what I like to refer to as "the Peace Corps spirit." More than that, you have acted like honest human beings. . . . I think it will all point to a better day for the people of Kili.[9]

Todd and Hope were not especially upset by the reprimands they received. "Officially, the Peace Corps had to slap us on the hand," says Todd. "The thing that surprised me the most was when these reporters and photographers showed up."

The White House had turned the embarrassment into a public relations coup. In August 1968, President Johnson announced that the people of Bikini could return home. "We were stunned," Jenkins said, when the news came over his shortwave radio. "Then, people were jumping and dancing and running around the island like it was New Year's Eve."

But the return home was nothing more than a week's excursion to Bikini to conduct a survey. "I think the reason that the survey was conducted," Todd wrote in his journal, "was to let the world know that the benevolent U.S. was now giving back Bikini to the rightful owners." As Todd noted, when High Commissioner Norwood came to Kili to formally invite the island leaders to participate in the survey, he suggested that he conduct the briefing outdoors for the benefit of the photographers.

"When we pulled into the lagoon, this was fabulous, you would want to call this looking like paradise," Todd wrote in his journal of their arrival at Bikini. "But one guy was crying when we pulled in because his island was completely gone, blown away. [Three of Bikini's twenty islets were vaporized.] He was an old man and he was sitting there at the railing and these tears came down his face. It wasn't going to be a simple matter of getting in a boat and going back."

At a flag-raising ceremony on the Bikini shoreline, a trust territory official offered "thanks to the U.S., where 200 million people can give back Bikini to 300 Bikinians. May the flag on the left (American) always protect flag on the right (Micronesian). . . . Phony as hell," Todd wrote.

After the Bikini trip, the Peace Corps' regional office notified the Jenkinses that they were being transferred from Kili to Majuro, the Marshall Islands district center, because Hope was about two months pregnant and therefore considered "physically vulnerable." When sufficient housing could not be secured, the Jenkinses had no choice but to resign.

## Todd Jenkins

Because the Peace Corps was upset about the "political incident," they were not assisting us in getting housing. We found three places on our own and asked the Peace Corps to approve them, but something would always happen and the arrangements would fall through. We were due to go on vacation then and we told the staff that if there was housing available when we got back, we'd stay, but if there wasn't, we'd resign. When we returned from our vacation I asked the staff person, "Do you have a house for us?" "No," he said. So I said, "We're leaving."

Even when we left the Peace Corps, we still thought it was very worthwhile, and we thought our writing to the UN was a good thing. It got a lot of reaction. The government had to do something. The Kili people had to do something. They had to go back, see what was left, and open their eyes. It's not paradise.

☆

In 1969, 145 Bikinians resettled but in 1978 they were found to have unsafe levels of cesium, a radioactive metal, in their systems and were evacuated. "Maybe Todd's petition made it possible for those one hundred forty-five to return," says John Pincetich. "But at best it appears to have been a mixed blessing with a high price tag." In April 1988, ground-breaking ceremonies were held on Bikini to inaugurate a $30-million construction program that will eventually lead to resettlement. High levels of cesium are still concentrated in the soil and vegetation, and ways of removing it—either by potassium inputs or stripping off the topsoil, or a combination of the two—are being considered.

A Navy lawyer, Lieutenant Commander Howard Hills, working with the State Department Office on Pacific Island Affairs, said at the time of the ground-breaking that it was "time the Bikinians became self-reliant and stopped being the perpetual victims." The Reagan administration, he said, was seeking to end "handouts" to the Bikinians and allow them to plan their resettlement and pay for it themselves with a government-furnished trust fund.[10]

*Chapter 4*

☆===

# *The Dominican Republic, 1965: The Peace Corps Versus the War Corps*

In May 1965, when the people of Santo Domingo, the capital of the Dominican Republic, took to the streets in an attempt to overthrow the military-backed government of Reid Cabral and reinstate exiled President Juan Bosch, the State Department advised the White House that the uprising was the work of communist insurgents. President Johnson called out the Marines to assist the right-wing military leaders in preventing "another Cuba." The preventive measure lasted four months and cost the Dominican Republic 2,850 lives and the United States 28 lives.

Rather than evacuate, Peace Corps volunteers and staff stayed in Santo Domingo during the uprising, literally dodging bullets as they cared for their wounded Dominican friends in the city's hospitals. To volunteer Kirby Jones, this commitment proved that "the Peace Corps idea worked, that American kids had something different to offer." In the Peace Corps' *Volunteer* magazine, the agency congratulated itself for "demonstrating that it could cross battle lines in war as it had previously crossed ideological lines in peace."[1]

While the Peace Corps was proud of its volunteers' heroism in the Dominican Republic, many of these same volunteers thought that President Johnson's decision to intervene on the side of the military commanders was a grave mistake, and they were shocked and ashamed to be administering medical help to Dominicans who had been wounded by American soldiers. Volunteers were aghast when President Johnson explained that the United States had intervened because a popular democratic revolution had been pirated by Communist conspirators. Backing his explanation, the CIA produced a list of fifty-eight suspected plotters. "The list really burned me," says Associate Peace Corps Director B. J. Warren. "The head of the maternity hospital was on it, and several of the others on the list were dead, in jail, or out of the country."

The Marine intervention, said Peace Corps nurse Alice Meehan to a reporter, "has set back by 50 years the image of the United States we were trying to build."[2] One *Washington Post* story quoted a volunteer's estimate that 90 percent of their contingent regarded the intervention as a terrible blunder.[3]

President Johnson was furious over volunteers' criticism of the intervention. Yet at the same time, State Department officials were deeply impressed by the ease with which volunteers mixed among "the unclean Bosch crowd."* They hit upon the idea of teaming Corpsmen with their own personnel to travel around the country and collect information on Dominican sentiment after the uprising. Sargent Shriver rejected the proposal.

Following the uprising, the phrase "the Peace Corps versus the war corps" caught on around agency headquarters, and Shriver jumped at the suggestion made by two former State Department advisers that the Peace Corps dispatch legions of volunteers to compensate for the military intervention. Officials discussed sending one thousand volunteers, which would have been the Corps' largest contingent anywhere, to one of the smallest countries in which it operated. The idea, however, was scrapped quickly. Despite the volunteers' heroic efforts during the civil war, Dominican affection for the Peace Corps was waning. "Our pupils are scared to work with us," said one volunteer following the invasion. "It isn't considered proper now to associate with Americans." Another volunteer told a reporter, "Before we were very popular. Now people won't even talk to us."[4]

---

*"The unclean Bosch crowd" was a derogatory expression used by the United States embassy officials in Santo Domingo to describe the barrio residents who supported the return of Juan Bosch.

## *Hazel Vespa (Dominican Republic, 1963–65)*

(The following passage is from a letter Vespa wrote to her parents six weeks after arriving in Santo Domingo.)

Our humility as Americans is . . . aroused by our daily experiences in this country of chaotic transition between a thirty-three-year-old despotism and a vision of political-economic democracy. . . . We work in urban squatter neighborhoods in which our goal is to help residents identify, rank, and solve what they consider to be their own community problems—where there are four thousand people living in six to nine square blocks of one-story wood, cement, tin, cardboard, and banana-leaf houses. This neighborhood has only about five public water faucets, one five-room school for two thousand school-aged children, no recreational facilities, no accessible medical facilities, few electric lights, and only about sixty to one hundred dollars a month family income. . . . The destiny of these people will be determined not nearly so much by us, as by the political and economic policies of the United States, Dominican Republic, Common Market, and Communist nations.

## *Karen Clough (Dominican Republic, 1963–65)*

I was first assigned to be the string bassist in the Dominican Republic National Symphony, but as it turned out, I would have been taking a job from a Dominican musician so I was assigned to do community development in Santo Domingo. The Peace Corps gave me a volleyball and told me to go play with the children in order to ingratiate myself in the barrio. I got rid of the volleyball and used the skills I had as a musician. I had an alto recorder with me and since it was just after Christmas I started playing "Jingle Bells." That's how I made my breakthrough in the community, singing "Jingle Bells" in Spanish.

Soon after that I became interested in public health because I got very ill there myself. I wrote songs about parasites and we made a little filmstrip about them. For another project, I gave some parasite medicine to the mother of the child with the biggest belly I could find [a distended stomach is symptomatic of parasites], and I told her that I wanted that parasite when it came out. She thought I was nuts, but she brought over the worm, which was at least a foot long. I put it in a jar of formalin and hauled it around to show people. It was a very successful campaign.

## Hazel Vespa

There was a Dominican lady named Lucy who lived a couple houses from us in the barrio and she had a dream of teaching cooking and sewing to young girls, ten- to thirteen-year-olds. I worked with her and we started a very basic cooking class. Cooking over charcoal, I figured out how to make pancakes and then banana pancakes and then banana doughnuts, which were a bit hit. She got the sewing class together with her one sewing machine and I helped her write a grant application to the Dominican department of education for two more sewing machines.

They subsequently invited her to a one-week training course in home economics. There happened to be a *publico* [communal taxi] strike the week of the course, so she walked the five miles each way to get to the classes.

The girls in her sewing class wanted to make maternity clothes for their first project. I was constantly writing home, for example: "The next time you go shopping would you look for maternity patterns, and since cloth is very expensive here, please look for the ones with the least amount of cloth."

## Lynda Edwards (Dominican Republic, 1964–66)

The people in my barrio thought I must be a prostitute since prostitutes are the only women who live by themselves. One day a delegation of three women came to visit me and said, "Although you're a prostitute, you never get pregnant." A light bulb went on in my head and I decided that I would play along. "I have a special method," I told them, "a saline-soaked sponge." I also told them about the well-baby clinic which gave out these things and I explained the rhythm method.

After that day, the neighborhood women would come to my house one or two at a time. Some would come right out with it and ask, "Where's the clinic?" But most were a little embarrassed. "We heard that you could tell us some things about health," they would say. So we'd make small talk for a while before they broached the topic. We would talk about the weather and then get to how hard it was to feed so many children and get them all through school. "Sometimes you can limit a family," I would say. "Isn't that good?" Some women didn't know how you got pregnant. They thought you'd get pregnant if you ate spaghetti with lemon. When I explained it to them, they thought it was a tremendous joke.

Volunteers were prohibited from talking about birth control but I was discreet. If the Peace Corps told me to stop, I don't think I would have and I might have been sent home.

☆

The Dominican Republic had gone through seven governments since Rafael Leonidas Trujillo's CIA-assisted assassination in 1961. The administration of President Reid Cabral, the last before the uprising, was squeezing an already impoverished country with strict austerity measures and provoking the army by slashing defense spending and cracking down on corruption.

On the morning of April 24, 1965, a group of young army officers rebelled. They took over the government-run radio and television stations and announced the demise of the Cabral government, and the imminent return of their exiled president, Juan Bosch. In the barriors of Santo Domingo, the news was cause for celebration. "The men in my neighborhood drink this rum called Old Stick," recalls Karen Clough. "They said, 'Come on and have some.' That was the first hint I got that there was a revolution going on. Everyone was happy."

The pro-Bosch officers distributed an estimated twenty thousand guns to the people of Santo Domingo, who took to the streets to defend Bosch's return against the Loyalist officers and troops led by Colonel Elias Wessin y Wessin, who had led the 1963 ouster of President Bosch. "There were twelve-year-olds walking around with guns," recalls one volunteer.

### Kirby Jones (Dominican Republic, 1963–65)

It was just like in the movies, people were crouching behind telephone poles shooting at the police station. You could hear machine-gun fire and you could see Wessin's planes dive-bombing the Duarte Bridge. [The Duarte Bridge crossed the Ozama River, which separated the rebel-controlled downtown area of Santo Domingo from Wessin's stronghold, the San Isidro air force base on the opposite side.]

### B.J. Warren (Associate Peace Corps Director, Dominican Republic, 1964–67)

As more and more firearms got passed out, we manned the Peace Corps office twenty-four hours a day. We joked about whether to sleep on the first floor and possibly get caught in a crossfire, or sleep on the second floor and get caught in the strafing runs.

We got a lot of calls from Dominicans asking us to please send in the Marines. I assumed, as did the volunteers, that if the Marines did come in, they would land on the side of the constitutionalist [pro-Bosch] forces because the U.S. government had put so much effort into helping the Bosch government [through President Kennedy's Latin American aid program, the Alliance for Progress]. I figured we'd want to back our investment. But it was clear which side the Marines were on because they landed at San Isidro. I was mad when I learned this and felt very betrayed. It made me embarrassed to be an American official.

At one point, the staff had to work out of the embassy offices because there was too much fighting where the Peace Corps offices were. I recall stepping outside the embassy building once and all of a sudden these two Dominican women came running up carrying a sheet between them with a little twelve-year-old boy in it, dead. The Marines had opened fire and shot this little guy.

### Lynda Edwards

My neighbors were at my house watching Wessin y Wessin's planes strafing the city. Then we saw these two huge troop carrier planes coming and we knew it could only be the U.S. My neighbors were so happy. "The Americans are coming to help us," they said. But I knew the United States was going to come down on the wrong side. I felt my heart break.

☆

In six days the United States military presence in the Dominican Republic increased from 405 to 14,000. "I remember seeing 'Go Home, Yankee,' scrawled on the walls that week," remembers Peace Corps staff member Steve Honore. "I'd never seen anything like that. It made me feel terrible."

### Lynda Edwards

It was not good to be an American in Santo Domingo at that time, and I didn't think there was any way I was going to get out of the barrio. But Steve Honore, one of the Peace Corps staff people, came to collect us. He dressed as a Red Cross technician. It took a lot of guts, though, because it was a scary time to be out.

I was told later by my neighbors that after I had left the barrio, a group of angry Dominicans had come for me. Perhaps they wouldn't have hurt me, but I wouldn't want to bet on it.

## Hazel Vespa

(From a letter to her parents dated May 2, 1965)

We're told that you have received at least three telegrams informing you of our safety here in the Dominican Republic, where a popular (though somewhat lawless) revolution is now being crushed by the U.S. Marines helping the powerful Dominican Air Force and Navy. . . . Though we were often close to centers of fighting and concerned that either we or our Dominican friends might be injured accidentally, we wanted to stay in the barrio for as long as practical because we wanted to let [our Dominican neighbors] know that we were fully behind their struggle for social justice no matter what other Americans or our government said or did.

## Kirby Jones

Word had come that there were going to be anti-American demonstrations in the area of the city where I was. The Peace Corps told me, "Go to the nearest hospital," their theory being that hospitals were safe places to be. The hospital closest to me was a mile and a half away and I knew that once I left my neighborhood, where people knew me, it would become very dicey. So I made a red cross, put on a white coat, and carried my Peace Corps medical kit, hoping that I'd be taken for a doctor. It worked.

The hospital scene was unbelievable. There were shot-up bodies wall to wall, in the corridors, on the stairs, some dead, some half-alive, with every range of injury. Other volunteers were already there when I arrived. We did everything from making and folding bandages to carrying the dead down to the morgue. Most of the time there was no electricity, so I was holding flashlights over the operating table while the doctors tried to find the bullets. I remember holding the flashlight while some guy had his leg amputated.

## Lynda Edwards

We were treating people who were horribly wounded. I saw a lot of gore but I just didn't look much. I picked up the bedpans and the dressing pans and rinsed them out. I never understood the expression "the smell of blood" until that experience.

## Karen Clough

A Dominican at the hospital said to me, "This is our revolution. What are you doing here?"

A shell came through the window and my head happened to be tilted to one side. Otherwise I would have been hit. I worked in the operating room holding flashlights and at one point, the surgeon asked me if I'd like to do some suturing.

I never panicked, although I did feel queasy when a man whose leg had been shot off was brought in. The severed leg was lying right there beside him on the stretcher. One of the volunteers who was working at the hospital had a breakdown and had to be airlifted out. A man brought in his son who had a bad head injury; his brain was coming out. The father said, "Let me take him and put him in a coffin." We had to keep telling him, "He's not dead yet."

All the volunteers had caffeine addictions because we were too lazy to boil our water. So we just drank Coke and coffee to keep ourselves going. Then all the female volunteers started menstruating at the same time and none of us had any Tampax. We were also all out of cigarettes. We tried to bathe in the hospital and since we had no clean clothes to put on, we walked around wrapped in sheets.

☆

While on a brief trip to Puerto Rico from his assignment in the Dominican Republic, *New York Times* reporter Tad Szulc shopped for "under-clothes—brassieres and panties and what-have-you" for the volunteers working in the hospitals. He later dedicated his book on the uprising, *Dominican Diary*, "to the Peace Corps volunteers of Santo Domingo."[5]

## Kirby Jones

I had been at the hospital six days when about ten new wounded were brought in. Among them was this one girl, about eleven or twelve years old, whose hand was shot half off. At that point I knew I'd had it. I could not take this anymore. The Peace Corps office was rotating volunteers in and out of the hospitals so I called up and said I wanted to leave on the next jeep out. They said, "Okay, we'll put you in another hospital." I said, "No, I'm not going to another hospital."

## Steve Honore (Associate Peace Corps Director, Dominican Republic, 1963–66)

At one point we thought the hospitals might not be safe very much longer, so I was ordered to collect the volunteers. But most of them refused to leave, and when the Dominican doctors found out what I was doing they practically surrounded me and said, "You can't take these girls. If they leave, we might as well close the hospital down." I explained my orders and that the volunteers might be in danger. They said they wouldn't be in danger because they don't allow anyone in the building with arms. "Even if somebody did come in to harm them," they said, "we would protect them with our own lives."

## Kirby Jones

A bunch of volunteers were staying in an abandoned girls' boarding school for the duration of the fighting and we were looking for something to do. Wessin's forces had cut off all traffic into the city which cut off the food supply in the barrios. Four of us took a couple of Peace Corps trucks and went down to the AID and CARE warehouses, loaded up with these huge bags of grain, and drove out to the barrios. Francisco Caamaño, leader of the pro-Bosch faction, had heard about the volunteers' work in the hospitals and announced on the radio that we were the only Americans who would be allowed in areas of the city controlled by his forces.

Those food runs to the barrios made us much more aware of what was really going on. To get to the barrios we had to pass through several U.S. and rebel checkpoints, and we saw for ourselves that what the U.S. said it was doing—remaining neutral in the conflict—was totally at odds with what was actually happening.* U.S. forces were allowing Wessin's men to pass through U.S. checkpoints and enter the rebel-held areas of the city. I watched this happen at one checkpoint and then later that day I heard an army press officer categorically deny it.

## Lynda Edwards

We felt the need to make a protest, that the invasion was a mistake. And who better than we to make that point publicly? We were right there with

---

*The official explanation for the Marines' presence was as a peacekeeping body, to protect American property, and to evacuate Americans and other foreign nationals who wished to leave.

the people and we knew they wanted their constitutionally elected president back and their constitutional government back.

☆

The following is an excerpt from a letter sent to President Johnson and Sargent Shriver from a group of volunteers in Santo Domingo. The group also planned to release it to the press.

> We the undersigned Peace Corps Volunteers have been living and working with the Dominican populace in order to facilitate democratic institutions and to encourage the yearning for social justice. . . . Our Dominican experience convinces us that the Constitutionalist Forces have overwhelming popular sympathy. . . . Though few persons disagreed with sending a limited contingent of U.S. troops to evacuate foreigners and protect the embassy, it has seemed from the beginning that the U.S. military action has backed the rightist military juntas. . . . We are firmly convinced that for both the United States and the Dominican Republic, U.S. commitment to the Dominican Constitutionalists fulfills long-range mutual self-interest.

When the letter arrived at the White House, Frank Mankiewicz, Peace Corps regional director for Latin America, recalls that President Johnson's aide Bill Moyers phoned him and said, "You better go down there and shut those [Peace Corps] guys up, or the President's going to pull them all out."[6] Mankiewicz flew down to the Dominican Republic, and, as Kirby Jones recalls, told the volunteers that "the President knew how we felt, and that if we released our letter to the press he'd pull us out. Mankiewicz left the decision to us and we didn't release the letter. Maybe we were chickenshit, but I felt very satisfied after the meeting. I shook Mankiewicz's hand at the door."

## Lynda Edwards

I had nothing but contempt for Frank Mankiewicz. I had heard him say more than once that if there was ever a revolution, he expected to see the volunteers on the barricades. I later understood that he was keeping us from getting kicked out, but at the time I thought he was a hypocrite and a windbag. It must have been very difficult for him to ask us not to give the letter to the press.

## Fran Johnson (Dominican Republic, 1963–65)

I refused to sign the letter to President Johnson. I felt we didn't know everything about the situation and why the United States had intervened. I felt Caamaño [leader of the pro-Bosch faction] was a Communist. Other volunteers didn't speak Spanish as well as I. The Dominicans I talked to thought the Americans did the right thing. They thought the rebels were a lot of hotbloods who had ties to Cuba. The other volunteers wouldn't speak to me or eat dinner with me. It was fashionable to be anti-American. That was part of it.

## Karen Clough

I was working in a hospital when I heard about the letter to President Johnson but I didn't really care about the more esoteric parts of the war. I was more concerned with our patients and preserving my own life. I thought about the Monroe Doctrine, though. Here we were, the big hotshit country and the Monroe Doctrine says that we'll go into Latin America and we take care of them and conquer them when we have to. I wondered if we really have any right to do that. But then I thought, "The Marines are the ones with the food," which I needed, so I wanted to make friends with them.*

☆

After four months of sporadic fighting, the rebels were exhausted and the United States finally cut off the flow of money and arms that sustained Wessin's forces. The Organization of American States designated Hector Garcia-Godoy, a Dominican businessman and diplomat, as provisional president.

## Hazel Vespa

When we went back to our barrio, we found that our house was being occupied by one of Wessin's officers. One of the families I was closest to had been killed, the parents and all seven children.

The army had come through and arrested all the boys between thirteen

---

*The Marines delivered rations and medical supplies to volunteers working in the city's hospitals.

and nineteen. Many of them had been in the scout troop my husband worked with. We got a family we knew to cook a lunch for us to take to the prison. My husband brought it inside and was gone two hours. As it turned out, the prison officials decided to release five of the boys to him. We brought them back to the barrio and their mothers were crying. That was our last night in the Dominican Republic.

It was hard to decide if what we had accomplished was of any consequence in light of the civil war and the U.S. intervention. Then we learned that the Peace Corps was going to send in a thousand volunteers as a response to those events. It was hard to decipher what those thousand volunteers really signified.

*Chapter 5*

☆═══

# *Exporting the American Revolution: The Peace Corps and the Nigerian-Biafran War*

In 1960, seventeen European colonies in Africa declared independence. The nationalist movement sweeping across the continent in the 1950s and 1960s drew much of its inspiration from the American struggle for independence from Great Britain, and Sargent Shriver believed that Peace Corps volunteers in Africa were helping to pass the torch of freedom. "The President is counting on you," he told the first group of volunteers headed for Ghana and Tanganyika.* "It's up to you to prove that the concepts and ideals of the American Revolution are still alive."[1]

Until the early 1960s, Africa was of marginal interest to Washington. During the Eisenhower years, fewer than fifty American diplomats were stationed on the continent, and in its few dealings with Africa, the State Department routinely deferred to the policies of the European colonial powers. But in 1961, Sargent Shriver told the heads of state of the newly independent nations of Americans' eagerness to come live among their

---

*Tanganyika, a UN trust territory under the stewardship of Great Britain and Zanzibar, was a British protectorate. Zanzibar achieved independence in 1963, Tanganyika in 1964, and together they became the new country Tanzania.

hat they know. Two years later, over one thousand
rs were participating intimately in the day-to-day life
endent or soon to be independent African countries.
volunteers in Africa were assigned to teach in high
n which Peace Corps officials took great pride. By
ty of nascent governments to educate their citizens,
the Corps was playing a vital role in the postcolonial era. Providing teachers "was just the kind of assistance to a country that wants to move fast and far and wide which the Peace Corps was born for," said one country director in Africa at the time.[2] Shriver didn't hesitate to boast about how much the volunteer teachers were appreciated. "Ethiopians say the Peace Corps can have more effect on that country than anything in the last four hundred years," he stated in a 1962 interview. "It can be the catalyst for the greatest change in Ethiopia's modern history."[3]

The Peace Corps also predicted that volunteer teachers would make a significant contribution to newly independent Nigeria. A nation of 56 million people, with a parliamentary government and a sound economy based on petroleum, palm oil, and cocoa exports, Nigeria, in 1961, seemed poised for a rapid and distinguished entrance into the world community. By 1966, Nigeria hosted 742 volunteers, the largest Peace Corps contingent in Africa.

Peace Corps teachers tried to introduce independent thinking in their classrooms and wean their students from British rote methods that, despite independence, were standard practice. Many of them also attempted to amend those syllabuses that acculturated African students to British civilization.

Nigeria's chief obstacle to progress was, in fact, its colonial legacy. When European rulers staked out their African holdings, Nigeria's borders were drawn around three distinct tribal nations: the Ibo in the south and east, the Hausa in the north, and the Yoruba in the west. After Nigeria declared its independence from England in 1960, tensions between the Hausas and the Ibos strained the new country's tenuous national unity. In 1966, thousands of Ibos were massacred. Then, finally, there was a two and a half year civil war. "I was heartbroken," remembers Jon Kwitny (Nigeria, 1965–67), "not only for these people, but what was happening to the country. It was the demise of what we went over there to try to help build."

Depending on where volunteers lived in Nigeria they took the side of either the Ibos or the Hausas, and it was not uncommon for them to develop prejudices. "The volunteers from the north discounted the fact of the massacres," says Janis Bianchi (Nigeria, 1965–67), who served in the eastern region. "They wanted to sweep it under the rug and say it really wasn't as bad as everybody said it was, and that the Ibos brought it on themselves." Another volunteer who served in the eastern region recalls that a friend serving in the north stopped writing to her "because if I supported them [the Ibos], then I wasn't being a reasonable person, so there was no sense in pursuing this friendship."

Seething hostility burst forth in January 1966 when Ibo army officers murdered Nigeria's Hausa leaders and established a provisional military government. Six months later, Hausa officers ousted the new Ibo government. When reconciliation talks failed, the Ibo homeland seceded from Nigeria and declared itself the Independent Republic of Biafra. Civil war broke out and over two hundred Peace Corps volunteers in the eastern and midwest regions had to evacuate.

Over the next few years, as the war continued, Nigeria requested fewer volunteers. Safety considerations warranted prudence, but it was political tit for tat that ultimately led to the program's demise. The United States government had refused to sell arms to Nigeria, and the American public was squarely on the side of Biafra. The exhilaration of sharing one's Revolutionary heritage and advancing African independence turned into dejection as volunteers watched from the sidelines as far greater forces determined Nigeria's future.

## Monica Greeley (Nigeria, 1966–67)

We got to Nigeria the day after the first coup, but my eagerness to get to my site overshadowed the political situation. My site was so remote that volunteers from other organizations had turned it down. As I was driving in, people along the road would wave and call out "Father" because the only other white people they had ever seen before were missionaries.

The teachers and students were extraordinarily gracious and outgoing. On Saturday mornings a few girls would sit outside my front door and study quietly till I got up. They were very grateful that I was there. The school was only three years old and my being there meant there would be a third and fourth form. Since the building was still under construction when I arrived, there wasn't even a classroom for me to use, so I would teach on the grass in one-hundred-degree sun.

## Jonathan Kwitny (Nigeria, 1965–67)

I was assigned to teach English and literature in forms four and five, which are the last two grades before graduation. These years are spent studying for the West African school certificate exams. We were assigned four books to read over the two years: a play by Shakespeare which had to be analyzed line by line, a novel by Dickens or Jane Austen, some poetry, and maybe something more modern and African.

I really wanted the students to read something that was written in a more current use of English because you'd get in their essays, "I take pen in hand in the year of our lord . . ." If that's what they're reading and we're calling that great literature, that's what comes back. So the next year I taught forms two and three, which had no obligatory reading lists. I set up a syllabus that met my two criteria: first, that you read quickly, as you would for enjoyment; and second, that you read only books that are written as you would speak.

## Janis Bianchi (Nigeria, 1965–67)

The town of Nimo had a feeling more like a county than a town. There were a lot of palm trees and rolling hills. It was hot but not unbearable and there was a breeze. There was a little market that I visited once a week, and there was a post office and bar and the rest of it was farmland.

My house was a concrete-block duplex in the boys school compound. I had a steward who shopped and cooked for me. I had to insist that he prepare some African dishes for me. He considered his European cooking a skill, but not his African cooking. He'd make the same things I would eat at home: fried chicken, vegetables, pork chops.

We didn't have a library at the school but we got a bunch of British and American books from Canada, maybe two thousand, new and used, and we created a library. The boys complained when we had to read poetry, but they absolutely loved Dickens. They would take nicknames from characters. Lots of kids were called the Artful Dodger. They would change their names from month to month.

## Bunny Meyer (Nigeria, 1967–70)

I was completely comfortable when I traveled around in the north. I never worried about my safety. When I traveled down in the south, which was much more Westernized, I was nervous. There's an oversimplification of northern Nigeria as backward and southern Nigeria as progressive. The north was steeped in tradition that wasn't erased by the influence of Christianity or Western thought.* It's a much quieter and simpler way of life.

There was something about the beauty of the little things in life that really came home to me. The woman who was my closest friend lived with her husband and his three other wives. In a traditional Islamic society, women in their childbearing years stay within the family compound during the day. I remember thinking that was terrible and that it must feel like prison. But she was a very joyous and loving woman who just lived very differently.

### Bill Brownell (Nigeria, 1965–66)

My personal allegiance was to the Ibos. They were the most American in their attitudes towards life. They were aggressive in business and had a keenness about education. Hausas were extremely alien.

I was hitching in the eastern region and an Ibo pharmacist picked me up in his Mercedes. We became close friends. He was thirty-three years old and a hard-core capitalist. He used to pop amphetamines to keep going. He lived in a two-story house, which was unusual in Aba [a town in the eastern region], and he had a TV and a stereo. We talked about his business and his concern about his kids' education. He wanted to know what it was like to grow up in the United States. We used to get very drunk on palm wine, which cost about twenty-five cents a gallon and tasted like oranges and coconuts.

☆

After Hausa army officers removed the short-lived Ibo government in July 1966, Hausa resentment against the Ibos touched off a series of massacres. According to one estimate, thirty thousand Ibos were killed and one million fled back to their homeland in the eastern region.

### Tom McGrew (Nigeria, 1964–67)

The Hausas, at first, were docile about the Ibos murdering their leaders in the first coup. I didn't see how upset they were for a couple of months, when they began expressing their thoughts about "the damn Ibos."

---

*Missionaries to Nigeria concentrated their efforts in the eastern region.

Everyone knew there would be trouble for the Ibos. The word was all over town. Initially, it was just going to be a demonstration, but it turned into an organized mob of hundreds of people going through the Ibo quarter beating up shopkeepers, stoning their children, looting, and threatening their lives. I actually stood within feet of the stone throwing.

It wasn't scary—it was sad. I came to Africa with a whole lot of very idealistic fantasies about what the Peace Corps could do and what Nigeria could do for itself. After that day, a new section opened in the market where they sold the stuff that had been looted. In a month's time there were no Ibos. They had fled for their lives.

### Jonathan Kwitny

When the Ibo shops started to close up, you realized all the people you had been depending on were Ibos, like the man who delivered the gas canister and who sold candles when the electricity went out. Things just ground to a halt. Reuben, an Ibo carpenter who was making a box for me to take my stuff home in, broke down and cried in my house about what was happening. I offered to let him stay with me but he had a big contract he had to finish and then he was going to get out. He'd lived in Benin City for years and suddenly, because he was an Ibo, he had to go.

Many of my students helped their Ibo friends get out. Others wound up in the army shooting them. There were Ibo students I never heard from again. Sam O'Feeley was maybe the best student I had: He was brilliant, clever, courteous, and an athlete. I was told he was literally fleeing on foot.

There was a gas station a hundred yards from my house and these big trucks would pull up, some crammed with as many as eighty people, all of them Ibos coming from the north and heading toward the eastern region. I'd hear these stories about crowds chasing them, chanting anti-Ibo slogans, and routing them out in the middle of the night, jumping out the back window carrying the baby. It was horrifying and tragic. We loved Nigeria and had such hopes for the country. It was a second home.

### Robert Feldman (Nigeria, 1967; Kenya, 1967–68)

I grew up in a kosher home in a Jewish neighborhood in Brooklyn. I was bar mitzvahed there and went to Brooklyn College. I didn't want to be in a Jewish environment anymore so I went to Nigeria.

I discovered that in parts of Nigeria, the stereotype of the Ibo was very similar to the stereotype of Jews in New York: They worked too hard to make money and tried to cheat people. In fact, it was usually an Ibo who owned the "cold store," the one store in town that had a refrigerator. Having grown up in New York, I also understood tribalism. The blacks, the Puerto Ricans, the Irish, the Italians, and the Jews each had their own areas and each thought they were better than the others. It was the same in Nigeria.

I then saw this booklet, "Nigeria Pogrom: Crisis 1966," which contained photos of the atrocities [taking place in the north]. It reminded me of the fact that my grandparents fled the pogrom in Russia in 1905.

The similarities between the Ibos in Nigeria and the Jews in Nazi Germany were also very real to me. What if I were confronted with an Ibo in jeopardy? Would I be heroic and risk my life to hide an Ibo? I became more positive about Judaism as a result.

## Carl White (Nigeria, 1964–66)*

I worked in a government social services office in Kano [a city in the north] and heard murmurings among the Hausa administrators that they felt like the losers after the first coup. After the second coup, Hausa troops and civilians sought retribution. I recall the day that soldiers boarded a British Airways jet waiting to take off and removed all the Ibo passengers. Then they lined them up on the runway and shot them. After that, they went to the Ibo section of the city and started killing. We could hear the shooting and screaming.

The next morning, as I rode into the city on my motorcycle, I saw corpses lying in the streets and lots of Hausas walking along with loads of furniture and household things. They had been looting the Ibo quarters. As I came through the hospital gates that morning, I saw rows of twenty or thirty bodies lined up and garbage trucks were pulling up filled with still more bodies. It was the worst thing I have ever witnessed. I heard that a thousand people had been killed.

There were mobs of people at the train station trying to get away, so I went to try to help in some way. It was total chaos; hundreds of people were literally climbing over each other to get on the trains. People were hysterical and frightened to death they wouldn't be able to get out. I gave people money for tickets, and located kids who got separated from their parents in the crowd.

The following day, the Ibo quarter was completely empty. It used to

---

*To protect current business interests in Nigeria, the volunteer requested that his real name not be used.

be bustling with activity. In the rest of the city, life went back to normal. The Hausas wanted to put it behind them.

I didn't root for either side. The issues were extremely complex and I didn't feel I knew them well enough to take sides. I just hoped it would be over soon.

## Ned Greeley (Nigeria, 1966–67)

(Ned Greeley and Monica Newland were married shortly after their return from Nigeria.)

There was a systematic attempt at my school to drum into the students, all of whom were Ibo, the threat they were living under. The message was "We're going through a period of trouble. We're probably going to have to fight and you have to get ready." The whole school would go to these rallies where they were taught civil rights songs like "We Shall Overcome."

I was very pro-Biafra, but at the same time I thought it was terrible that Nigeria had to be in this situation.

## Monica Greeley

The children at the church-run girls school where I taught in the eastern region were protected from the conflict until they were told during the morning prayers that they could poison little Hausa girls the same way anybody else might and that they had a special role to play. This didn't go on very long because the school closed when the fighting was about to break out.

We were hoping to make some contribution, but in this situation we had absolutely no voice whatsoever. We weren't symbols to them, and they certainly weren't asking our advice on instructing kids in how to kill other kids.

## Janis Bianchi

We evacuated in August, just as the Biafran troops were invading the midwest.* We had a couple of hours to get our stuff out. It wasn't unex-

---

*The first major offensive of the war came in August 1967, when Biafran forces moved into the neighboring midwest region in order to prevent the Nigerian government's use of that area as a staging ground for attacks on Biafra.

pected: The Peace Corps staff had been telling us not to go very far from our sites and to let them know where we were. On the other hand, the Peace Corps had told the government of Biafra that we would not leave unless our security was jeopardized, that we would stay despite secession. A lot of volunteers got angry because they didn't think we were in any danger. We felt a great loyalty to the Ibos. We also had these somewhat romantic notions that we could set up first aid stations and be useful in some way, like Ernest Hemingway running around Spain.

## Ned Greeley

The Peace Corps gave me a van and told me to pick up six volunteers within a sixty-mile area. The war had just broken out and all the people were scared. There was a roadblock at every intersection and I had to get out of the van at each one and explain that I was a teacher in a school in that area and that I was going to pick up these people. "Please let me go," I would say. One of the volunteers I picked up had been beaten up a little bit in the market. The people were mad that he was being pulled out. Seeing the Peace Corps leave was a sign that something really serious was happening.

The most difficult part was getting from Enugu [the capital city of the eastern region] to Port Harcourt on the Atlantic coast [a distance of almost two hundred miles]. We had a convoy of forty jeeps and we had to get through several dozen roadblocks. The local peasants who manned them were drinking palm wine all day and could be pretty excitable. A couple of times we had guns pointing at us.

I was reassigned to a rural development post in Niger, but when I got there I realized I had such an emotional investment in Biafra that I just didn't have the energy to plug into another country. Around that time I saw pictures of Detroit burning, and I asked myself, "How can I be out here when things are going so badly in the States?"

## Monica Greeley

One of the Peace Corps staff people came to my site and told me that they were a little worried about what might happen over the coming weekend and suggested I pack a small bag and stay with a friend. That Sunday afternoon, we received word that the volunteers were supposed to go to Port Harcourt and prepare for departure from the east. When we got there I was quite vocal about having been conned out of my home without being able to say good-bye or pack some things that were important to me. One of my most treasured possessions was a bust of John F. Kennedy. They told me I couldn't go back because I might not be able to get out again.

☆

Even though the volunteers felt helpless during the civil war, their commitment to Biafra continued after their Peace Corps service. "I knew what happened to my site from watching the news," recalls Monica Greeley. "They'd show maps of the areas where people were starving and I tried to pick out my students in the pictures I saw." Ned Greeley and Jon Kwitny testified before Congress about supplying aid to Biafra, and Janis Bianchi worked for the Committee for Nigerian Biafran Relief with other former volunteers. "The library I started was destroyed," says Bianchi, "and a fair number of my students were killed fighting with the Biafran Army." Bill Brownell sent his friend the pharmacist an invitation to his wedding but it was returned. "I never found out what happened to him," Brownell says.

# Part Three

## The Vietnam Era

# Introduction

In 1966, as the United States dramatically escalated its forces in Vietnam, the Peace Corps planted a flag in its fiftieth country and reached a peak enrollment of 15,556 volunteers. Among those who served in 1966 were the last to sign up while President Kennedy was still alive and the first to join in search of draft deferments.

The formidable and enduring impact of the Vietnam War on the Peace Corps cut across both the Johnson and Nixon administrations—from the controversial 1967 dismissal of Bruce Murray (Chile, 1965–67), who wrote an antiwar letter published in a Chilean newspaper, to the takeover in 1970 of the Peace Corps building in Washington by an organization of radicalized ex-volunteers.

As early as 1965, the war began to cast a shadow over the Peace Corps' halo. At the University of California, Berkeley, antiwar activists were encouraging students *not* to join the Peace Corps as a show of protest. And the following year, a student at New York's Queens College wrote in the school's underground paper: "By joining the Peace Corps, one consciously and voluntarily associates himself with the same government, and becomes part of the same long-range foreign policy that daily commits unspeakable atrocities in Vietnam. . . . On a small scale the Peace Corps does fine work, but it is simultaneously a P.R. cover-up for America's international rape."[1]

Through both the Johnson and Nixon administrations, Peace Corps officials tried strenuously to safeguard the agency from the multiple shocks of the war. Jack Vaughn, Peace Corps director from 1966 to 1969, attempted to bolster waning enthusiasm for the Corps by insisting that the war in Vietnam made the Peace Corps "more real, more relevant, more urgent than it has ever been. . . . What our volunteers are doing is participating in the efforts of 56 countries to become, often against long odds, masters of their fate, rather than victims of it like Vietnam."[2]

Joe Blatchford, Vaughn's successor in the Nixon administration, tried to appease members of the House Foreign Affairs Committee who were fed up with volunteers' antiwar protests by explaining that the Corps had "inherited a very difficult situation resulting from volunteers just out of college with strong liberal views." The Peace Corps, he promised, would "weed out" these types by instituting better screening.[3]

How the war affected volunteers' experiences overseas varied from country to country. "In Nepal, the Vietnam War was just an article in *Time* magazine which we got late," says Vicki Elmer, who served in the remote kingdom from 1965 to 1967. "But when I finished my two years, an incoming trainee told me, 'It's not the way you think it is. The U.S. is really doing something wrong in Vietnam.' I was stunned." In Thailand and the Philippines, volunteers were reminded of the war, sometimes every day, by the roar of B-52 bombers flying in and out of nearby American military installations.

Elsewhere, it was the reactions of nationals and host governments to the war that had the most dramatic impact on the volunteers. Tanzania president Julius Nyerere ordered the Peace Corps to leave his country. In Ethiopia, it was not uncommon for students to ridicule volunteers as agents of cultural imperialism and accuse them of secretly working for the CIA. Some were even pelted with rocks and provoked into fistfights. The harassment got so intense that a group of volunteers wrote to the trainees preparing for Ethiopia advising them not to come. In one six-month period, 92 out of 235 Peace Corps teachers in Ethiopia had resigned.[4]

The war in Vietnam penetrated the Peace Corps' every quarter. But three distinct factors—volunteers' antiwar protests, the draft, and the Committee of Returned Volunteers (CRV)—had the most impact. Together, they would challenge many of the assumptions that had come to define the Peace Corps, and raise doubts about its unquestioned altruism.

When the Peace Corps dismissed Bruce Murray and tried to squelch antiwar protests by other volunteers, the liberals at home and Corps members around the world began to question the extent to which the organization really was, as officials insisted, a uniquely independent agency of the federal government, untainted by politics.

The war diminished the Peace Corps' glowing reputation for attracting Americans dedicated to helping others overseas, as thousands of draft-eligible men enrolled as a means of avoiding Vietnam.

The CRV, the first national organization of Peace Corps alumni, also contributed to the Corps' changing image. Founded in 1966 as a discussion group, the CRV surged to the forefront of the antiwar movement and advanced the impression that the Peace Corps was replete with hippies and radicals.

For those caught up in the antiwar movement, the urgency of stopping the war pushed the government-sponsored Peace Corps into irrelevance. For those who cherished patriotic values, the Peace Corps, with its protestors and draft dodgers, was suddenly no longer showing the world America's best.

*Chapter 6*

☆═══

# *Volunteer Protest: "Peace Is a Silent Passion"*

"What the hell is going on here?" Richard Becker (Brazil, 1966–68) wrote in an open letter to his fellow volunteers in June 1967. Becker had just received a Peace Corps bulletin stating that volunteers were prohibited from expressing themselves publicly on foreign policy issues of the United States or any other country. Although no elaboration was provided, Becker connected the bulletin to a controversy brewing in Chile. Almost a third of the volunteers there had signed an antiwar petition that they were about to send to the White House and the media. Director Jack Vaughn notified them that they would face disciplinary charges if they proceeded.

According to Peace Corps policy, volunteers could communicate their opinions on any subject to the White House, the media, and members of Congress as long as they did not in any way identify themselves as Peace Corps volunteers. In a letter to the group in Chile, Vaughn explained that their expressions "cannot include your Peace Corps connection or your foreign address, since the latter makes identification almost inevitable. Such messages," Vaughn suggested, "could be sent to your family or friends for forwarding from U.S. post offices." [1]

Becker was deeply disturbed by the policy. "For our work to have any meaning," he says, "we had to establish for ourselves that the Peace Corps wasn't just another arm of American foreign policy. There was a fear among us that we were being used as public relations." The volunteers in Chile never released the petition, but one of them, music teacher

Bruce Murray (Chile, 1965–67), was so incensed over what he felt was a violation of their First Amendment rights that he wrote a letter criticizing the Peace Corps' policy as well as the United States' involvement in Vietnam. The letter was published in a Chilean newspaper and Murray was dismissed. His expulsion from the Corps became a watershed in the organization's history.

Until the Vietnam War, the Peace Corps policy on public expression had yet to be tested. In the early 1960s, such an issue would not have even occurred to the agency's administrators. Indeed, Sargent Shriver had often gloated that the volunteers' freedom of movement and discourse was the best advertisement for the American way of life. As the war in Vietnam intensified, volunteers chose different ways of expressing their disapproval, most often in petitions to the White House and the media. More dramatic forms of protest were also employed. In Tunisia, for instance, volunteers turned their backs on Secretary of State William Rogers as he made a speech at an embassy reception. In the Dominican Republic, they marched down the main artery of the capital and bought a full-page newspaper ad for their antiwar petition. In Ethiopia, they staged a day-long vigil in front of the U.S. embassy. And volunteers in Panama, South Korea, and Venezuela chipped in to send representatives to Washington to voice their disapproval in person to members of Congress.

The tone of their petitions ranged from conciliatory—the war in Vietnam was "incompatible with the fundamental ideas underlying our service in the Peace Corps. . . . We find it increasingly difficult to represent Americans to Kenyans," read a letter to President Nixon[2]—to unrestrained contempt. "The President's verbal endorsement of the accomplishments and ideals of the Peace Corps is a hypocritical use of this organization. The government is using us as apologists for policies that run counter to the reasons for our service and the original reasons for the agency's existence," read a joint petition from volunteers in Guatemala, the Dominican Republic, Panama, and South Korea.[3]

Not all volunteers were against the war, however. Letters on file at the Lyndon Baines Johnson Library in Austin, Texas, express admiration for the President's policies in Southeast Asia and a few Peace Corps alumni signed up eagerly for the Army. Brian Walsh (Guatemala, 1965–67) felt he "owed America something" and believed that communism would spread throughout Southeast Asia if the United States didn't prevent it. David Livingston (Liberia, 1962–64), said, "Given the choice of using a piece of chalk and a blackboard in the bush, or using an M-16, I'll chose the M-16. It's a better convincer. It convinces them to do what my nation thinks is right."[4]

The Peace Corps felt compelled to squelch volunteers' protests through all manner of threats, policies, and appeals. Jack Vaughn tried to convince them that public expression of their antiwar sentiments was not a constructive way of promoting peace. "Peace is a silent passion," he wrote in the *Saturday Review* in 1968. "It is a one-on-one relationship, a quiet persuasion. Totally, it is self-discipline and self–control. In the pursuit of peace you bite your tongue 100 times for every time you speak a word."[5]

In more forceful terms, Vaughn explained that antiwar protests violated the Peace Corps' charter and jeopardized the agency's efforts. In his letter to the volunteers in Chile, Vaughn wrote:

> The Peace Corps was established as an apolitical organization and it has been our firm belief that preservation of that character is essential to its effectiveness. This has meant that . . . we avoid any official or seemingly official involvement in political matters. . . . To seek or permit such identification as a means of enhancing the significance of one's words or actions is to exploit the unique status and respect which the Peace Corps has achieved over the past six years.[6]

It became clear to many volunteers that their director's reasoning obscured the simple truth that as an agency of the executive branch, funded by Congress, the Peace Corps really wasn't an apolitical organization. When Bruce Murray was dismissed, five volunteers in Ecuador wrote to *The New York Times:* "We have been ordered to support the war in Vietnam—with our silence. . . . We have been partially deprived of our status as free agents, as representatives of the American people rather than the American government."[7]

Indeed, members of Congress on both sides of the aisle didn't share Shriver's enthusiasm about volunteers' freedom of discourse. E. Ross Adair (R-Ind.) said, "If there is a person in the Peace Corps who feels he cannot support U.S. foreign policy then he ought not to be in the Peace Corps."[8] Congressman Wayne Hays (D-Ohio) asked if American taxpayers should pay for volunteers who "make a general practice of talking against the United States."[9] Congressman Thomas E. Morgan (D-Pa.) asked if there should not be some restraints on volunteers' freedom of speech.[10] Jack Vaughn says he received "a lot of static and flak from every corner." Joe Blatchford, Peace Corps director under President Nixon, was told by the administration to quiet protests. In addition to straining relations with Congress and the White House, Peace Corps officials feared that volunteers' protests might make convenient propaganda for the government of North Vietnam, and could strain diplomatic relations by inspiring protest movements in those host countries ruled by less tolerant governments.[11]

The Peace Corps' crackdown on protests opened a breach between volunteers and officials in Washington who suspected them of using their Peace Corps affiliation as a tactic "to get publicity."[12] Meanwhile, many on staff also wanted to make known their own objections to the war. They too signed antiwar petitions and one country director in Africa was fired after he helped organize a 1969 moratorium demonstration on the lawn of the U.S. embassy.

Vaughn backed down from the first such staff-organized protest. Kirby Jones (Dominican Republic, 1963–65) was the desk officer for Ecuador in the spring of 1967 when he was approached by prominent antiwar organizer Allard Lowenstein.

## *Kirby Jones (Dominican Republic, 1963–65)*

I had lunch on the lawn in Lafayette Park [across the street from Peace Corps headquarters, just a few blocks from the White House] with Lowenstein and two or three other people. Lowenstein had organized student body presidents and Rhodes scholars in letter campaigns to President Johnson protesting the war. He wanted to work on ex-Peace Corps volunteers. I said, "Okay, let's do it." We drafted a nonconfrontational letter and I began organizing meetings and calling people around the country who started collecting signatures.

When Jack Vaughn found out, he called me up to his office and said, "You've got to stop." I said, "I can't stop." Then he went through this long song and dance about how long it had taken him to establish credibility in the White House, since Johnson had always thought of the Peace Corps as a Kennedy creation, full of Kennedyites, and that this was going to adversely affect the relationship between the Peace Corps and the White House. That didn't impress me a whole lot. Then he said it was a question of loyalty to the President. I said, "I'm sorry you feel that way, and you're going to have to fire me because I'm not going to stop."

Vaughn didn't fire me because we liked each other. I thought he was a real good Peace Corps director. If he did fire me, I would have been really ticked off and I don't think I would have silently crept away. He wouldn't have prevented anything by firing me because the letter was already well under way and it might have created an incident. He just swallowed it.

☆

Attempts were made by the Peace Corps to foil the letter campaign. The Peace Corps General Counsel Office warned one of the groups collecting signatures, the Peace Corps Committee for Peace, that use of the name Peace Corps was illegal and punishable by fine and imprisonment. And a Peace Corps spokesperson told the *Baltimore Sun* that the vast majority of former volunteers who had been approached about the letter refused to sign it.

A few months later, when 92 out of 317 volunteers in Chile signed an antiwar petition, the Peace Corps reacted decisively. Its handling of "the Bruce Murray case," as it was later referred to, ultimately cost the Peace Corps more in lost trust than it gained in appeasing the White House and Congress.

### Bruce Murray (Chile, 1965–67)

I signed the petition along with one hundred or so others. When Peace Corps administrators in Santiago found out about it, they called a meeting and told us that we couldn't sign it identifying ourselves as Peace Corps volunteers because we were employees of the United States government. I questioned this, pointing out that it was our constitutional right to sign the petition. But they were having none of that.

☆

U.S. Ambassador Ralph Dungan also met with the petition's organizers and told them that if they couldn't abide by this stipulation they should resign. The petition never appeared publicly, but Bruce Murray wrote to Jack Vaughn, Peace Corps officials in Chile, and *The New York Times* stating his objection to the Peace Corps' policy and his opposition to the war.

### Bruce Murray

*The New York Times* didn't publish my letter but UPI somehow picked up on it and wrote a story about the Peace Corps' policy on political expression which ran in *El Sur*, one of the major daily newspapers in Chile. I thought the Peace Corps had made some outrageous comments in the UPI story, so I translated into Spanish the letter I had written to the *Times*, brought it over to *El Sur*, and they published it.

(The following is an excerpt from Murray's letter:)

The volunteer, although a representative of and paid by the United States government, does not, upon entrance into the Peace Corps, automatically forfeit any of his rights under the First Amendment. . . . Also, the First Amendment does not restrict a person from using the position in which he is employed, be it Peace Corps volunteer or any other employment, on a petition or any other form of protest.

Part of the job of a Peace Corps volunteer is to give an opportunity to citizens of a foreign country to know an American citizen in all the varied aspects of his personality including his thoughts on important issues. The better understanding that can result from this interchange of ideas can be a great factor in leading to peace in the world. I find it a contradiction for the Peace Corps to try to suppress any part of the personality of the volunteer in this fashion, and I shall not tolerate such repression.

I thought the Peace Corps might get a little upset about this, but I thought it was fair to present another point of view. People who study music in school, as opposed to those who study political science, are a little more naive.

☆

The day after the letter appeared, Murray, a university music instructor, was called out of an orchestra rehearsal and given a message to go to Santiago, the capital, and report to Peace Corps country director Paul Bell immediately. Bell informed Murray that the following day he would be flying to Washington for "consultations."

## Bruce Murray

Paul and I had a very amicable discussion. I asked if I was being "terminated" and he stressed that I wasn't. I assumed I would be returning to Chile until I got off the plane in Washington. My luggage had gotten lost, so I had to fill out some forms for the airline. As I started writing down my address in Chile, the Peace Corps rep who had met my flight said, "No. Don't do that. You're not going back."

I thought he didn't know what he was talking about. But then, when I got to Peace Corps headquarters, the Chile desk officer said I *was* there for termination. This was when I got mad. It was explained to us in training that being apolitical meant that you didn't mingle in the politics of the host country. If I had been campaigning for the Christian Democratic party, I would be violating the rules. But being apolitical hardly means that you give up any interest in what your own country is doing. Vaughn told me that he had no options whatsoever and that I could not go back to Chile. I met with several other officials but they had already made up their minds. They made me feel like I was a big disappointment.

I was very distraught. I really loved Chile and I wanted to stay another year. Besides teaching at the university, I went to the city prison once a week to the section set aside for boys six to eighteen. We sang or I brought records. I also visited an orphanage every Sunday.

People at the university were upset, too, because my dismissal was a contradiction of everything the Peace Corps had been saying—that we were independent agents and not called upon to toe the government line. I had voiced a protest and was gone—in the middle of a semester.

☆

Murray's expulsion received national coverage. As one former volunteer wrote to *The Washington Post:* "When an organization that purports to represent not the State Department but the people of the United States cannot tolerate freedom of expression from its own members, then that organization has betrayed the ideals from which it was conceived and violated the essence of democracy."[13]

The Peace Corps released the following statement to the press:

> We are terminating Bruce Murray because he insisted on writing a letter to a Chilean newspaper dealing with his personal political views on the Vietnam war, using his position as a Peace Corps volunteer to get publicity for these views. Our decision would be the same whether he was for or against the Vietnam war. . . . Politics and the Peace Corps don't mix. If a volunteer insists on getting into politics when he is overseas, then he should get out of the Peace Corps."[14]

In a lengthy letter to Murray, which discussed why he was terminated, Vaughn quoted a passage from the volunteer handbook that explained how the Peace Corps' apolitical nature allowed it to carry out its work in countries regardless of "[volunteers'] own or host country opinions of U.S. policy of the moment; there has been no better evidence of the genuine commitment of the U.S. to humanitarian principles."[15] Meanwhile, students at the university where Murray had taught held a demonstration to protest his dismissal and the university decided not to accept any new Peace Corps volunteers.

### Bruce Murray

The Peace Corps was using me as an example. They could nip these protests in the bud by showing they were going to get tough. The official explanations for my dismissal were really stretching it. Vietnam was an issue in Chile in the sense that it was a reflection of American foreign policy and there was some general antagonism towards the United States. The Peace Corps needed to justify my dismissal because it did not serve the purpose of the government to have Peace Corps volunteers protesting the war.

If there was an apolitical volunteer in Chile, I was it. Writing that letter was the first time I'd ever done anything like that. Even in graduate school I never got involved in the antiwar stuff. The church group I belonged to was upset about discrimination at the sorority houses, but I'd never even been to a demonstration.

☆

"I felt that we shouldn't terminate Murray until we made doubly sure we knew the facts," says Jack Vaughn today. "And that's why I sent somebody down there to find out what really happened. We learned that Murray was making placards and having meetings and so forth. In effect, he had left his job to be a full-time propagandist." The letter Vaughn wrote to Murray explaining why he was dismissed made no mention of meetings or placards.

A Peace Corps regional director in Chile described Murray's letter as an example of "childish petulance." Many of the volunteers, he says "sought confrontation; for the most part they were bored and wanted some excitement. And they wanted to hit the Peace Corps hard."

Murray's dismissal ended his colleagues' appetites for a skirmish. "It would have been great if a lot of volunteers had risen up and really protested my dismissal," says Murray, "but they didn't."

### David Elder (Chile, 1966–70)

We were definitely not representatives of the government, like the diplomatic corps, and we didn't have to agree with our government. I never felt I had to defend what we were doing in Vietnam. The thing Bruce did that upset the staff so much was that he put "Peace Corps" after his name. I felt they were right in expelling him because he came off as if he were a spokesman for the Peace Corps.

### Jean Ann Hale (Chile, 1966–68)

The Peace Corps policy against involvement in host country politics went with the territory and we accepted it. That was bullshit, though, about

Vietnam being an issue in Chilean politics. I think we thought it was unfair that Murray was fired, but things often are. I was sorry it happened, but I expected it.

I stayed in Chile after my two years with the Peace Corps and worked for the university I had been with as a volunteer. I felt much more comfortable without those ties to the Peace Corps and the U.S. government. I was free to speak as I wished and I didn't have to be concerned with stepping out of line.


## *John Ridgway (Chile, 1965–68)*

I knew the Peace Corps policy was that we were not to get involved in political issues, and I thought it was a good policy. It wasn't the mission of the Peace Corps to get involved in politics. I had deep admiration for Bruce's courage and straightforwardness, and I was terrifically disappointed that he was kicked out. Underneath though, I wished he hadn't bucked the Peace Corps system and the authorities.

☆

After a month of intense media attention and institutional soul-searching, the Peace Corps announced a "clarification" of its policy on volunteers' rights of expression. The prohibition against volunteers' stating their Peace Corps affiliation in letters or petitions to U.S. publications was lifted, although volunteers were still prohibited from publishing in host country publications.

The new, more liberal policy was a smart move. By permitting protests in the stateside press, the Peace Corps created a safety valve that prevented additional negative publicity being caused by the dismissal of other volunteers. The new policy also confined the embarrassment of volunteers' protests to the domestic scene.

Considerable damage, though, was already done. While a 1966 Harris poll had found that only 3 percent of college seniors interviewed believed that the Peace Corps limited the volunteers' freedom of speech, the same question posed in 1969 found that 70 percent believed it.

Murray was the only volunteer terminated for antiwar protest during the Johnson administration. His expulsion may have served as an example to other volunteers—particularly those whose dismissals would have made them eligible for the draft—and the "clarification" may have provided volunteers with a sufficient outlet. That Murray's case was unique indicates that volunteers at that time were, perhaps, more involved in the

Peace Corps experience and politically more conservative than is generally assumed.

Bruce Murray's troubles, meanwhile, were only beginning. When he arrived in Washington "for consultations" he phoned his mother in Rhode Island and learned that two days earlier—the same day he spoke to country director Paul Bell—the secretary at Murray's local draft board had called to tell her that Bruce had been reclassified 1-A. Mrs. Murray asked the secretary to send the notice of reclassification to her son in Chile. The secretary replied that she would mail it to Murray's Rhode Island address, since Bruce was on his way home.

When he received his induction notice, which ordered him to report three weeks before his twenty-sixth birthday, Murray applied for both conscientious objector status and a national interest occupation deferment to allow him to teach music as a member of the faculty, not of the Peace Corps, at the university in Concepción, Chile. The local board refused to consider his request and Murray was indicted for refusing to be inducted.

## Bruce Murray

I was stunned. How did the draft board know I was coming home before I knew myself? It appeared that there was collusion between the Peace Corps and the draft board. I couldn't figure out any other explanation. I stopped off in New York City on my way home from Washington and someone put me in touch with the American Civil Liberties Union. They filed a lawsuit on my behalf against the Peace Corps for wrongful termination, violation of constitutional rights, and conspiracy between the Peace Corps and the Selective Service.

☆

Murray's case came to trial in United States district court in Rhode Island in the fall of 1969. The trial revealed that the Peace Corps and the Rhode Island draft board moved with deliberate haste to remove Murray from Chile and induct him into the armed forces. Paul Bell, the country director who told Murray he was going to Washington "for consultations," testified that he had recommended to his superiors that Murray be terminated even before his conversation with him. The Peace Corps employee who handled the paperwork on the dismissal admitted that she falsified forms to indicate that all termination procedures had been completed.

The Peace Corps' defense was dealt a severe blow by the U.S. Ambassador to Chile Ralph Dungan, who volunteered to testify at his own expense. Dungan told the court that country director Bell informed him that the petition was circulating and they agreed that they "had to take action to forestall any reaction adverse to the United States." Furthermore, Dungan said, Murray's offense was not that he had involved himself in host country politics, but that by writing his letter he had disobeyed a directive not to attach his name to a political expression.[16]

Judge Raymond J. Pettine ruled that the Peace Corps had violated the due process guarantee of the First Amendment. "It is clear," Pettine wrote in his opinion, "that the involved agency has violated its own regulatory framework for termination." The judge also confirmed that Murray's selective service rights were unlawfully denied by his local board, and he enjoined prosecution of the indictment.[17]

Jack Vaughn's successor, Joe Blatchford, maintained Vaughn's policy permitting volunteers to write to American newspapers and state their Peace Corps affiliation. But, elaborating on this policy, Blatchford suggested to volunteers that they express their grievances to the U.S. ambassador in their country and request the ambassador to forward their petitions to the White House.

Blatchford says that during his watch, from 1969 to 1971, no volunteers were dismissed over protest issues. The Associated Press reported in March 1970 that twelve volunteers had been dismissed over the previous four months for publicly stating their opposition to the Vietnam War. These dismissals were already less newsworthy than Murray's.

# Chapter 7

☆

# *A Haven for Draft Dodgers*

Richard Nixon was right about the Peace Corps. Back in the 1960 presidential campaign, when John F. Kennedy proposed the idea, Nixon had predicted that the program would become a haven for draft dodgers. By the time Nixon won the White House in 1968, that was precisely what had happened. The Peace Corps did not keep records of how many men signed up to avoid going to Vietnam—as that was not information the Corps was anxious to collect—so there are no precise statistics to *prove* they had done so. But the dramatic shift in the ratio of male to female volunteers between 1965 and 1970, from 55–45 to 70–30, and the preponderance of volunteers who readily acknowledge that avoiding the draft was their main reason for joining the Corps suggest that Nixon was indeed correct.

Of the many ways of avoiding military service during the Vietnam War, joining the Peace Corps was one of the more obscure, and probably accounted for a very small percentage of those who evaded the draft. More common options were fleeing to Sweden or Canada, joining the National Guard, or getting married. Nevertheless, the draft resulted in a preponderance of volunteers who were motivated more by opportunism than altruism. "I had no grand illusions about saving the world," says Guy Baehr (Dominican Republic, 1968–71). "If we can do good, fine; at least we're saving our asses."

For young men unwilling to go to Vietnam, a stint as a volunteer could get them a deferment for two years of their draftable lives (ages eighteen to twenty-six). "A lot of guys left when they turned twenty-six, or extended till they turned twenty-six," says Ed Lanzner (Panama, 1968–69).

112

The Peace Corps, however, wasn't certain protection from the draft. The Peace Corps Act stated that volunteers would not be *exempt* from their military obligation. Service in the Peace Corps, however, was deemed by Selective Service Director General Lewis Hershey to be an occupation that served the national interest—and therefore a volunteer's military obligation could be *deferred*. But whether or not individual volunteers were granted deferments was left up to the local draft boards.

If one's draft board looked positively on the Peace Corps and had a large enough pool of eligible men from which to fill its quota, the volunteer would get a deferment. "I went to see one of the members of my draft board," recalls Jim Clarke (Marshall Islands, 1967–68). "I told him that I had three options: report for my physical, go to graduate school on the deferment I'd received, or join the Peace Corps. He said, 'Two years in the Peace Corps is a better service to your country than the military.' " Tom McGinley (Marshall Islands, 1968–69), had the opposite experience with his draft board: "I fought very hard to stay in the Peace Corps. I'm from a small town in Texas and my board's feeling was, 'None of this Peace Corps shit. You go fight like a man.' " Some Peace Corps applicants had a more difficult time obtaining a deferment if they happened to be registered with a draft board in a middle-class or upper-middle-class communities, since most of the draft-eligible men in those areas had the means to seek out options, like graduate school, that qualified for deferments.

For some volunteers, the deferment may have been a reprieve from the draft, but not from their conscience. "I took this stuff more seriously than some of the others," says Lowell Wiley (Marshall Islands, 1968–69). "I felt guilty having beaten the draft. While the other guys were dying for me, there I was—out in paradise. I decided to go back and put myself on the line." During his Peace Corps training in Maine, Bill Broyles realized that "it was more wrong for me to avoid the draft and let somebody else go fight in my place than it was for me to go."[1] He dropped out of the training program and enlisted in the Marines.

Some volunteers also felt a certain amount of pressure to perform brilliantly in their assignments or risk getting sent home and losing their deferment. One volunteer in Peru was so distraught because his job wasn't going well that he did not attend one of the Corps' conferences. His friends went out to his site to investigate and found him sitting, dazed, in his room, which he had painted black.

Many of those volunteers who went into the Peace Corps without deferments devised tricks to either delay or disqualify themselves from the Army when their induction notices arrived. Some would deliberately contract malaria simply by not taking malaria prophylactics. One volunteer in North Africa faked a mental breakdown. Others flew home and sought the advice of draft counselors. "Because I wear glasses, the counselor sent me to an ophthalmologist who coached me in how to flunk the Army's eye exam. I was reclassified and went right back to Africa."

While Peace Corps headquarters in Washington insisted that the agency was not swelling with draft dodgers, the Peace Corps field staff had no qualms about it. "In the early sixties the word was, 'Don't mention the draft. You're here to be a volunteer so keep quiet,' " says Roger Flather, who held various overseas positions from 1962 to 1969. "As the war picked up, it was all right for the person to say, 'I don't want to go to Vietnam. I'd rather spend my two years this way.' "

Not only were they sympathetic, many staff members actually helped volunteers avoid the draft when their induction notices arrived overseas. "I spent thirty percent of my time writing letters to draft boards which had sent notices to volunteers," says Ann Morgan, who was deputy country director in Thailand from 1968 to 1971. But letters of commendation sometimes failed to win the draft boards' understanding. "One of the best volunteers I had ever worked with was drafted out," says Morgan. "He was killed shortly after he got to Vietnam." A staff person in Micronesia worked out a system whereby volunteers would "miss" their induction date: "When mail arrived at the Peace Corps office, I would open everything from the draft boards. Then I radioed the guys who had received induction notices and told them when the boat carrying their mail was due to arrive at their island. The volunteer would make sure to be 'accidentally' on another island, unable to get on the boat and head home. He'd be safe for at least another few months."

Jack Vaughn and his successor, Joe Blatchford, tried to shield the Peace Corps from the impact of the draft by appealing to the White House to maintain the volunteers' eligibility for national interest occupation deferments. If enrollment dwindled, as volunteers were drafted out, the Corps' prestige would slip. Yanking volunteers from their assignments—for example, teachers in the middle of the school year, or agricultural specialists in the middle of planting season—could damage diplomatic relations by indicating to host country governments that the United States was not interested in honoring its agreements.[2] They also argued that if volunteers were drafted out of their posts, the taxpayers' money that had paid for their training and transportation would be wasted. It was "unfair to the nation, the host country, the Peace Corps and the individual," said Jack Vaughn.[3] The White House granted their requests and national interest deferments for Peace Corps service remained available for the duration of the draft.

The Peace Corps tried to demonstrate that its ranks were not swelling with draft dodgers. In November 1966, an agency press release stated that "it is possible to identify those people whose prime motive is draft avoidance." According to the release, volunteers' Spartan living conditions probably discourage those who "merely want to come in out of the cold of the draft." (Vaughn admits today that he could not pick out those individuals whose sole motivation was to stay out of Vietnam.) The release also stated that the draft "had no discernible impact" on college recruitment since the ratio of men to women (60–40) was consistent with previous years, despite the need for increasing numbers of troops in Vietnam.[4]* Of course, this logic failed to take into account the reasons why men signed up. In 1970 male volunteers accounted for 70 percent of the Corps' enrollment, and when the draft ended, Peace Corps officials complained that recruiting had become more difficult.[5]

## *Michael Rich (Niger, 1967; Senegal, 1968–70)*

I quit graduate school because you were automatically refused a deferment if you took more than four years to finish your undergraduate education, and I had taken more than four years. The Peace Corps was the only option I could see. I could get a deferment for teaching but I didn't feel like staying in the U.S. to be a teacher, and going to Canada had a stigma about it. The Peace Corps, though, was considered quite respectable.

I got my induction notice the day I left for Peace Corps training. The mail arrived as I was bringing my suitcases to the car. I handed it to my father and said, "This didn't arrive today."

I was at Kennedy Airport, just about to leave for Africa when I was paged and told not to get on the plane. I had informed the Peace Corps that I received an induction notice and that I had hired a lawyer to appeal it and get me a deferment. Nevertheless, they called me to Washington to discuss my situation. They said, "It's stupid to send you over because you're not going to win your case and we don't want to waste the money."

---

*The ratios cited previously, for 1965 and 1970, were contained in the Peace Corps 1981 Annual Report, p. 19. The ratio above, for 1966, was contained in the press release discussed.

I finally convinced them to let me go. It felt like I was fighting for my life.

When I got to Africa, I had a hard time fully adjusting because I never felt like I was really there. I thought that any day it would be pulled away from me. I wanted to come down with some illness that would keep me out of the Army, so I stopped taking my malaria suppressants and got malaria.

I was assigned to work with a counterpart in a government-sponsored literacy program. The man turned out to be an alcoholic and I didn't want to be responsible for keeping him sober. I stuck it out for about ten months and then asked to be reassigned to a teaching position that had opened up. Around the same time, I found out that the appeal my lawyer had been working on failed, and a few weeks later I got a new induction notice. At this point I contacted my congressman and asked for his help.

In the meantime, the Peace Corps said that until my draft situation was cleared up they weren't going to give me a new assignment. So I worked in the Peace Corps office in the capital and tutored the president of Niger in English. I'd go to the palace a couple days a week and talk to him in English for about an hour. Sometimes I went to the palace at night to see the movies they showed for the palace employees and their families. On the weekends I'd go with the president and his wife to their farm across the river from the capital.

After a few months of this, the country director decided he was going to send me home because I still hadn't gotten a deferment and the teaching job I wanted had been filled. I told him that if he didn't recommend me for another position in another country I would go to Washington and complain about him. I was bound and determined that his caprice wasn't going to send me to Vietnam.

He transferred me to Senegal, and soon after I heard from my draft board. Thanks to my congressman, I was granted a one-year deferment. I ended up teaching school in a prosperous little town located right on the ocean, which was a pleasure after being in the middle of the Sahara Desert. I wrote my draft board, as was required, to tell them my new address and when I expected to finish my stint with the Peace Corps. A year later, they sent me a renewal of the deferment—unsolicited. When I turned twenty-six, the other volunteers asked me, "Why are you staying?" It was the middle of the school year and I was quite comfortable. I had made a circle of friends and I had a nice home. I didn't see any reason to leave.

## Robert Marshall (Libya, 1968–69; Tunisia, 1969–70)

Everyone at Harvard was very eager to find something that would get them out of the draft. Joining the reserve units was very common. Some of my friends were gorging themselves on chocolate to make their acne worse so they could get exempted on skin problems. Another guy was working on his flat feet. The Peace Corps was one of the easier options and also a noble one. It was very popular at Harvard because of the Kennedy legacy. That spirit was still around.

When I applied to the Peace Corps, I requested Thailand, the Philippines, or Malaysia because I had lived in Japan as an exchange student during my senior year in high school and had taken courses in Asian history. But I was assigned to Libya, which nobody had ever heard of at that time. Other than people in the oil business, no one had ever gone there.

I was posted to the most isolated site in the country. It took me two weeks to get there. I hitched a ride on a Land-Rover which the Ministry of Education was sending out to deliver some school books. We kept getting stuck in the sand, and since there were no roads in the desert— you follow truck tracks and the lights marking the oil fields—we got lost a couple of times.

The town of three thousand had three public buildings: the town hall, the hospital, and the schoolhouse. The Libyan government had decided that every fifth-grade student in the country was going to have two hours a day of English instruction and they invited the Peace Corps to fill those spots. That was my assignment. I lived in a room in the school and wore a suit every day, even though I had to walk three miles between the two schools where I taught.

The first month everyone in the town invited me to their homes because they felt this obligation to have me over and give me dinner. They all served spaghetti with tomato sauce and a piece of mutton. The hot spices made me sick every time. They thought I must be lonely so they'd come by and just sit in my room for hours. I resented the intrusion upon my time. I wanted to be a Peace Corps volunteer and relate to the society from nine to five. But after five, I wanted to do my own thing: prepare lessons, correct papers, listen to the BBC, read novels, and take care of my room. But time just doesn't exist for people in the desert. They'd just sit and not say anything. Sometimes they'd nibble on some sunflower seeds or I'd offer them a little can of apricot nectar and that would be my big social obligation.

I discovered the stars there. The desert is the best place to look at stars. There's no electricity so there are no lights competing with them. You see stars down to the horizon. That was exhilarating. The mail would come every two or three weeks. Those were wonderful moments, when the mail would arrive. That kept me busy for a couple of days, reading mail and writing letters. I had one visit from a Peace Corps staff member. We played whiffle ball in the desert. The Libyans thought we were crazy.

All the men in the town worked in the oil fields. When one of the American foremen there learned I was living in this town, he asked one of the workers to bring me out on my day off. They couldn't believe an American was actually living with the Libyans. After that, I'd go out to the oil field once a month and they'd bring me into the commissary and let me take anything I wanted. Every day they'd give the workers some canned goods and a fresh loaf of bread to bring me. After a while they were sending me steaks.

[Marshall's sojourn on the Libyan desert was cut short when Colonel Muammar al-Qadaffi overthrew King Yidris in 1969. Qadaffi set out to erase Western influences and reestablish Libya as a Muslim society. The Peace Corps was asked to leave and Marshall was reassigned to teach in a boarding school in Tunisia.]

I wasn't all that sorry I didn't have a second year in Libya. My life in Tunisia was luxurious compared to what I'd been through in Libya. I lived in the teachers dorm, which had running water and electricity, and I ate in the student dining hall. The Tunisia volunteers were different from the Libya volunteers. They smoked dope and read Marxist literature. A friend of mine who lived in Tunis had a nice house and a housekeeper who came in every day to clean and cook his dinner. He taught English at an adult school to very wealthy people and he spent his free time reading and sitting in a café. His life there was such that he could have been in Paris.

I like to think I would have gone into the Peace Corps even if there hadn't been a Vietnam War. I had that international interest and was in no hurry to start a career. The idea of national service has always appealed to me. I think everybody should spend two years after college doing something for society.

I was proud I did the Peace Corps. I still am. I feel different. Everyone's a lawyer or an investment banker. Not everyone can go around saying, "I taught English in the Sahara Desert."

## Murray Cox (Western Samoa, 1969)

The year I graduated from college was the year they initiated the lottery. Because of the number I drew, I knew I would be called as soon as I graduated. I applied for conscientious objector status but was rejected because by 1969, so many people had tried to get COs that they had really clamped down.

The Peace Corps was a very practical way to get out of the draft. But there was also an allure. It was a glorified thing when I was growing up. My college roommate, who later joined the Weathermen, thought my going into the Peace Corps was a total cop-out. I told him I was doing something very constructive by going to another country to help my fellow man. But I knew I was serving myself.

I dropped my first acid during Peace Corps training in Hawaii. We had an afternoon off and a few of us climbed up this hill which overlooked the channel between Maui and Molokai. I was positive that I could see beneath the water and watch the currents between the islands.

The program I was involved in was called Rural Health and Sanitation. During the training period, we had language instruction in the morning and in the afternoons we were taught how to build latrines. I asked the training staff, "When do we get instruction in rural health? Are we going to learn basic first aid and how to give injections?" But no one was up front with us.

At some point in the training we heard that the Samoan government wanted to increase their tourist trade, but couldn't do it with the island's sanitation facilities, which consisted of these traditional sea latrines. You couldn't have people shitting in the same water you want the tourists to swim in. So the government banned the traditional latrine and brought in the Peace Corps to build new latrines, which the Samoans called the "Peecee Co-ah."

When we first got to Samoa, we were assigned to a family to live with. One night at supper the father and mother of the family I lived with got into this heated discussion. I couldn't understand very much of their conversation but I heard the word "peecee co-ah" flying back and forth. Finally, the mother said with great contempt the word "slime." One of the kids told me later that their mother was just infuriated that this new latrine, which they didn't even want, was being foisted on them.

I wanted to transfer into another program but this was against the Peace Corps' rules. You lived with your assignment or you went home. I loved Samoa itself. The Samoan guys would take me out to the reef in these dugout canoes and the porpoises would jump alongside us. It was truly idyllic.

But I couldn't spend two years doing something that these people didn't want. The more disillusioned I became, the more willing I was to take the chance of facing the draft or just dropping out completely and living on a commune, getting high and getting spiritual.

A number of other volunteers in that program were not very happy, either. One of my friends said he could put up with it, though, because he just wasn't ready to face the draft. One volunteer got into surfing, did the least amount of work, and had a great time.

[Murray Cox received an induction notice six weeks after leaving Western Samoa but he did not report for about a year. He dieted to below the minimum weight and presented letters from two psychiatrists stating that he was emotionally unfit for military service. Cox was classified 4-F (not qualified for any military service).]

☆

Between July 1969 and July 1970, 150 out of 7,800 male volunteers were drafted out of their assignments. George McDaniel was one of them.

## George McDaniel (Togo, 1968)

I was in medical school but had problems fitting in. I had taught high school previously, and was told by my draft board that if I returned to teaching, went to grad school, or joined VISTA, they'd draft me. They would not draft me if I went into the Peace Corps. I had no problem serving my country, but I was against the war.

As it turned out, the other guys in my training group for Togo, West Africa, felt the same way; they were willing to serve their country but in the Peace Corps, not the military.

Two weeks before I left for Africa, in the spring of 1968, I got a notice from my draft board classifying me 1-A [available for military service]. I wrote to them, and they answered that there'd been a bureaucratic snafu and not to worry.

When I got to Togo, we had in-country training, and then I was assigned to Niamtougou, a crossroads town of about five hundred people, about two hundred fifty miles from the capital. I had arrived at the beginning of the rainy season, so I couldn't actually begin working. But I was assigned to a Togolese counterpart, and we started planning projects. We spoke with the village chief, the governor of the province, and others in the village. They wanted to build a community center by the marketplace where they could hold meetings and have programs in public health, agriculture, and that sort of thing. We were also going to construct a screened-in butcher shop in the marketplace, since the fresh meat was otherwise sold in the open air and flies got on it. When the dry season arrived, we hoped to build culverts to prevent the dirt roads that led back to isolated villages from being washed out in the rainy seasons.

I was in Niamtougou just a month when I got a letter from my draft board officially declaring me 1-A. The Peace Corps said they would take my case to the Selective Service Board of Appeals of Georgia. I'll never forget when the telegram arrived from Secretary of State Dean Rusk, notifying me that my appeal was denied. The Peace Corps then took my case to the President's Board of Appeals.

In the meantime, the rainy season was ending, and I wanted to start our projects, but I couldn't. The Peace Corps had emphasized that it was critical for volunteers to establish a foundation of trust, and if I left with projects uncompleted, the next volunteer would have a hard time getting the villagers' support. I was very bitter that my government was putting me in this position. I was playing by the rules, and my government was betraying me.

As I was waiting around, I wondered what would be the right thing to do. I didn't want to go to jail for refusing to be inducted because I hated confinement and knew I'd lose my mind. I didn't want to go to Canada because I didn't want to be prevented from ever going home. If I went to Vietnam, though, I could at least have it behind me. I could also get killed, but I had been reading Hemingway, Faulkner, the existentialist writers, and *All Quiet on the Western Front,* and I wasn't afraid of death. I thought war could be a way to confront and understand oneself, even if I ended up dying.

In October 1968, I got a telegram saying that I'd lost the presidential appeal. I wrote a nasty letter to my draft board, telling them to come and get me, and resigned from the Peace Corps. I flew to East Africa and hitchhiked around Kenya and Tanzania. I saw the lions and wildebeests on the Serengeti Plain, visited settlements of the Masai, and climbed Mount Kilimanjaro. I came home in time for Christmas and a month later was inducted.

Since I knew French and had been learning an African language, I scored high on the language aptitude test in basic training. They were going to place me in a Vietnamese language program, and I thought that would be great because I could then read the writings of Ho Chi Minh in the original and gain a better understanding for teaching history in the future. But my security check showed that I'd been in the Peace Corps and had also demonstrated against the war. I was classified "Code Z" and was disqualified not only from language school, but from Officers Candidate School, even from Noncommissioned Officers School.*

The only thing I was qualified for was the infantry. I was frightened but in some strange way, I was also looking forward to it. After all the rifle and hand-to-hand training and the harassment of drill sergeants, you get psyched up. And by that time, I had become pretty tough. I still thought Vietnam was an immoral war, but wanted to find out what it was like.

I was assigned to the First Infantry Division—the "Big Red One"—we operated between Saigon and Cambodia. We were just north of the Twenty-fifth Division, the unit in the movie *Platoon*. My experiences and the changes I underwent left an indelible imprint. In one ambush, a VC was crawling up on our position and I threw a grenade that landed on his back. We then followed the blood trails of wounded VC. They were very young, mostly teenagers. I found one, lying facedown by some bushes, and thought he might be armed, waiting to kill an American passing by, so I was going to finish him off. I radioed to my lieutenant to tell him what the rifle fire was going to be, and he said not to, so I circled past. When we returned to him, I cocked my rifle next to his head, and we rolled him over and saw that he didn't have a gun or grenade. He was terrified. I tried to comfort him. His legs were scrambled. We shot him up with morphine, and I carried him in my arms to a chopper. I tried to tell him he'd be alright. He didn't understand English, but I think my voice conveyed comfort.

On a reconnaissance mission, my squad leader was twenty yards ahead of me when he stepped on a booby-trapped mortar round. I would have been cut in two, but I was caught by some "wait a minute" vines that grew up after Agent Orange defoliated the vegetation. The explosion was so huge, though, that I was thrown like a chip of wood. I'll never forget the leaves floating down gently in this tall cloud of black smoke. Both his legs were broken like toothpicks, and the bones cut through the skin. I could have been choppered out too because I had shrapnel in my face. But I wanted to stay with my unit. I wasn't going to leave more of a load on someone else.

---

*Personnel enrolled in the Army language-training programs are often recruited for intelligence work. Former Peace Corps volunteers are barred from such work for five years after their service.

I got an Army Commendation for Valor. I thought it was undeserved because it was really just a bureaucratic thing—we all got medals. When I came back to the States, I realized that I should try to help break stereotypes—commies, gooks, niggers, Jews, pigs, rednecks. Once we stereotype a person, they become nonhuman and we can mistreat or kill them. That's the process we went through in training for Vietnam. We were killing gooks, not people.

I also came to respect the VC. They hung in there day in and day out, and believed in what they were fighting for—to run their own country.

In looking back on the two services, the Peace Corps and the Army, the Peace Corps was far more efficient. The Peace Corps trained us to learn about people, to try to think as they do in order to understand problems and solve them. But the military distanced themselves from people and did not demand the truth. *We* were right. *They* were gooks. But of course, they won.

*Chapter 8*

☆≡≡≡

# *The Committee of Returned Volunteers: "Confessions of an Imperialist Lackey"* *

We went abroad to help Asians, Africans, and Latin Americans develop their resources and become free people. Once abroad, we discovered that we were part of the U.S. worldwide pacification program. We found that U.S. projects in these countries are designed to achieve political control and economic exploitation: to build an Empire for the U.S. As volunteers we were part of that strategy; we were the Marines in velvet gloves.

> —*From a leaflet distributed by the Committee of Returned Volunteers in front of the Peace Corps building in May, 1970*

This statement, drafted by the same people who a few years earlier proudly served their country in the Peace Corps, reflected the antagonism toward American foreign policy shared by a growing number of returned volunteers. But it was the Committee of Returned Volunteers (CRV), an organization of former Peace Corps volunteers and alumni of other overseas volunteer programs, who brought this rancor to its apex.

When it was founded in 1966, the CRV—the first national organization of Peace Corps alumni—was a forum for discussion of United States policies toward the third world. "Some people thought it would be okay to have an alumni association, but not a body that was going to make

---

*The chapter heading is the title of an essay written by Tom Newman, a former Peace Corps volunteer and staff member.[1]

*124*

political statements because we might embarrass the government," recalls Alice Hageman, one of the CRV's early organizers. However, those who propelled the group had begun to be disillusioned by their country's policies while overseas, and their doubts were confirmed as the war in Vietnam intensified. In a year's time, the CRV's restraint gave way to a rebelliousness that carried its members to the streets of Chicago for the 1968 Democratic National Convention, to the sugarcane harvest in Cuba, and to North Vietnam with other activists for so-called peace delegations. The FBI kept careful surveillance on the group, and one congressman ranked it among the ten most subversive organizations in the country. Finally, the CRV brought their radicalization to the Peace Corps in May 1970 when they occupied the agency's headquarters in Washington, D.C., to protest the invasion of Cambodia and the killing of four students at Kent State University in Ohio and two students at Jackson State University in Mississippi by National Guardsmen.

The story of the CRV illustrates how the Vietnam War helped rob many volunteers, and to an extent the Peace Corps itself, of its innocence. "I think the people who were in the CRV were very bright, thoughtful, and compassionate," says Hageman. "They were the kind of people who wanted to spend two years of their lives helping others." Adds Margot Jones (Ecuador, 1965–67), "The CRV was full of idealists who felt very committed and somewhat betrayed."

## Aubrey Brown (Nigeria, 1961–63)

In 1960, I helped the Kennedy campaign in my area by handing out brochures outside polling places. When the Peace Corps was announced, I was more than ready for the idea. I thought it was a marvelous change in U.S. policy. For once we were doing something that was right, and I wanted to be a part of it.

One of the things that bothered me about the Peace Corps was the relative passivity expected of the volunteers. I had assumed that we'd have more of a role in figuring out what we were going to do overseas. I also felt that the Peace Corps limited the volunteers' experience because it was an all-inclusive institution that took care of all your needs. I think people had much broader and richer experiences when they ventured outside the Peace Corps' parameters.

When I came back and went to graduate school at Columbia, I attended a wide variety of meetings and listened to people who had been to demonstrations in Washington and had gone to Selma, Alabama.* I also met a lot of people who had overseas experiences similar to mine but who hadn't been in the Peace Corps. I realized that the Peace Corps wasn't the be-all and end-all.

## Joe Stork (Turkey, 1964–66)

I graduated from a small Catholic college in Pittsburgh in 1964 and I saw the Peace Corps as a way to travel, and a great first job for an internationalist career. The idea of service appealed to me, as well.

Being in Turkey exposed me to other ways of looking at the world. There was a great deal of antipathy towards America in the little town where I taught English. They saw the United States as this colossus that routinely fucked over other countries. They were very warm and hospitable, but they saw me as representing those U.S. policies. I agreed with them about U.S. policy but I argued that the Peace Corps was very different and not a typical government agency.

But after a year in Turkey, I began to see the political angle. While I was there, the number of volunteers in Turkey grew by about fifty percent. [The contingent in Turkey increased from 319 in 1964 to 447 in 1966.] A lot of us were teaching English in the public school system, which I didn't think was a very constructive assignment. We had classes of sixty students, very few of whom derived any benefit from it. I quickly came to see myself as a baby-sitter, not a teacher, and I concluded that the Peace Corps was pretty much for the benefit of the volunteers and the United States rather than for the Turks.

When I came home in the summer of 1966, I was ready for something like the CRV. I met Aubrey [Brown] in the swimming pool at Columbia Teachers College. It was an opportunity to touch base with others who had a similar experience and I threw myself into it.

## Marlyn Dalsimer (Côte d'Ivoire, 1962–64)

The French expatriate teachers in the school where I taught were very hostile towards Americans. They used to ask me about Vietnam and it was embarrassing because I was completely ignorant about it. They were bitter and resentful about their defeat there and they felt the United States had sort of horned in on them. Vietnam was *their* territory.

---

*Brown is referring to the 1965 fifty-four-mile march led by the Reverend Martin Luther King, Jr., from Selma to the state capital in Montgomery.

But I believed that if the U.S. was in Vietnam, it was only for good reasons, to help and be generous. I was also very glad that the United States was not a colonial power because the guiding principle of the Ivory Coast's school system was that French culture was superior to African cultures, and that the people of the Ivory Coast should try to be like the French. [The Ivory Coast had been a French protectorate until it achieved independence in 1960.] I would be ashamed to be from a country that did that to other people.

Then I visited Liberia, which, unbeknownst to me, had been basically an American colony for years.* I was struck when I saw about two hundred fifty American jeeps parked behind this government building in the capital, loaded with all this riot gear. I was so disillusioned and angry that this was the kind of aid America was sending. The intent was to keep the ruling class in power and beat the heads of poor Liberians. Of all the things people need—food, education, housing—to send all that hardware really made me sick.

When I went to Liberia, I wasn't critical of my country but over the two years the Peace Corps provided me with the opportunity to see imperialism, racism, the effects of domination, and terrible poverty. I came back with a much more sophisticated view of the world and the United States' complicity in all this stuff.

I started thinking the Peace Corps was kind of wishy-washy, so I wrote Jack Vaughn that I had observed his never having made a public statement about the war in Vietnam. I told him that as head of an organization with "peace" in its name, I expected him to. We always hoped the Peace Corps would be different. But at that time I didn't understand that it's a part of government and people like Jack Vaughn have to fall in line behind administration policy.

☆

In December 1966, seventy-five people who had served in the Peace Corps and other overseas programs founded the CRV at a meeting at Columbia University. According to its statement of purpose, the CRV would be "well informed about events in developing countries and U.S. policy toward them. The organization would bring our concerns before the public and communicate them to the administration, Congress, and others who influence U.S. policy toward Asia, Africa, and Latin America."[2] It was suggested that the group give special focus to the war in Vietnam. The idea

---

*Founded in 1822 by freed American slaves, Liberia has enjoyed generous U.S. aid for years and has been one of the United States' most loyal allies in Africa.

was voted down. "In the beginning, we decided to shy away from Vietnam," says Aubrey Brown, the group's first chairman. "But we compromised by setting up these committees that would study and report on different areas of the world and one of them worked on Vietnam."

That winter the antiwar movement surged through the Columbia campus and the Vietnam committee began working on a paper that discussed the war from the viewpoint of those who had served overseas.

In the summer of 1967, two events consolidated the CRV's position on the war and fostered an increasingly skeptical view of the Peace Corps. The first event was the expulsion of volunteer Bruce Murray, which "raised questions," says Aubrey Brown. "Peace Corps officials had always paraded around the notion that the Peace Corps was apolitical, but we began to realize that its political dimension was actually quite substantial."

The second event was the August 1967 publication of the Vietnam committee's paper in *Ramparts,* with 659 names endorsing it.* The paper drew a vivid contrast between the government's simultaneous support of the Peace Corps and the ongoing destruction in Vietnam. The paper struck a nerve. As Aubrey Brown recalls, "People called up asking, 'What can I do to get my name on it?' We got stacks and stacks of mail, some containing unsolicited contributions. One guy sent us three hundred dollars."

The following excerpts are from the paper:

It has often been said that those who serve abroad will make their most important contribution when they return, by helping the United States understand other nations. It is on the basis of our experience overseas, our perceptions about the lives and aspirations of other peoples, our hopes for the future of the world and our nation's place in it, that we now speak. . . .

The increasing destruction wrought by U.S. forces in Vietnam reveals a basic contradiction in our nation's policies overseas, a contradiction between that which builds up and that which destroys. For those of us who worked to build a school or dispensary, for those of us who saw dysentery decrease because we helped the people dig a well, for those of us who helped a village realize its ambition to have a bridge to get its goods to market, for those of us who helped a child discover the meaning of electricity, each bomb in Vietnam that destroys a school, a well, a bridge or a child destroys the very kinds of things which we considered most important in our service as volunteers. We are therefore led to

---

*Ramparts* was a leading journal of New Left politics most noted for its March 1967 exposé of CIA funding of the National Student Association.

question whether the United States really values the goals towards which we worked while overseas. We who served overseas did so in part because we wanted to construct, not only schools and roads and sanitation systems, but also dialogue among men of differing cultures. Each bomb that we drop, each villager whom we kill, increases the hatred of Asians for the American intruders. Rather than opening up communication, our actions in Vietnam leave us with a legacy of bitterness, the burden of which we must carry into the future. . . . .

The paper went on to call for the withdrawal of U.S. troops from South Vietnam, to criticize Washington's support for the self-serving corrupt regimes of South Vietnam, and to oppose the United States' practice of crushing nationalist movements in the name of containing communism.

The paper's conclusion moderates in tone, reflecting idealism and patriotism:

To admit that we have made a tragic mistake will require great courage. Nevertheless, we believe that U.S. withdrawal at this point, rather than undermining the honor of this nation, on the contrary will be a sign of its strength and health. . . . We believe that our nation can show its true greatness by responding to the appeals for peace which come from all around the world.[3]

The huge response to the *Ramparts* paper—about seven CRV chapters sprung up around the country, bringing membership, eventually, to two thousand—demonstrated that the CRV could contribute a significant voice to the antiwar movement. But the group hesitated. "A lot of members didn't want to take that strong a stand against the war," recalls Elaine Fuller (Colombia, 1963–65), who worked for a New Left newspaper, the *Washington Free Press*, and lived in a communal house with members of Students for a Democratic Society. "To us it seemed that CRV was all very nice, but it wasn't really where the action was."

Aubrey Brown observes that many members of the CRV, and Peace Corps alumni in general, preferred "very Milquetoast kinds of organizations and protests." Brown believes that while the overseas experience might have been an enlightening one, the Peace Corps itself precluded volunteers from considering drastic political viewpoints. "The experience of identifying with oppressed people is a potentially very explosive one," says Brown, "and those folks who have any honesty will move to very radical positions. The Peace Corps prevented that from happening by keeping the terms short, by allowing people relatively little say-so about what they did, and by laying on a heavy trip that the Peace Corps was not political."

By early 1968, the CRV's leaders began to adopt increasingly radical points of view. Specifically, they rejected the widely held notion, which was incorporated in the *Ramparts* statement, that United States involvement in Vietnam was a "tragic mistake." Their new contention was that America's intervention was a deliberate attempt to manipulate events in the third world for its own benefit. "This idea was shocking to some people," recalls CRV member Bob Love (Philippines, 1963–66). "A couple of former volunteers thought there was something almost treasonous about the direction CRV was going in." Says former CRV leader Gerry Schwinn (Nigeria, 1961–63), "As soon as things started sounding too radical, people dropped out."

CRV members were becoming active, highly visible participants in the antiwar movement, burning their draft cards and attending rallies with their huge banner held aloft. Several were arrested in the 1968 takeover and strike at Columbia University, and "there wasn't any question that CRV wouldn't be in Chicago [for the 1968 Democratic National Convention]," says Gerry Schwinn. Opposing chapters debated whether the CRV should back liberal Democratic candidate Eugene McCarthy for President, or take part by simply addressing the issues. Finally, Aubrey Brown recalls, it was decided that "we were going to be 'in the streets.' "

## Alice Hageman

(Hageman served with the Frontier Interns, a program similar to the Peace Corps, that was sponsored by the Presbyterian Church, U.S.A. She was assigned as a representative to the United Nations Educational, Scientific, and Cultural Organization in Paris, France, from 1962 to 1965.)

I remember thinking, somewhat melodramatically, "I don't want to do this if they're going to gas us. But Jesus was only thirty-three when he died and I was thirty-three," so I thought, "if Jesus could do it, I could do it."

We were well prepared for a difficult time. We organized ourselves in groups of four to keep track of each other and we designated a central place where people could phone in if we got separated. It was a sort of check-in system so we'd know if anyone was missing. We were at Lincoln Park when Dick Gregory started a march by saying, "I live in Chicago and I have a right to have my friends come visit me. You're all invited over." The whole crowd began to move.

### Aubrey Brown

We realized we were one of very few organized constituencies there. We had a loudspeaker and a banner that stretched across the street, and we found ourselves leading this march of a couple thousand people down Michigan Avenue.

☆

Harris Wofford, who joined the CRV contingent, recalls that the group managed to keep the marchers on the sidewalks and obeying traffic lights in order to avoid provoking the police and National Guardsmen. Instead of taunting the police, as many demonstrators did by calling them "pigs," the CRV, according to Wofford, chanted, "More pay for cops."[4] The CRV led another march in Chicago, which was halted by a military barricade and exploded into a police riot.

### Bob Love (Philippines, 1963–66)

We came to this overpass and just beyond it was a crossroads. Suddenly, from around the corner, under the overpass, came all these armored personnel carriers rigged in barbed wire with soldiers standing on the back gripping what looked like machine guns. It was terrifying. We just came to a standstill and sat down. We were trying to figure out if we should attempt to disperse or go back to Lincoln Park when the police started lobbing tear gas canisters into the crowd and people began falling down because they couldn't see.

### Alice Hageman

Tear gas is terrible, especially if you wear contact lenses. The tear gas clings to them. There were medics around who had ketchup bottles full of water that they would put in your eyes. I had a canteen of water, a handkerchief to wet down if we got gassed, and a hat because it provided a little protection if we got clubbed.

### Aubrey Brown

We were within inches of the billy clubs but none of us was hurt. We helped raise the chant, "The whole world is watching." We had a lot of attachment to our banner but as the tear gas began to fall we cut it apart, soaked the pieces in water and distributed them to the people around us.

☆

1969 was perhaps the CRV's busiest year. CRV leaders met with representatives of the National Liberation Front, and a CRV contingent of seventy-five marched in the presidential *counter*inaugural parade carrying posters of North Vietnamese leaders. The Washington, D.C., chapter held a teach-in on South Africa to commemorate the ninth anniversary of the Sharpeville massacre and sponsored a Cuban film festival. The Seattle chapter joined a demonstration against United Fruit recruiters at the University of Washington. In San Francisco and Milwaukee, CRV members gave radio interviews denouncing the Peace Corps, and at an Earth Day festival in upstate New York, the CRV's New York chapter staged a dramatization of how napalm was destroying the environment in Vietnam.

In the summer of 1969, thirty-nine CRV members spent six weeks in Cuba to "experience an alternative model of development and evaluate its effects. Through our trip we may be better able to understand the concept of world revolution and its implications for international relations and domestic change in the U.S."[5] Participants helped cut sugarcane, picked fruit, met with Cuban officials, and visited hospitals and schools that had been built since Fidel Castro came to power.

After the Cuba sojourns, the CRV issued a position paper that stated that "real development is often impossible without a revolution which carries out an equitable redistribution of economic and political power."[6] The Peace Corps, they concluded, prevented revolution and should therefore be abolished for the following reasons:

• It gives legitimacy, through its very presence, to the local power structure which invited it. This elite, typically in collaboration with powerful U.S. financial interests, indulges its narrow self-interest at the expense of the common people.

• It provides an illusion of progress by helping to coax out of an obsolete and inadequate politico-economic system some token social projects (a school here, a health center there). . . .

• It makes friends for America abroad who will become the future supporters of and apologists for U.S. policy in the third world. . . .

• It capitalizes on the idealism of U.S. youth and on the good will of the people of the U.S. to present a false image of the U.S. presence in the third world.[7]

In a compilation of essays entitled *Volunteer?* CRV members examined the Peace Corps from the perspective of "having been used as pawns in the game of imperialism." In one essay, "Confessions of an Imperialist Lackey," former Philippines volunteer Tom Newman states his contention that

> Most of us, I'm sure, are by this time bored with the idea of the Peace Corps if not downright ashamed of our participation in it. . . . We may even desire to repress our identity as returned volunteers. We must resist that desire. . . . Nobody else can reveal the hypocrisy of the Peace Corps as well as we can. . . . Is the sincere young man sitting with his local friends and holding the little black child in his arms really an agent of American imperialism? You bet he is.[8]

In May 1970, when President Nixon announced the United States' invasion of Cambodia and National Guardsmen killed four students at Kent State University in Ohio and two students at Jackson State University in Mississippi, the New Mobilization Committee to End the War in Vietnam (MOBE) called for a demonstration in Washington the weekend of May 10. An estimated 100,000 people came to hear speakers Coretta Scott King, Dave Dellinger (Chicago Seven defendant and veteran pacifist), Dr. Benjamin Spock, and Jane Fonda. The White House was ringed with buses in the event of a siege and the city girded itself with a force of 7,500 police, Army troops and National Guardsmen.

CRV members distributed leaflets to Peace Corps staffers that week, encouraging them to go on strike in protest against the Cambodia incursion and the Kent State and Jackson State killings. When it became clear that the staff would not go on strike, the CRV adopted a favored tactic of the antiwar movement: They would take over the Peace Corps building. "It was two blocks from the White House, a very strategic location," notes Alice Hageman. And there was still some residual feeling about volunteers being these wonderful, idealistic people. So to have some of them take over the building had some mileage."

Dressed as if they worked there, about a dozen CRV members entered the building in twos and threes early that Friday morning. They convened in the stairwell outside the fourth floor and at eight-fifteen burst into the Southeast Asia offices chanting, "Ho, Ho, Ho Chi Minh—NLF is gonna win." They escorted Peace Corps staff out of the building, hung signs out the window (LIBERATION NOT PACIFICATION and CHE LIVES) as well as a nine- by fifteen-foot Vietcong flag. A team downstairs on the sidewalk

took their places on a picket line and distributed a printed statement to
passersby that read:

> In recent weeks we have seen the invasion of Cambodia, renewed bomb-
> ings of North Vietnam, further attempts to exterminate the Black Panth-
> ers, murders at Kent State. . . . These events have left no doubt about
> the U.S.'s continued commitment to the goal of worldwide domination.
> They have forced us to take an action we have postponed too long.

Meanwhile, the contingent inside the building phoned *The New York
Times* and taped the windows "in case they tried to hurl in tear gas canisters," says Elaine Fuller. The fourth floor and sidewalk contingents
communicated with walkie-talkies, speaking Turkish to foil police inter-
ception. "We had people at the ready to talk in Malay if the Turkish
broke down," Aubrey Brown recalls. A pulley was rigged and at ten o'clock,
the sidewalk crew sent up a basket of doughnuts and coffee.

Peace Corps Director Joe Blatchford was under the impression that
"the group occupying the building was coordinated by the Weathermen.
They were trying to provoke a Chicago-type situation where heads are
smashed by the police in front of TV cameras. I didn't want to give them
that opportunity," says Blatchford, who refused to call in the police. "I
didn't want another Chicago on the administration."

There's evidence, however, that the administration wouldn't have been
disturbed by some head smashing, as long as it was not provoked by the
police. "Bust the Peace Corps—get it rough," H. R. Haldeman wrote in
his notes from his meeting with the President that day. "No soldiers do
anything—let the kids break windows," he jotted. And then, the last item
in his notes, "get Peace Corps out."[9] While Blatchford was trying to protect the administration from the specter of the police clubbing Peace Corps
volunteers, the President may have regarded the situation as an opportunity for the public to see that the organization had turned into a league
for wild-eyed radicals, and this would make the task of dismantling it
easier.

## Bob Love

People were quite surprised to see the Vietcong flag flying outside the
Peace Corps building. Some of them thought it was great and others were
very perplexed. College students came up to me on the picket line and

told me they were thinking of joining the Peace Corps because they thought it was the one good thing the U.S. government had going. I told them that I had felt the same way when I was a volunteer, that I wanted to let people in the third world know that the United States had friendly feelings towards them and that we commiserate with their poverty. But I had discovered that our country was part of the reason for that poverty. American corporations' need for cheap labor and the desire to maintain stability in those countries at all costs were issues that the Peace Corps didn't even address. I told these students that the best thing they could do for people in the third world was to stay at home and do something about American foreign policy.

Later on Friday afternoon, MOBE organizers asked if someone from CRV would address the crowd and somehow I was designated to do it. I had never seen such a sea of people. It was as if the crowd went on forever. I explained that we were occupying the Peace Corps building to drive home the point that just as American involvement in Vietnam was not an exception to foreign policy, the Peace Corps was not an exception to the various branches of government. It just sugarcoated a rather bitter pill. After I gave my speech, Abbie Hoffman gave me a great big hug.

☆

That evening, Dave Dellinger asked the crowd to protect the occupiers at the Peace Corps from the police by maintaining a presence there through the night. "People we never heard of came and slept out in front of the building," recalls Aubrey Brown.

The following day, the focal point of the demonstration was at the Ellipse, on the opposite side of the White House from the Peace Corps. "The CRV ended up being all by their lonesome selves," Blatchford recalls. "All their friends from all over the country were a half a mile away. I thought that was hilarious. I called them up Saturday afternoon and asked, 'Aren't you guys a little itchy? You know, Jane Fonda's giving a speech. You're missing it all.' "

The occupiers left the building Saturday evening, around nine o'clock, after thirty-six hours inside. The decision to leave, says Aubrey Brown, had more to do with safety concerns than the desire to join the crowds on the Ellipse. "The cops came down very harshly to clear the streets Saturday evening," recalls Brown, who manned the picket line. "We weren't sure we could protect them much longer."

### Elaine Fuller (Colombia, 1963–65)

We thought we'd made our point. We wouldn't have gained anything more by staying over another night or getting arrested. We just slipped away and went to Gerry Schwinn's house to relax and have something to eat. I remember I had a terrific headache. The next day a bunch of us went out and had a picnic on the Potomac. We thought we'd done a good thing.

### Aubrey Brown

I was quite pleased with the way things went. The occupation probably would have had more of an impact if there had been violence. It's a reflection of how radical we were at that point. I wasn't strong enough to have said, "Look, we could really set this whole thing off," but I don't know that I would have actively opposed anything that might have gone in that direction. Joe Blatchford obviously saw the potential.

☆

A Peace Corps spokesperson told a reporter that the occupation was "a failure because they didn't attract the attention here they wanted." [10] But *The New York Times* gave it front-page coverage, and *The Washington Post* devoted ten column inches and ran a huge photo of a Peace Corps official hanging out a window trying to remove the Vietcong flag. While on his way back from a peace delegation to North Vietnam, Gerry Schwinn read about the occupation in a Philippines newspaper.

"The occupation was the beginning of the end. It was the last major thing CRV did," says Alice Hageman. The CRV was, in fact, losing its direction as new issues emerged. In 1969, its national board had decided that the CRV should try to redirect MOBE's focus from protesting the war to combatting imperialism. At the same time, the female members of the CRV were discussing chauvinism within the organization and "women's lib in a third world context." [11] In 1970, it was decided that the CRV's directorship should be shared by one male and one female. Gerry Schwinn offered to stay on past his term as chairperson until the newly elected cochairs could assume their positions. "That arrangement only lasted for a week," Schwinn says, "because there was a coup. The women in the New York chapter came into the office one day and told me to leave. They just took over." The women then handed over the leadership a few weeks later when the cochairs were ready to go to work. Six months into his tenure in office the male cochair decided that he could make his most valuable contribution to the antiwar effort by organizing protests within the military. He resigned his post and enlisted in the Army.

No elections were held to fill the vacant spot. "It was a flurry of phone calls to see who was available," says Elaine Fuller, who took the job in April of 1971. A short time later, it became clear to Fuller that the spirit propelling the CRV had become too diffuse to perpetuate it. "The dominent figures in the CRV started spouting Mao and no longer saw the organization as being responsible to some constituency," says Fuller. "It was just this group of revolutionaries and that's what destroyed it."

The CRV's last "action" took place in the spring of 1971 at the Cherry Blossom Festival in Washington, D.C. Amid the celebrations, five members in long white gowns donned coolie hats and then poured "blood" from small bottles on themselves. They shouted "U.S out of Vietnam," were arrested, and were taken away.

That summer, the CRV held its last conference in Colorado, and members ceremonially burned the bylaws, which, according to Fuller, were seen by the CRV's radical contingent as "just so much bourgeois foolishness."

President Kennedy receives a group of Peace Corps trainees on the White House south lawn. *John F. Kennedy Library*

"They were barely able to grasp the notion that I had come from far away to help them," says Thaine Allison (Borneo, 1962–64) (*center*), "and there I was, asking them to plant their rows straight."

Elaine Fuller (Colombia, 1963–65) (*center*) distributes farm supplies from CARE to *campesinos*. "It was good public relations, and the farmers needed the material support," says Fuller, "but they treated me with a deference which was really undeserved. I was just a kid."

Volunteer newlyweds Ann and Mike Moore (Togo, 1962–64) spent a vacation backpacking. The Moores visit the home of Adam, their guide (*third from left*), and two of his four wives (*at right*).

Robert Borkhardt (Iran, 1962–64) (*third from right*) and fellow volunteers are welcomed by the shah of Iran, Muhammad Reza Pahlevi (*second from left*).

Tom Scanlon (Chile, 1961–63) plays Chilean ballads on his violin for his co-workers at a retreat in the resort area of El Quizco.

"I used to take the kids for ice cream," says Marisue Zillig (Panama, 1965–67), "and then to the Peace Corps office, where they'd play with the toilet, which was quite a novelty to them."

In the Guayaquil barrio where she lived, Margot Jones (Ecuador, 1965–67) walks with young girls on their way home from school. "Although they came from very poor families, they were always well dressed and very neat."

LEFT: Todd and Hope Jenkins embarrassed the U.S. government with their activism in Micronesia (1967–68). After serving only one year, the Jenkinses settled in American Samoa with their sons, Misha, one, and Shem, four. *Department of Education, Government of American Samoa*

BELOW: Lynda Edwards (Dominican Republic, 1964–66) (*right*) teaching an adult literacy course

LEFT: "The ladies in the barrio thought I was too *rubia* [fairskinned] to carry water," says Karen Hahn Clough (Dominican Republic, 1963–65). "They permitted me to carry water only late at night. Finally, I was allowed to carry water in the daylight."

BELOW: Kirby Jones (Dominican Republic, 1963–65) poses in front of the community center he helped organize in the Santo Domingo barrio of Simón Bolívar. Jones lived in a room in the back of the building.

TOP: Jon Kwitny (Nigeria, 1965–67) made frequent weekend and holiday motorcycle trips to remote villages, pursuing his interest in indigenous music and handcrafts.

BOTTOM: Bunny Meyer (Nigeria, 1967–70) (*second row center*) with the Bichi Teachers' Training College drama troupe, which translated family folktales into English and performed them in primary schools.

LEFT: "In training we were told we wouldn't have to tow the government line," says Bruce Murray (Chile, 1965–67). "My dismissal was a contradiction of that."

BELOW: Bill Brownell (Nigeria, 1965–66) (*center*) poses with his cook-steward Patrick and Patrick's friend James. The Nigerians' watches are conspicuous, in keeping with the custom of displaying personal possessions in photos. *Ukwu's Photos, Ewohimi, Nigeria*

RIGHT: George McDaniel (Togo, 1968) (*right*) and his colleague Ta Ta Norbert, a rural community development agent for the Togolese government

BELOW: Drafted out of the Corps, McDaniel served with the First Infantry Division in Vietnam.

"Some people thought it would be okay to have an alumni association, but not a body that was going to make political statements," says Alice Hageman, one of the founders of the Committee of Returned Volunteers (C.R.V.), who went to Cuba in 1969 to help with the banana harvest.

LEFT: "One of the things that bothered me about the Peace Corps was the relative passivity expected of the volunteers," says C.R.V. cofounder Aubrey Brown (Nigeria, 1961–63).

ABOVE: In May 1970 the C.R.V. took over Peace Corps headquarters to protest the bombing of Cambodia and the killings at Kent State. They flew the Vietcong flag and taped the windows to protect themselves from a tear gas attack. *Arthur Ellis*/The Washington Post

RIGHT: Urged by antiwar organizer Dave Dellinger to protect the occupiers from a middle-of-the-night police raid, fellow demonstrators camped out in front of the Peace Corps building.

ABOVE: Peace Corps director Joe Blatchford (*center*) welcomes a contingent of Peace Corps families before they leave for Ghana.

LEFT: "I loved being in Morocco; what I didn't like was the Peace Corps," says Linda Bridges (Morocco, 1970–72), who is pictured here with her children (*left to right*), Michael, four, and Lydia, eight, buying fruit for her family in the open market in Rabat.

BELOW: Meredith McGehee (Niger, 1978–80) tosses a jump ball between students Fatou Outarra and Fati Idi in an intramural basketball tournament.

LEFT: Philip Karp (Togo, 1978–80) (*third from right*) and young men of the rural village Titigbe (population, 400) place a supporting pillar in the foundation of a three-room cement-and-tin schoolhouse, which replaced the previous straw-roofed school.

BELOW: "When I first arrived, I thought the village women were boring," says Cherie Lockett (Senegal, 1979–81) (*left, with a friend*). "But I was wrong. As it happens, the engines of change were among the women."

RIGHT: "The attitude towards children in Niger is 'survival of the fittest,' " says Becky Raymond (Niger, 1978–81), who is pictured here showing a young mother in the village of Guidan Roumdji how to prepare a nutritious porridge for her baby.

Celebrating the Peace Corps' twenty-fifth anniversary in 1986, six thousand returned volunteers marched from the Lincoln Memorial to Arlington National Cemetery, where they laid a wreath at President Kennedy's grave and attended a service for volunteers who died overseas. *Al Stephenson*

LEFT: Barcia Miller (Dominican Republic, 1984–86) with the Asociación de Artesanos Don Bosco. Miller showed them basic marketing techniques, and, five years later, Miller reports, the group's crafts are selling in Dominican and Puerto Rican gift shops.

ABOVE: "I saw a window of opportunity with the Caribbean Basin Initiative," says Bruce Burton (Honduras, 1983–85) (*second from left*), who helped a farmers' co-op export thirty-five thousand pounds of snow peas to the United States.

RIGHT: One farmer I worked with couldn't figure out the logistics of building a well (as shown) and he didn't have the confidence to learn how to do it," says Billy Fanjoy (Mali, 1988–90) (*center rear*). "For years, volunteers read the metric tape for him." *Karen Schwarz*

# Part Four

# The Nixon-Ford Years, 1969-77

# Part Four

☆

# The Nixon-Ford Years, 1969-77

# Introduction

☆═══

Joe Blatchford, President Nixon's Peace Corps director, recalls his predecessor, Jack Vaughn, telling him that volunteers' use of marijuana was the Peace Corps' toughest problem.* But after his first trip overseas, Blatchford was not especially worried about it. The Corps' real troubles, he felt, were much more serious. "I inherited an institution that was going out of business," Blatchford recalls. "I kept hearing from host country officials, 'We like your boys and girls very much, but don't you have any mechanics, businesspeople, farmers, biology teachers, and foresters? We have problems out here and you keep sending us English teachers!' Things had changed, but the Peace Corps kept doing the same things as when it first started."

To revive the Peace Corps, Blatchford focused on increasing the percentage of volunteers who possessed the specific skills that countries were seeking. Peace Corps veterans say they thought that bringing in skilled recruits was stupid at best and downright devious at worst. It was widely known in the agency that the few technically skilled volunteers whom the Peace Corps had provided in the past were older, and could not learn the languages or adapt to the rigors of life in the third world as easily as the recent college grad. Blatchford's initiative, they concluded, was a discreet way to replace the war protestors with Silent Majority types. " 'Technically qualified' was a euphemism for 'not liberal,' " explains Charlie Pe-

---

*Vaughn says he did not speak with Blatchford at all during the transition. "It was total cold turkey."

157

ters, who headed the Peace Corps' evaluation division from 1961 to 1968. Staff and volunteers nurtured a contempt for Blatchford, who was variously thought of as "the worst thing that ever happened to the Peace Corps," "Nixon's way of saying 'Fuck you' to the Peace Corps," "a horse's ass," and "a superficial, publicity-hungry pretty boy."

The resistance to Blatchford's idea revealed how set in its ways the Peace Corps had become. Host country requests for skilled volunteers—ranging from carpenters and diesel mechanics to air traffic controllers—were nothing new. But since the beginning, the Peace Corps could fill only a tiny percentage of those types of positions, and the agency focused its recruiting efforts on the most receptive constituency, college students in their senior year. By 1964, recruiting techniques had become tailored so precisely to the college grad that those who might have valuable skills but lacked a college degree were discouraged from applying.[1] In fact, by the mid-1960s the pool of applicants had become almost completely homogenized. "The group I went to Thailand with," recalls a former volunteer, "had only one or two people who had not come from Ivy League, Big Ten, or Seven Sisters colleges. The Peace Corps was an extension of junior year abroad." This situation was brought to Shriver's attention five years before Blatchford came along. "Shall we remain essentially an organization of the college elite," an adviser wrote, "or shall the Peace Corps open its doors more widely to the qualified and dedicated non-college Americans, thereby transforming the Peace Corps into a broad-based organization with volunteers from a more representative cross section of American life?"[2]

While holdovers from the Kennedy and Johnson administrations wrung their hands over Blatchford's purge of youthful idealists, the disadvantages of volunteers in their mid-twenties with no specific skills were becoming clear. Host countries knew their needs and were no longer impressed by evocations of President Kennedy and America's beneficence to the struggling countries of the third world.

In June 1969, Nixon aide Alexander Butterfield reported to National Security Adviser Henry Kissinger that there was "an increasing feeling among many of the African nations that the Peace Corps volunteers are a mixed blessing. . . . A frequent complaint is that Peace Corps volunteers have been ill-prepared to endure the stresses and strains of living in a developing country."[3] Even Liberia, then one of the United States' most loyal allies in black Africa, questioned the value of "needless proliferation [of volunteers] as it contributes little of substance to national development efforts."[4]

Between 1969 and 1971, as they grew disillusioned with the volunteers, the governments of Somalia, Turkey, and Bolivia expelled the Peace Corps as a convenient means of appeasing anti-American sentiment or, as in the case of Tanzania, to show disdain for United States involvement in Vietnam. "You can use something as a political football if it has little value to you," said William Dyal, a Peace Corps regional director at the time.[5]

A change in recruitment strategy was further justified by the fact that volunteers of the late 1960s lacked the dedication of the earlier groups. "The wonderful thing about them is that they had tremendous guts," says Charlie Peters. "They stuck it out." Peters notes that by 1969, the early termination rate was almost 60 percent. "An attitude was forming in the late sixties," adds Norman Bramble, a training officer in India, "that when you volunteer you get to do the kind of work you want. When we told the trainees what the host government wanted them to do, they'd say, 'Oh, that's not what I wanted to do,' and a lot of them went home."

Volunteers' grooming and dress habits strained the Peace Corps' welcome in host countries. "A beard was seen as a pretense of poverty. To the Indians, volunteers were mocking them," says Bramble. "The volunteer's usual response to the suggestion that he shave was, 'If I shave I'm going against my principles.' " Volunteers' long hair and short skirts so offended Malawi President Hastings Banda that in 1969 he asked the Peace Corps to leave.

Despite its troubles, and contrary to the fears of the staff that he would gleefully eliminate it, President Nixon showed considerable respect for the Peace Corps, at least in the beginning of his first term. Instead of plowing it under, or leaving it to die of neglect in the hands of a hack political appointee, the White House looked for a Republican with legitimate credentials for the job of director. Two of the three candidates on the short list were eliminated because they lacked relevant experience, even though both had played fairly important roles in the presidential campaign. One of them had actually sought out the position. The third candidate, Joseph Blatchford, also had solid Republican credentials, but his other qualifications clinched his appointment. While in law school in 1959, Blatchford founded an organization similar to the Peace Corps called ACCION (Americans for Community Cooperation in Other Nations). Blatchford's ACCION, however, was privately funded, chiefly by IBM, because he believed that a grass roots volunteer program should not be tied to the political process.

Administration support began to sour on a Sunday morning in September 1969. That day, President Nixon hosted a White House breakfast for Peace Corps country directors. As he said good-bye to his guests, members of the Committee of Returned Volunteers assembled across the street in Lafayette Park and treated the President, his guests, and reporters to a bit of guerrilla theater: In their dramatization, Uncle Sam sent out a Green Beret to beat up a third world peasant as a chorus sang the Marine Hymn. Then, a Peace Corps volunteer entered bearing Nutrition, symbolized by a Coke bottle, and Education, symbolized by a copy of *Time* magazine. The chorus chanted, "Gosh, Golly, Gee whiz, Wow." The play concluded with the peasants kicking out the volunteer as the chorus egged them on with songs about revolution.

The White House was further antagonized by the Peace Corps when volunteers around the world joined in the 1969 Vietnam moratoriums on October 15 and again on November 15. To show their objection to the continuation of the Vietnam war, they staged sit-ins and candlelight vigils in front of American embassies, circulated petitions, and took out ads in national newspapers. It was now clear to the White House that Blatchford's plan to whip the Peace Corps into shape with plumbers and electricians would not erase the deep-rooted antipathy to the war.

According to documents in the National Archives, Nixon aide and speechwriter Pat Buchanan was assigned to "investigate the Peace Corps' egregious blunders overseas with an eye, as we understand it, to doing away with the thing." Buchanan wrote to the President that "I would not counsel such drastic action. It would put us crosswise with a number of our friends who have swallowed the propaganda that this is the greatest thing since sliced bread."[6] Instead, Buchanan suggested a strategy to discredit the Peace Corps: "Exposure of Peace Corps blunders—turning them over to our Republicans on the Hill to investigate . . . while we perhaps leaked the blunders again and again" in order to influence public opinion against the Peace Corps.[7] Two weeks later, Buchanan submitted to the President a detailed chronology of volunteers' antiwar demonstrations and embarrassing run-ins with host country governments. He theorized that "while the number of political incidents in the nine-year existence of the Peace Corps is relatively small, the increased open defiance of Peace Corps rules is an indication that there could be serious troubles ahead."[8]

In this second memo, Buchanan advised more direct action: first, that the administration make drastic cuts in the Peace Corps budget; and second, that the White House instruct Blatchford to work toward "minimizing these disturbances, getting rid of the troublemakers, reducing the size of the Peace Corps—and changing its nature to a more mature, altruistic outfit than it seems to be today with the young leftists dominant."[9]

Nixon agreed that the Peace Corps needed an overhaul and wrote back to Buchanan that Blatchford was "a good man—work with him on this." He also approved Buchanan's suggestion of arranging some negative publicity to pave the way for cuts in the Peace Corps' budget. "I think a speech (Senate) or article putting all the incidents on record would be a good starter."[10]

Two weeks after receiving Buchanan's second memo, President Nixon soured further on the Peace Corps, and he decided that the organization should be phased out entirely. The impetus for this decision was a lengthy editorial in *The Wall Street Journal* arguing that the war in Vietnam was sapping the Peace Corps' lifeblood—idealism and naïveté. The editorial stated: "The public identity of the Peace Corps still lies with the Kennedy concept, and for an agency so involved with human idealism, evolution away from it is a powerful problem."[11] The day after the piece ran, one of Nixon's aides wrote to John Ehrlichman and Henry Kissinger that "the president noted that he feels a quiet phasing out of the Peace Corps and VISTA [Volunteers in Service to America] is in order. He notes that the place to begin is to get the appropriations cut."[12] (From that point, the White House's request to Congress for Peace Corps funding dropped each year for the next four years, from $109.8 million for fiscal year 1970 to $77 million for 1974.)

As the Peace Corps grew poorer, it could no longer afford to maintain the improvements in training and programming that had been initiated by Jack Vaughn during the Johnson administration. Joe Blatchford's optimistic plan for retooling the Peace Corps with skilled volunteers was executed on the cheap. "We'd take a volunteer who was an agronomist and have him instruct trainees who might have had some farming experience," says one former country director. "We were able to wire together a modicum of skill, but I wasn't pleased with it. I think we were kidding ourselves."

The final crippling blow came in the spring of 1971, when President Nixon announced that as part of his government reorganization plan the Peace Corps would be installed in a new superagency called Action, which would house all the federally sponsored volunteer programs scattered among several different agencies.* According to the President, Action would be a more efficient way of "enlisting the dedication and idealism of those young Americans who want to serve their fellow man."[13] But Democrats

---

*The following volunteer programs were moved into Action: the Office of Volunteer Action, formerly in the Department of Housing and Urban Development; Teachers Corps and Retired Senior Volunteer Program, both formerly in the Department of Health, Education and Welfare; VISTA and Foster Grandparents, both formerly in the Office of Economic Opportunity; and the Service Corps of Retired Executives, formerly in the Small Business Administration.

in Congress, the Peace Corps staff, and some volunteers were convinced that Action (originally titled Third Century for the upcoming bicentennial) was contrived by the administration as a way of submerging the Peace Corps in a "bureaucratic swamp" and ultimately drowning it.[14] "It would be very hard for Nixon to kill the Peace Corps because it had an apple-pie reputation," says Jim Greene (Peru, 1970–72). "It might not be that hard, though, to phase out something with a different name."

The impact of Action's absorption of the Peace Corps was felt almost immediately. The Action bureaucracy slowed the Peace Corps' day-to-day operations as its various functions—recruitment, training, and congressional liaison, for example—were swallowed by centralized offices. The Corps' visibility diminished as public relations and advertising departments promoted Action instead. "You couldn't find the Peace Corps in the phone book," recalls Sargent Shriver. Even the agency's letterhead was replaced by Action's, and the Peace Corps director's title became Associate Director of Action for International Operations.

The Peace Corps' relocation under the Action umbrella also had repercussions for the Corps' overseas operations. "The Peace Corps bureaucracy just sort of went to sleep on India," said Daniel Patrick Moynihan, ambassador to India in the early 1970s. "What is it doing if it can't fill a quota of 50 [volunteers]?"[15] And when a *Washington Post* correspondent asked a spokesperson from Brazil's foreign ministry for a comment on Peace Corps activities he was told, "I asked around and nobody knew whether we were for the Peace Corps or against it. In fact, hardly anybody remembered it was still here."[16]

The impact of budget slashes and the plunge into organizational chaos was compounded when Action filled up its senior positions with incompetent patronage appointments. Volunteers in Peru were so appalled when a favorite staffer was "reassigned to Washington" and replaced by one of Blatchford's fraternity brothers—a self-made millionaire who spoke no Spanish and had no experience in Latin America—that they organized to have him removed. "I have a very sad feeling every time I think about what they have done," Linda Hatch (Peru, 1970–72) wrote home. "There may be a mass resignation in December. . . . I certainly am not proud to be a member of Blatchford's political action corps."*

Blatchford resigned after the 1972 election. His successor, Michael Balzano, the White House's liaison to ethnic groups, attributed the Peace

---

*Volunteers considered threatening a mass resignation but never carried it out. A number of staff members in Peru, however, did resign over their associate's "reassignment" and other contentious issues.

Corps' decline to the following factors: the increasing number of host country requests for highly skilled volunteers; requests that stipulated males only; the surge in nationalism; and the growing suspicion that volunteers engaged in intelligence work.[17]

The wounds inflicted by the Nixon administration weakened the Peace Corps for years to come. But it also forced the Corps to break with the past. At its tenth anniversary, the organization could hardly afford to rest on the laurels earned in the days of Camelot. Blatchford blasted the outdated reverence for college grads and initiated an invigorating debate. By trying to recruit skilled volunteers, the Corps demonstrated to its hosts a sensitivity to and respect for their needs. Critics charged that Blatchford cast aside the Peace Corps' cross-cultural goals by recruiting skilled individuals who didn't learn the language or appreciate the native customs. But he actually expanded upon these goals by sending mid-career professionals and blue-collar technicians. They, too, could show the developing world what life in America was about, and they, too, could bring home to the United States valuable lessons about the developing world.

# Chapter 9

☆════

# *The Peace Corps Meets the Brady Bunch: Skilled Volunteers and Families*

In the fall of 1970, Joe Blatchford called reporters to come to meet a new group of volunteers before they left for Ghana. Except for the sea of luggage, the lobby of Washington's National Hotel looked more like an audition for *Romper Room* than a Peace Corps send-off. A dozen moms and dads in sport coats and tasteful coordinates smiled for pictures while their children made faces at the TV cameras. These were the new volunteers: six families and twenty-five children ranging in age from two months to eighteen years.

In his quest to increase the number of skilled volunteers, Blatchford sought out older applicants and invited them to bring their families. The Peace Corps got much good press with this initiative, but more important, the corps was able to provide host countries with skilled technicians such as plumbers, carpenters, and electricians, and professionals such as architects, financial analysts, and civil engineers. But the families program was not all *Leave It to Beaver*. Overseas staff, accustomed to dealing with single volunteers with minimal needs, now had to worry about allergy shots, good school systems, baby-food shipments, and orthopedic shoes arriving by diplomatic pouch.

The difficulties were such that two thirds of the overseas staff were "negatively disposed toward family placements," according to a study of the program conducted just two years after it was first announced in 1969.[1]

"The families program was a big bust," says Robert Currie, a former staff member in Micronesia. "A lot of the children couldn't adjust and many of the men couldn't be effective in their assignments while dealing with the trauma their families were going through." A former country director in Africa says that fathers were not comfortable with their seemingly subordinate status. "They really didn't see themselves as volunteers," he recalls. "They all seemed to think they should have my job. A lot of them were pains in the ass and much more trouble than they were worth." The wives, too, presented the Peace Corps with unanticipated problems. The nonmatrixed spouse, as the wives were called, was told that after they settled their families the overseas staff would assist them in finding work. But more often than not, the wives were left on their own and improvised assignments at local schools or orphanages.

In some cases, husbands and wives were both given substantial assignments. In 1970, Nancy Lassus and her then-husband George took their two daughters, ages six and eight, to Nairobi, Kenya, where Nancy filled the Kenyan government's request for a diabetes education specialist, and went on to establish the East Africa Diabetes Society. George Lassus worked for the Kenya Ministry of Works developing a system for amortizing the cost of construction equipment purchased with foreign-aid monies.

Accommodating families was also expensive. A 1972 internal report estimated that a family of four cost over three times as much to maintain as a single volunteer for one year. The expense seemed excessive, considering that the corps got only one full-time volunteer per family. Just two years after the families program was announced, the Peace Corps scaled it back. Recruiting policies were revised to stipulate that only family heads with "scarce skills" and a maximum of two children should be accepted. By 1976, the criterion was an "extremely scarce skill," although the maximum number of children was raised to three.[2]

The Peace Corps also attempted to bring in skilled applicants by recruiting through professional associations and trade unions. One of the more successful efforts was conducted with The Smithsonian Institution, which supplied the Peace Corps with about seven hundred fifty zoologists, botanists, and environmental scientists between 1971 and 1977.

The type of work performed by these volunteers departed dramatically from that of the hordes of starry-eyed, B.A.-wielding idealists who taught English or grappled with "community development." A husband-and-wife team of zoologists, for example, studied the daily and seasonal movements of an endangered species of sheep in the Lake Urmia region of Iran. And in Costa Rica, a botanist worked for a national park, identifying and cataloging plant species.

Critics of the trend toward more skilled volunteers contended that these recruits would not fulfill the Peace Corps' less tangible objectives. Their skills, it was argued, were far too sophisticated to be learned by uneducated host country nationals. Cross-cultural exchange, they charged, was minimized because the skilled volunteers worked in either desolate locations or in government offices.

The advantage in sending skilled volunteers was readily apparent to the new recruits who found great satisfaction in their work, in marked contrast to the frustration they observed among the younger volunteers. "The specialists' jobs were much better defined because they were tailored to their skills," says Dick Jachowski, a placement officer at Peace Corps headquarters back then. "It wasn't a shotgun approach."

## Joanne Hauler (Côte d'Ivoire, 1973–76)

I was thirty-three years old when I joined the Peace Corps and I was a nun. I was working as a supervisor in the chemistry section in a large hospital laboratory when I saw an ad in *Laboratory Medicine* magazine which said the Peace Corps was looking for people with technical skills. The head of my order told me that if I wanted to go overseas I should work with one of the missions. But I thought I'd be lost in the great conglomerate of the Dominican sisters. I spent the night praying over it, and the next morning I wrote her a letter saying, "I cannot accept your decision. I'm going anyway."

The Peace Corps told us we were an experimental group. We had people with degrees in agriculture, range management, and animal husbandry. A psychologist interviewed each of us to make sure that we would go overseas with an open mind, and be willing to work with whatever facilities were available. They didn't want to send anyone who thought they could bring the most recent technological advances to the poor impoverished natives.

I was assigned to teach at two schools for laboratory professionals. What made my job especially challenging was the lack of technical vocabulary in the French instruction we received in training. So in my classes I had to say things like, "Take this thing here and that thing there and do this."

Most of our group fit into the academic setting really well. We were working with the rest of the faculty just as we did at home, only they were

African. In fact, I got the sense that if anything, because we were a little older, we tended to be more eager to learn from them, than the younger volunteers who thought they were bringing all the good of America to the Ivoirians.

The younger volunteers tended to be more impatient. I was riding a bus to northern Ghana with about twelve other volunteers and the bus broke down at this crossroads where there was nothing but one village and a lot of monkeys. The driver took off to get help and never came back. The younger volunteers could hardly stand the fact that we were abandoned for the night by this roadside. The other passengers made the best of it. We sat in a circle around a little fire, kept the children warm, and sang songs.

I lived in an apartment in a section of Abidjan that was a mix of Ivoirian and non-Ivoirian people, but largely Ivoirian professionals. I would compare it to lower-income apartments in an American city. Most of the time there was no hot water and I used the electricity only when I could afford it. I was friends with some UN volunteers, and some of the other teachers who were French, Lebanese and Ivoirian. They'd come over and we'd buy a few bottles of cheap beer, talk politics, make popcorn, or listen to music. Sometimes we'd chip in for a taxi and go to the discos. Our African friends would try to teach us this dance that can be very erotic. They'd laugh at us because we didn't do it the way they did. Sometimes the Ivoirian teachers invited me to go home to their villages for the weekends. I extended my service for a year but I could have stayed in the Côte d'Ivoire for the rest of my life. My parents were up in years, though, and I promised I would spend some time with them.

## *Ralph Smith (Botswana, 1972–74)**

I had been teaching basic biology for seven years at the University of Michigan and my wife and I decided that if I didn't get tenure we were going to travel and have fun. When I didn't get it, a friend who did consulting for the Peace Corps suggested I apply for the Smithsonian program. I disagreed with the idea of running overseas to help out in any way possible. Just building chicken coops didn't help. I felt that you had to work on a higher level to have any impact.

As it turned out, the Botswana Ministry of Wildlife had asked for a mature, experienced volunteer to start a conservation education depart-

*The name of this volunteer and some identifying details have been changed to protect his privacy.

ment. A significant percentage of the Botswana economy depended on tourism and wildlife, but the government had allowed the country to turn into a Rachel Carson disaster area. The government welcomed anything that would help make money, like cattle ranching or mining, without looking at the consequences for the environment. In addition to having taught, I had done some conservation work for the U.S. Forest Service and the National Park Service in the early 1960s.

My job at the Ministry of Wildlife was basically doing public relations. I wrote for the government's daily paper and the monthly government-published magazine about the value of wildlife and how the environment is easily abused. I took high school students on trips out to the desert and I escorted Marlin Perkins around when he came to do a show. I also did a weekly radio show on different aspects of Botswana ecology. We'd dramatize poaching scenes by recording trucks screeching and people getting caught by the police. I put together a slide show with a script for schoolteachers on how the environment was being slowly degraded. I also assembled a wildlife exhibit that explained the country's game laws and took it to various agricultural fairs.

The Peace Corps was my first time going overseas. I hadn't known anyone who had been to Botswana, and I hadn't heard anything positive about it—just the illnesses you could contract, and that it was a hellhole of starving people. As it turned out, the only hardship we faced was the few bugs that came through our screen windows. We had a fully furnished home with electricity, hot water, and flush toilet. We hired a woman to clean and do the laundry and we also had a boy cut the grass.

We hung out with expatriates, British and Canadian volunteers, and some people from the United Nations Development Program. We had some of the Africans I worked with over for dinner but they wouldn't invite us to their homes. They never initiated any social activity, although we had a great time together on field trips.

My wife was a psychiatric nurse and taught basic psychology at the nursing school in the capital. But she got very frustrated with it because her students couldn't grasp the notion of a subconscious. In her second year, she worked with a women's sewing cooperative. The Peace Corps kept saying they'd find her something else more appropriate to her skills, but they never did. She wasn't that thrilled about the whole thing to begin with. She also missed her friends and we weren't having fun as a couple. Our marriage was rocky anyway and it completely deteriorated in Africa. She was alone for weeks at a time while I was in the field, and I met other, more exciting women. We separated four months before we finished our two years.

I can't tell how much impact my work had. The teachers always thanked me for my classroom presentations and they always asked me to come back, maybe just to give themselves a break during the school day. The students I worked with were very polite and said they learned a lot. I like to think some were moved.

## Richard Klukas (Colombia, 1972–74)

My wife and I had been accepted by the Peace Corps for Chile in 1961 but we didn't go because we were still in college. We started thinking about it again in 1970. By that time we had two sons and we were ready for a change of scene. I was working for the U.S. Park Service and a memo came around describing the Peace Corps' Smithsonian program and stating that the Park Service would grant two-year leaves.

Colombia wanted to attract more tourism by developing national parks that offered skiing, hiking, and horseback riding. I was assigned to plan one of these parks but there had been a major flood right before I got there so the funds that would have gone into developing the park were diverted to rebuilding roads.

The Peace Corps reassigned me to an agricultural extension job at a state agency. I studied the impact of the coffee industry on the rivers. It turned out that washing the beans in the river increased the level of acidity and was killing the fish. I worked on introducing rainbow trout in streams for recreational fishing and I experimented with different species of trees for reforestation purposes since the jungle was being destroyed for cattle grazing. I worked with species like black walnut that would not only slow the erosion caused by the disappearing jungle but would also be valuable as lumber. I was also asked to make a list of birds in the area so they could promote bird-watching.

There was a limited budget for equipment. We had to make do with what was available. I would have to drive five hours each time I wanted to take a water sample instead of having a device set up that reads the water conditions continuously over a period of time. A microscope also would have been nice too, but I had to forget about doing things that required one. At the time, the hippie culture was to hang loose, so that's what I did.

The young liberal arts volunteers seemed more frustrated than us and they were dropping out. They seemed to be searching for meaning in their lives and weren't as concerned with the Colombians.

## Gary and Julie Brusca (Mauritius, 1972–74)

(The Bruscas brought their three children, ages eight, seven, and three.)

### Julie Brusca

Mauritius is a resort island for Europeans, South Africans, and Australians. We lived in a vacation bungalow on a bay and the white sand beach came right up to our garden wall. We had a flush toilet because the Peace Corps was very concerned about our living standards but since our rent was guaranteed for two years, our landlord never fixed anything. So we lost the hot water and our stove. Our kids went to a convent school on the European part of the island. We were concerned about their education because there are twenty-three public holidays a year, three weeks off for Easter, and a summer and winter vacation each two months long. We thought they'd have to go back in grades when we got back, but they came home fluent in French and Creole.

The Peace Corps told me they were hiring my husband but they promised me a job, too, although they never did anything about it. I found work at a convent training the girls from a very poor village so they could work as maids and cooks at the tourist hotels.

### Gary Brusca

I had been teaching college since 1964. When friends came back very excited from their Peace Corps assignments in Tonga, we started thinking maybe we could do it, too. I took a two-year leave without pay and I lost seniority, but it was probably the best experience of our lives. The country director told us that he was against our coming. He had been a volunteer in Nigeria and was of the old school, that volunteers should be young B.A. generalists without spouses or children.

My job description sounded thrilling. I was replacing someone from the UN's Food and Agricultural Organization who had established an oyster farm. The farm was supposed to lead to the development of cooperative units with local families who would sell the oysters to the hotels on the island. The project turned out to be a bust. When I arrived, all the oysters were dying.

My immediate boss was the head of the Mauritius government's fisheries program and he didn't want to hear about this because they had sunk a lot of money into it. I tried different ways to keep the oysters alive: We built oyster-rafts out in the ocean; we tried working in shallow water, deep water, cold water, and hanging them in racks and trays but nothing worked. They all died.

I then turned to raising green sea turtles. Mauritius used to be a nesting ground for the species but they had been overfished. We brought in sixty turtles from another island and raised them until they could be released into the ocean. The turtles were doing well but they kept disappearing. Then I learned that the night guards at the research station were letting people steal the turtles for the shells which were sold to the tourists at the airport. We were down to the last nine turtles when a cyclone hit the island and destroyed the pens. The turtles were lost.

My third project had the most potential. The reef around the island had been overfished, so I started a fishery. We trapped and collected lots of different kinds of fish and reared them in closed pens. A renewed fish supply would provide a local food source and a way for people to earn money. The station staff was very excited about it. But then we had a visit from the new minister of fisheries who brought some visiting dignitaries from India. When we showed them some of the fish we were raising, the fisheries minister ordered the workers to give the fish to his guests, the police escort, and the limo driver. That depleted our entire stock, and the men who worked for me at the station were devastated. These guys were called relief workers and were considered the bottom of the barrel. They were going to get their eighty cents a day whether they worked or not. But by the time I left, they were working extremely hard.

I didn't accomplish anything in my specific assignment. We weren't going to save the country with oysters. But I got a playground built in the village and set up a science club at the girls convent school. Those things were satisfying and I think they had some impact.

There's a greater chance for failure in a narrowly defined program like mine because all your eggs are in one basket. The countries might have expected miracles from the Smithsonian program because they were getting people who had Ph.D.'s. But the benefits to us as a family were far greater than anything my work might have contributed. We made a lot of friends and didn't want to go home. We toyed with the idea of staying for a third year but I couldn't get an extension on my leave.

## *Flo and David Wagner (Ghana, 1970–72)*

(The Wagners took their three sons, ages two, four, and five, and had a fourth child, a daughter, during their two years in the Peace Corps.)

## David Wagner

We were in our late twenties and had a very successful wholesale house-wares business in Huntington, New York. It looked like we had everything going for us: a ten-room house in the suburbs and two cars in the garage. But we knew there was more, we just didn't know what it was.

On the way home from visiting friends in upstate New York, we got stuck for hours in the traffic from the Woodstock festival. We sat there listening to the radio and a commercial came on saying that the Peace Corps was looking for families. That got us thinking. We had reservations about leaving the business, and our parents tried to give us guilt trips like, "We don't care what you do with yourselves, but what about your children?" We went anyway.

The Ghanaian government wanted to provide some kind of training in small business so that nationals could replace the British who ran most of the businesses in the country. So the Peace Corps recruited people who had run their own businesses and left it up to us to design something. We put together a small-business consulting agency within the Ghanaian Business Bureau.

I would be picked up by a driver every morning and when I got to my desk I would receive my daily allotment of four squares of toilet paper because it was so expensive. Local people would come into the agency with ideas for businesses and we'd help them write proposals which they could take to the bank for loans. We also held clinics in the evening on advertising, marketing, and accounting. After two years, the Ghanaian civil servants we worked with had pretty much taken it over and we felt we had been very successful.

We also set up our steward in his own cookie business. He made the best chocolate-chip cookies we'd ever tasted. We had an assembly line going in our house and his kids and our kids would go around selling them.

## Flo Wagner

When we got to Ghana, the men received two weeks of instruction in business consulting and the wives were taken on a bus tour. The Ghanaian men, with whom our husbands would be working, knew we needed more orientation than that so they paired each of their wives with the volunteer wives. My partner took me to the marketplace, which was a quite a shock. There's a lady nursing her baby while another child is urinating right next to the food I was about to buy. This was definitely not the A and P.

Our children adjusted beautifully to Ghana. Our five-year-old became friendly with a construction crew working nearby. He would take his sandwich and run down there every day to eat lunch and talk with them. He was also sneaking sandwiches for them to eat. Our four-year-old would go talk to our night watchman every night after dinner. The watchman didn't understand a word of English and our son didn't speak his tribal language, but they communicated in their own way and used to play games for hours.

My understanding was that the husbands were the primary volunteers and that the wives would get assignments once we were settled in Ghana, but that was a lot of bullshit. We had to find our own jobs. A nurse at the local orphanage said they were looking for help, so I worked there five days a week teaching English to these destitute tribal children. They learned to sing all the American nursery songs with a New York accent.

We didn't have any dealings with the Peace Corps, except when we needed to get shots. When I told the Peace Corps doctor I thought I was pregnant, he said, "But we have no regulations for you." I said, "But I'm still pregnant." I really wanted to have the baby in Ghana—I was Peace Corps and I was going to be like a villager—but my doctor in New York said under no circumstances should I give birth there. I flew to New York to have the baby and brought her back to Africa when she was nineteen days old.

We had an Ashanti naming ceremony. A traditional costume had been made for me and the whole ritual was done in Twi with an English interpreter. Her first name was Hebrew, Samanda, and her middle name, Adwoa, was Ashanti. It means "First Girl Born on a Monday."

## Alice Martin (Jamaica, 1972–74)*

(The Martins brought their three children, ages six, eight, and ten, to Jamaica where Alice's husband taught at an agricultural college.)

The Peace Corps was the hardest two years of my life but also two of the most valuable. We wanted our kids to experience something other than a typical middle-class white Protestant neighborhood. As it turned out, going into the Peace Corps gave my husband the opportunity to be

---

*Names and some identifying details have been changed to protect privacy.

twenty-two again. When our plane was delayed going down to Jamaica, Dennis said he was going to join the other volunteers in the airport cocktail lounge. I said that I would go and have my turn when he came back. He said, "No. You stay with the children."

A year after we were there, the Peace Corps asked me to fly back to the States to work with the families who were in training. It was very exciting to meet the new mothers. I was very positive about it and kept the stresses to myself. When I got back to Jamaica, the Peace Corps offered me a job assisting the other Peace Corps mothers. Dennis asked me not to do it. He said he couldn't be a volunteer if he was worrying about the kids. I didn't take a stand on it because I didn't want to get into a battle.

I can count the number of evenings I got to go out in the first year. The children and I gave my husband honor and prestige in the community but he felt we were like baggage. Dennis wanted to be a full-fledged volunteer with no restrictions imposed by his family. So he did what he wanted and went to the bars with the other volunteers while I baby-sat. I remember saying to myself, "He's spoiling this experience for me."

## Linda Bridges (Morocco, 1970–72)

(The Bridges were the first African-American family to join the Peace Corps. Linda Bridges was a dance therapist and her husband, Stan, was an administrator at a school for the blind in Los Angeles. They brought their four children, ages two, four, six, and eight.)

I didn't have any altruistic reasons for joining the Peace Corps. The city was planning a freeway through our neighborhood. We *had* to move whether we wanted to or not. I heard the Peace Corps was holding an orientation meeting and said to my husband, Stan, "Let's go. Maybe we'll get a trip out of this." And we did. They sent us to Morocco, where Stan did curriculum development for various schools for the blind and established a braille library.

I loved being in Morocco. What I didn't like was the Peace Corps. Our daughter Lydia caught a very bad cold and when her temperature got up to one hundred four, we took her to the hospital. It turned out that she had pleurisy. The Peace Corps nurse was out of town when this happened and when she came back, she called us to her office and said, "How dare you take Lydia to the hospital without asking my permission!" As I stood up to leave, I put my hand on her desk and she hit my fingers with her pencil as if I were a two-year-old. She was clearly a bigot. She used to wash her doorknob whenever a Moroccan had touched it.

The Peace Corps said that if I wanted to work, I'd have to find a job myself. One staff member told me about a private school for retarded children that might be able to use my services. I started working at the school and I also taught modern dance to Moroccan and French women. We gave a performance at the United States Information Agency building that was filmed for Moroccan television.

Morocco became home for me and I didn't want to move back to the United States. One of the women in my modern dance class was a senior official in the Moroccan government youth-sports program and she wanted me to stay in the country and work for her. She offered to pay for our children's schooling, our housing, and a generous salary. But Stan didn't have a position, other than his Peace Corps assignment. He also just wasn't as happy as I was in Morocco. I had a better grasp of Arabic than he did, so I was able to make more inroads socially. But I was traditional enough in my thinking to feel that it would cause problems if I was working and he wasn't.

I knew we had to leave when one of our sons became very ill. He liked to give food to the beggars and they got to like him so much that they started giving him things to eat, too. He developed pinworms, round-worms, and amebic dysentery, even though the Peace Corps nurse told us twice that his stool samples had tested negative. When we got back to the United States, he had to be hospitalized. The children also wanted to see their grandmother.

I think it's a wonderful idea for the Peace Corps to take families. I think our family brought a sense of stability to the program in Morocco. We had an easier time adjusting to life there because we had the support system of the mate and the children. There was never a feeling of loneliness for home. The other volunteers looked to us as their parents. They used to come by and talk to us about their problems.

# Part Five

# The Carter Years, 1977-81

*Chapter 10*

☆═══

# "The Hardest, Dirtiest Work There Is"

After Jimmy Carter's 1976 victory, a bedsheet unfurled from a window of the Peace Corps' headquarters in Washington declaring "We Won." Staff members were "out of their minds with joy to see the end of the Nixon era," recalls a Carter aide, anticipating that the new President, the son of former volunteer Lillian Carter (India, 1966–68), would restore the Peace Corps to its former glory. But the Corps' golden era would prove to be irretrievable, even with the help of a sympathetic administration.

For young Americans finishing college in the mid-1970s, the notion of serving in a government-sponsored volunteer program held little attraction. Unlike volunteers of the early and mid-1960s, who came of age trusting in America's benevolence to struggling countries, college grads of the mid-1970s had learned from the Vietnam War that their government's intentions overseas were not always honorable. For the "Me Generation," the idealism that had propelled individuals toward the Peace Corps ten years earlier seemed hopelessly naive. "Having a young President implicitly meant that if you were young you could make a difference," says Mary King, a veteran of the civil rights movement whom Carter appointed deputy director of Action in 1977. "That sense was gone by the 1970s. Young Americans couldn't believe the government could do anything good, that Washington would just as soon use its youth for cannon fodder."

In 1976, applications to the Peace Corps hit a record low of 13,908—

down from the record high of 45,653 in 1964. "I was very cynical and mistrusting about a lot of things the government was doing," says David Lowe (Kenya, 1978–81). "I had the sense that the Peace Corps was a tool of American imperialism." Lowe's father summed it up well when he said to his son, "The Peace Corps? Nobody does that anymore."

For the American public, the Peace Corps was not only dated but somewhat nebulous. "I traveled in Mexico for a month after graduating from college," recalls Keith Mendelson (Togo, 1976–79). "That's where the idea dawned on me that the Peace Corps might be an interesting thing to do, but I had no idea what the Peace Corps did."

Neither did the Peace Corps. Despite Joe Blatchford's aggressive leadership, the agency never fully refurbished itself with technically sophisticated volunteers, and when Blatchford was named director of Action in 1971, the reins of the Peace Corps were passed to a succession of caretaker administrators, four in all, in just four years. By the time of Carter's inauguration, "there was no vision about what kinds of programs Peace Corps volunteers might be best at and what kinds of programs might best contribute to development," recalls a former staff member. "There was just a sense of sending people out there."

The demoralized staff looked to the new administration to reinvigorate the agency. When President Carter appointed as director of Action prominent antiwar activist Sam Brown—who cut his political teeth on Eugene McCarthy's primary campaign in 1968—"we all thought he was going to be our savior," said one official.[1] While his credentials were politically correct, his dogmatic approach—Theodore White described Brown as "armored with unshakable righteousness"[2]—ultimately alienated the staff and delayed a much-needed housecleaning.

To run the Peace Corps, Brown sought out a woman and a member of a minority. After a six-month search, he appointed Carolyn Payton, a fifty-two-year-old psychology professor who headed Howard University's student counseling service and had worked for the Peace Corps in the 1960s. Payton and Brown agreed that the Corps' pursuit of skilled volunteers had drained the organization of its spiritual energy, leaving it as little more than an overseas placement service. According to Brown, "The volunteer experience often became a nine-to-five job rather than a fulltime commitment."[3] Payton, who was country director in the eastern Caribbean in 1969, recalls that Blatchford's announcement about skilled volunteers "was like a punch in the stomach. It went against my basic belief in what the Peace Corps is about," Payton says, "Having a sophisticated ability immediately makes you superior to the host-country person you're working with. I would rather send volunteers who recognize their deficits and therefore relate to the host nationals on a level of equality and egalitarianism."

Payton was determined to put the Peace Corps' house in order. She believed that comprehensive training and well-defined assignments were the basis for a successful operation. To help her overhaul training and programming—the process by which the Peace Corps determines what jobs should be performed in any given country—Payton hired David Levine, a former volunteer and staff person in Ethiopia, who was later dubbed the programming "guru." Levine believed that with the right volunteers, the Peace Corps could fill a specific niche in the development-assistance puzzle. "AID and the World Bank don't know how to link their efforts downward or get local activity to link upward," says Levine. "That's the magic the Peace Corps can do. You literally have people going over who say, 'Goddamn, it's nice to live in the mud and the shit. It's wonderful to be in this village.' "

Under Payton and Levine, B.A. generalists received greater respect than they had in years, but they also received greater scrutiny. Starting in 1978, applicants were put through a rigorous week-long screening process, called a CAST (Center for Assessment and Training).* Those who survived the CAST then entered an intensive training program, which, depending on the volunteer's destination and assignment, could last as long as four months.† "Rather than recruit an expert on silk culture," explains Mary King, "we would teach the generalist everything he or she needed to know about silk culture in the area to which they were going."

"For the first month of training we were at Howard University, where we had a crash course in biochemistry and nutrition," says Becky Raymond, who worked in a nutrition education program in Niger. "They also crammed in a lot of country-specific information at the same time. For the next three months we trained in-country, where we studied French and health issues specific to Niger. We also analyzed the Nigerian diet and the nutritional value of foods sold in the markets."

To make sure the new "skill-trained" volunteers, as they were called, could make full use of their know-how, Levine and Payton required more exacting work on the part of overseas staff. Instead of merely compiling

---

*Just a few years later, the CAST was deemed too stressful and was discontinued. In 1989, however, the CAST was revived in order to select the most qualified applicants for the Peace Corps' first program for China.

†In the Peace Corps' first ten years, training programs were usually about twelve weeks long. As the Corps' budget declined in the early and mid-1970s, training was gradually reduced sometimes by more than half.

shopping lists of job titles requested by host country governments, staff had to work closely with officials, analyzing the country's needs and identifying the specific skills required to address them. This, of course, entailed convincing host country officials that the B.A. generalist could perform specific tasks just as well as the practiced professionals the Peace Corps had been supplying, albeit in limited numbers.

"The Niger government requested that we send professional nutritionists," recalls former country director Phyllis Dichter, "but you don't need a master's degree to sit in a circle of mothers in a village and talk about why they should give their kids beans. I told the government that we would train the volunteers according to the skills they told us they needed." But it was difficult for the country directors to gain the confidence of host country officials in this new way of planning Peace Corps activities. After all, working relationships between the two groups had been minimal for several years. The challenge was further exacerbated by Brown's insistence that *all* assignments conform with "Basic Human Needs," the latest theory in the field of development assistance. Basic Human Needs maintained that foreign assistance efforts should address such fundamental problems as inadequate food, population growth, poor health, and lack of potable water. This bottom-up approach, which began to gain currency during the Nixon administration and was championed by President Carter, marked a dramatic departure from the previously held theory that foreign assistance should be directed at building the recipient's government infrastructure, economic institutions, and industries.

Of course, there had always been volunteers who dug wells, and preached sound nutrition and hygiene, but over half the corps' enrollment were assigned to teaching posts, and many volunteers performed work that was unrelated to survival issues. Brown's Basic Human Needs initiative directed a greater share of the Peace Corps' financial and human resources to projects that addressed critical survival issues.*

While Brown's championing of Basic Human Needs—"the hardest, dirtiest work there is"—revived a sense of romance and sacrifice about volunteer service, overseas staff weren't quite sure what the program meant.[4] "They told us what it wasn't," says John Chromy, who was country director in the eastern Caribbean at the time. "It wasn't teaching at a univer-

---

*Statistics show only slight change in distribution of volunteers among different assignments. In 1973, for instance, education assignments accounted for 48.4 percent. In 1979, education, renamed "knowledge and skills," accounted for 45 percent. Health increased from 8.8 percent in 1973 to 13 percent in 1979, and agriculture volunteers actually decreased slightly, from 22.3 percent in 1973 to 19 percent in 1979.

sity, playing in the national symphony, or teaching English to French-speaking Arab elites in Tunisia." A staff member in Lesotho recalls, "I used to call it 'earth, water, wind, and fire.'"

When it became clear that Basic Human Needs encompassed assignments relating to water supply, sanitation, health, and food production, the staff was still dubious about it, as those types of assignments were not necessarily appropriate in all the host countries. The Peace Corps, they felt, should respond to the needs of host countries as the host country, not the Corps, defined them.

One of the most contentious elements of the Basic Human Needs initiative was Brown's insistence on reducing the number of conventional teaching assignments, particularly English instruction. Brown maintained that such assignments made little real contribution because volunteers' students came from elite families and they would receive an education whether or not the Peace Corps supplied teachers.* He also contended that developing nations no longer considered traditional education a critical need. Pointing to Julius Nyerere's treatise, "Education for Self-reliance,"[5] Brown argued that "they do not want a mass of highly educated college graduates who cannot be employed because there are no jobs for them, or jobs they are unwilling to take because they are somehow beneath them."[6]

"Sam might have thought that," says Reginald Petty, country director in Swaziland and Kenya from 1978 to 1983, "but the governments were always asking us for teachers, teachers, teachers. Sam Brown just didn't understand the value of knowing English in these countries." Explains another official, "English is the only handle for social mobility, the only way someone can ever get to be middle-class. Suddenly you're employable. You can read the manual. You can communicate with the tourists."

To satisfy Brown *and* host country governments, overseas staff devised some artful programming tactics. "I used to tell the government ministers, 'If you let me bring in five skill-trained volunteers, I'll get you ten more English teachers,'" says Reginald Petty. The staff would also embellish teaching assignments with Basic Human Needs features. "We had a big English teaching program which the Togolese wanted to keep," says former country director Jody Olsen. "I told Washington that we were putting more teachers in remote villages and that they had secondary projects that were in keeping with Basic Human Needs."

This additional work was sometimes overwhelming. "The English

---

* A 1979 survey of volunteers in teaching assignments revealed that their students represented a mix of the country's socioeconomic layers.[7]

teachers probably put in more hours than other volunteers," recalls Meredith McGehee (Niger, 1978–80). They handled six or seven classes a day and prepared lessons and graded papers at night. They used to tell the staff, 'I'm already doing sixty hours a week and now you want me to go raise chickens?' The Niger government didn't understand why the teachers had to do this other stuff. They just wanted the teachers to teach."

Enthusiasm over Brown's appointment further waned when he raised unsettling questions about the disparity between the Peace Corps' humanitarian objectives and political realities. "On the one hand, it is hard to see how a Peace Corps volunteer teaching English or building a fish pond in a village someplace is making a political statement," Brown said at a State Department gathering in 1977. "On the other hand, we currently have a combined total of 68 volunteers in Jamaica and Tanzania [then under Socialist leaders Michael Manley and Julius Nyerere, respectively] and 490 in Korea and the Philippines [then under repressive right-wing leaders]. I think that makes a political statement which the rest of the world reads very clearly whether we want them to or not."[8]

Many Peace Corps veterans insisted that large programs were justified because volunteers had very good experiences in those countries, and that one of the intentions of the Corps was to provide these opportunities. "There were a lot of people at the agency who saw Peace Corps service as a very special time," says Mary King. "They didn't want to expose it to too much reality." But Brown's analysis was unavoidable in the fiscally conservative Carter administration. "We had to show that our spending was meaningful in terms of need," says King, "not in terms of the quality of the volunteers' experience."

To reaffirm the agency's commitment to apolitical humanitarian work, Brown announced plans to remove the Peace Corps from those countries that were not among the world's poorest nations—South Korea, Malaysia, the Côte d'Ivoire, and Brazil—and send volunteers to those countries in desperate straits, such as Bangladesh, Pakistan, Indonesia, and India. The news was greeted with skepticism. "It was incredibly myopic of Sam to assume that a relatively high GNP meant that everyone in the country was living well," says David Levine. "GNP doesn't reveal how the income is distributed." The abruptness of the action was particularly alarming. "We were going to *pull* out, not *phase* out," says Levine. "That was the direct antithesis of everything that the Peace Corps stood for, that you don't jerk the host country around and you don't make unilateral decisions."

"It's true that the Peace Corps had been concentrated in the southern-central part of Côte d'Ivoire, where people were better off," says Malcolm

Versel, a former training officer there. "But we were in the process of moving projects north where there was real need, particularly in food production. It was a stupid decision that really hurt America's image in the eyes of the Ivoirians. They were very offended. At least Washington could have consulted the Ivoirians, but the country director didn't even know about it. It was an order in a cable."

Finally, the tension over Brown's policies reached the boiling point. Peace Corps director Payton bitterly opposed many of Brown's "crackpot ideas"[9] and his meddling in policy decisions that would otherwise have been hers to make. "Leaving countries that are doing well and going into countries that are on the bottom is what the kneejerk liberal does," Payton says. "If you operate under the assumption that the Peace Corps is about Americans meeting internationals, then you don't exclude *any* countries. Whether or not we could find satisfactory jobs for volunteers was a better criterion than how much money a country has. I also thought Basic Human Needs stank. Every time there's a shift in administration the Peace Corps takes on a new slogan. It's offensive to me to tell a host country what their needs are." Payton resigned after one year on the job.

Coinciding with the internecine struggles were frequent criticisms of the Peace Corps in congressional studies and by the General Accounting Office. One report charged a lack of clear direction and leadership in Washington, a large percentage of volunteers of mediocre ability, and a high attrition rate.[10] Another study stated that some projects were of questionable value to the host country, and that volunteers lacked commitment.[11]

These problems, Congress felt, were the result of the Peace Corps' having to operate under the stultifying bureaucracy of Action. "Since its incorporation in Action in 1971, the Peace Corps has become a lackluster program," said Congressman Don Bonker (D-Wash.). "Under Action it lost its own unique sense of identity. . . . The Peace Corps' lifeblood is the vitality of its volunteers. Under Action, the GAO tells us that the drop-out rate of volunteers has risen from 10.9 percent in 1961 to 38 percent in 1975." Senator Hubert Humphrey asked "whether [the Peace Corps'] effectiveness is being jeopardized by its being administered under Action. . . . I fear that a shadow has been cast over the Peace Corps. It is not at all clear that it can still live up to its earlier aspirations."[12]

Brown offered three justifications for the Peace Corps' remaining within Action. First, he argued, the association with the government's other volunteer programs changed the overseas image of the Corps "from a sort of patronizing, 'well-we'll-send-a-bunch-of-people-abroad-for-a-sort-of-low-rent-Fulbright' . . . to 'Oh, you really take it seriously.' "[13] Second, "Our international and domestic programs can learn from each other ways to break the poverty cycle."[14] And third, keeping the Peace Corps within the federal fold* would demonstrate that "it is possible for the federal government to do something right—to do good . . . at a time when so many Americans are cynical and unwilling to believe that the government has any purpose other than complicating their lives."[15]

Payton thought Brown's rationale was groundless: "Host country nationals recognized our own poverty. I don't think it made one bit of difference to them that the Peace Corps was linked to VISTA [Volunteers in Service to America] under Action, and I never saw any sharing of knowledge between the two organizations." Others charged that Brown was territorial and therefore fighting hard to keep the Peace Corps, Action's flagship program, within his domain. "To tell [Mary King and Sam Brown] that they should . . . pluck the central diamond from the tiara just placed on their heads may be asking for an almost superhuman act of political modesty," wrote Harlan Cleveland of the Aspen Institute for Humanistic Studies, who authored a study for the Peace Corps on the agency's future.[16] "It was the sexiest part of Action, and I think Sam Brown wanted all that," says David Levine.

Mary King believes that the controversy over the Peace Corps' incorporation within Action had more to do with the Corps' collective ego than actual organizational problems. "There are lots of federal agencies with entities under them," King points out. "The fight over the Peace Corps being in Action was about emotionalism, and the desire for the restoration of lost glory. The argumentation that was used to remove the Peace Corps from Action masked the discomfort of having the Peace Corps so closely aligned with the domestic volunteer programs. Peace Corps volunteers and staff thought serving in a foreign culture was more difficult and required greater endurance and stamina than being a VISTA volunteer in Tulsa, Oklahoma."

To many on staff, it was the subordination of the Peace Corps to Action, not its association with VISTA, that they found repugnant. "The thought of the Peace Corps being under somebody's else's rubric, making it less than the idea that it was meant to be, was really galling and offensive," says Carol Czorek, deputy country director in Thailand in the late 1970s.

The controversy came to a head in early 1979 when Congress voted to remove the Peace Corps from Action and place it in a yet-to-be-created federal agency that would house all foreign assistance programs. After the

---

*Brown's remark refers to a bill that was before Congress which, if passed, would have reestablished the Peace Corps as a public corporation.

vote, the White House stepped in. By executive order, President Carter interdicted the Corps' departure from Action and reconstituted it as an autonomous agency *within* Action. In a letter to *The Washington Post,* Tom Scanlon (Chile, 1961–63) charged that the Carter administration "did nothing to undo this damage caused by the Peace Corps' placement in Action during the Nixon administration."[17] Others saw it as "better than we had before, a step in the right direction," Czorek recalls.

The Carter administration failed to deliver the hoped-for renaissance. While Brown's implementation of the Basic Human Needs initiative met with considerable resistance, the policy itself pushed officials to once again reconsider the role of the volunteer. With the adoption of Basic Human Needs, for example, the Smithsonian program [see p. 166] no longer seemed appropriate and the Peace Corps canceled its contract. In response to the cancellation, the secretary of the Smithsonian Institution, S. Dillon Ripley, pointed out that third world countries lack the funds to commission scientific and technical work, particularly as it relates to their environment, which is "key to all our future. . . . Ignoring basic ecological research while proclaiming to be interested in human needs is shortsighted. . . . I wish we Americans did not always see the world through such biased spectacles. Indeed, we are still 'Innocents Abroad.'"[18]

## Marina Baudoin (Zaire, 1978)

(In 1978, twenty-year-old Marina Baudoin went to Zaire as one of the Peace Corps' first female fisheries, or "fish farming," volunteers in that country. Until the mid-1970s, this job was considered to be a males-only assignment. Fisheries volunteers showed subsistence farmers how to build and stock artificial ponds, which provided them with a source of protein and supplemented their income. Under the Basic Human Needs initiative, fish farming was one of the areas in which the Peace Corps expanded, in terms of the number of volunteers assigned to the job and the number of host countries to which the Corps offered the program.)

Our training instructor told us he didn't think women belonged in the fisheries program. We should stay home and have babies. Even on our last day he said, "I still don't agree with you women going." When I got to Zaire, the male volunteers said they didn't think the women would have any chance of succeeding at all.

One of the sites for fisheries volunteers in Zaire was a Catholic mission which operated an agricultural school, girls school, and orphanage.

I asked not to be placed there because I wasn't particularly religious and was afraid I'd offend someone by accident. But I was the youngest one in the group and the Peace Corps staff person decided I should be near Westerners in case I needed help. The fathers accepted me right away but the nuns were a pain. They pressured me to work in the girls school. I was always knitting things or baking cookies for the parties they had for the kids. They didn't think I should be running around in jeans or riding a motorbike. [The Peace Corps issues each volunteer a motorbike.] One of the nuns, an American, told me, "They're going to attack you." I think they thought the Zairians were savages. I was more frightened of my motorbike.

To get myself started with the farmers in the area, I referred to the previous volunteer's log which told me how individual farmers were progressing with their ponds. I started with the better farmers who might set an example for the others. One of them refused to work with me because I was female, but after about eight months he asked me to talk to his four wives.

Most farmers weren't interested in building a pond if they didn't think they could make money by selling the fish. They don't understand what protein is or why they should eat the fish they raise since their parents and grandparents didn't have fish. I tried to explain that while manioc [a starchy root vegetable], their staple, fills you up, it doesn't do anything for you nutritionally. They think manioc is fine because their kids have big tummies. But this is usually a sign of parasites, not that they were healthy. They understand making money, though.

Some tried hard to get a pond going but ended up with mudholes because they just didn't understand what I was talking about. You have to approach them as you would a five-year-old. They've had very limited education or none at all. I tried to explain how the pond works by drawing pictures but they aren't used to learning from illustrations. I repeated things—like why the fish need to eat—several times. Talking to them about algae was ridiculous.

One man, whom I started from scratch, did very well. I knew only a few words of his dialect but I visited him week after week to see if he'd done what I said, and if he hadn't, I'd repeat it. He got the pond built and we left the fish in there for six months.

A whole lot of people came to his first harvest. Everyone stood around the pond as he emptied it. He sold most of the fish and kept some for his family. If a pond is successful, you'd get two-pound fish, and enough of them to eat one every night. They fried the fish in palm oil or cooked it in peanut sauce with hot peppers. I don't even like fish but I enjoyed it.

The farmers wanted me closer to them, so I moved off the mission and rented a concrete house which belonged to one of the farmers I worked with. A month after I moved in, the farmer raised my rent from about forty dollars a month to four hundred dollars because he needed to raise some money quickly. If I had agreed to the increase, I would have lost all my credibility with the other farmers. In their eyes, I would be just another rich white person. I had no choice but to move back to the mission.

By this time, it was the rainy season, which prevented me from getting out to the farmers on my motorbike. They were angry with me because they thought I was abandoning them. Then, the final straw was finding my dog, which the nuns hated, lying dead in a ditch from poisoning. I packed my bags and left for Kinshasa.

I asked to be assigned to another post but nothing was available. In the meantime, I worked in the Peace Corps office and started dating Harry Rea, the staff member in charge of the fisheries program. [Marina and Harry were married in 1981.] The country director made known his disapproval of our relationship, and a lot of the volunteers and staff thought that my leaving the mission was Harry's idea, and that he was taking advantage of me. So I quit the Peace Corps and stayed in Kinshasa with Harry and went to work for another development agency setting up health clinics in the city.

### Philip Karp (Togo, 1978–80)

The objective of our assignment, organizing school gardens, was to make Togolese education more relevant to the students' lives and provide another food source. We had learned in training that during the dry season, they had no green vegetables or fruit, just meat and sorghum which didn't provide any vitamins. A lot of the schools started a garden just because they wanted to please the white person or because the teachers thought I'd report back to their supervisor if they didn't.

The ones who really grasped the idea were those who saw that they could make money from it. I had thought the students and teachers would take home whatever the garden produced, or sell it in the local market, but they'd take everything to a hotel in the capital where they got a better price. I was put off by that at first. One girl took the lettuce we grew to the local market and sat with it all day. She didn't sell any. They were teaching me a lesson; no one liked lettuce enough to buy it, but they'd eat it if it was given to them. I ended up buying all of it myself and we had a party.

The Peace Corps gave us Burpee seeds, most of which could not grow in Togo. We spent two or three months tending the garden and when these nice big tomatoes started to ripen, the stems of the plants started rotting. The schools were excited about getting new okra seeds because their okra was very stringy. But the Burpee strain wasn't resistant to insects, and the plants were destroyed before we got the okra. I think I lost some credibility when the seeds didn't work. I'm sure people were thinking, "This guy's supposed to be an expert," and "What's the problem here?" The second time around, we planted what they knew they could raise and sell.

I think I did best with interpersonal relationships. I wouldn't be surprised to learn that the kids, who are now grown up, are using what they learned and that the community people, who saw the value of the school garden, pressured any subsequent school personnel to keep it up.

## Cherie Lockett (Senegal, 1979–81)

(A social worker from Boston, Lockett was a volunteer in the Peace Corps' animation program. Animation, a community development technique, typified the kind of village-based work that Basic Human Needs prescribed. The animation volunteer coaxed villagers to identify common problems, devise possible solutions and then take action.)

I felt isolated. It was scary and lonely. Learning the language and getting a sense of the community and its politics, was very difficult. It was also hard to be the only literate person for miles. Older men would point to my vagina and say, "If it's not watered, it'll die," and, "You need a good hard penis." At first, I was offended and angered by these comments. But I learned that these sexual jokes are perfectly acceptable and I learned to come back with something and parry with them.

I lived in a one-room thatch hut in a family compound. It took a long time for me to be accepted by the village as someone other than the visiting American. I had to prove myself as a woman—drawing water from a well, pounding millet, working in the fields picking peanuts. We were told in training that we might not be credible to the villagers on health matters because we didn't have husbands or children. The instructors suggested that we make up a story to overcome that. I told them that my husband and son had been killed in a car accident. I had reservations about lying but I stuck with it for two years. They didn't ask a lot of questions because they don't belabor death or take it as hard as we do since they live closer to it. I saw all the diseases you see in *National Geographic*. Every woman in my village had either miscarried or lost a child, usually to parasites.

When I first arrived, I thought the village women were boring. I assumed that when they got together they were just gossiping and had no interest in developing themselves. But I was wrong. In much of African village life, the engines of change are among the women. I got to know them by helping them treat their kids' diarrhea. I would visit a sick child and show the mother how to make a rehydration mix of rice, water, salt and sugar.

I finally felt at home after a year, when I got the language. I'd meet with groups of twenty to fifty people to talk about projects. At first, I thought I should set up a baby-weighing and nutrition program. But I couldn't teach them about nutrition if suitable food wasn't available. Then the idea of a garden came up. They ate millet three times a day, rice at celebrations, and chicken, rarely. They wanted a more varied diet but they also saw the garden as a way to earn money.

We took soil and water samples to an agricultural research station to find out what we could grow. The villagers had passed by the station hundreds of times and never thought of going in. The Senegalese civil servant who worked there addressed only me, and in French, because he thought the women weren't smart enough to understand the information. I asked him to talk to them in Wolof [a language indigenous to parts of West Africa] and *they'll* explain it to *me*.

I did a lot of the legwork to get the garden going and then stayed on the periphery of the actual building and planting. The garden was a little bigger than a basketball court.

We were disappointed that we didn't get a lot of vegetables from the garden. We knew from the start we were dealing with tough conditions. But what I tried to emphasize was the process: pulling together, organizing, and problem solving. Men and women started working together whereas traditionally they don't. The men also acknowledged the women's capabilities. It felt as if it I was just getting started when it was time to leave, but I believed we accomplished something.

☆

Meredith McGehee and Becky Raymond both served in Niger in the late seventies. On the southern edge of the Sahara, Niger is four fifths the size of Alaska, and only 3 percent of the land is arable. The average life expectancy is forty-four. Raymond taught nutrition to mothers of malnourished babies at a rural clinic and McGehee taught athletics at a girls high school in a large town. Raymond's work was the consummate Basic Human Needs assignment, and the stuff of heartwarming recruiting posters. Sending volunteers like McGehee to teach volleyball, or English for that matter, in a country unable to feed its own people seems like a cruel joke. The contrast between their assignments points out the disparity between American perceptions of need and those of the host country's. Host country governments have always asked the Peace Corps to send sports instructors for reasons that are incompatible with Western notions of the third world. "When your national identity isn't stable, sports is a good way to make sure people are rooting for the same thing," said McGehee in a recent report on sports in developing countries.[19] "It was an imperialist mindset that viewed sports instruction as unnecessary." McGehee says today, "The Nigerians would argue, 'Why shouldn't we have as good an education as Americans?' "

### *Meredith McGehee (Niger, 1978–80)*

I looked into the Peace Corps while I was in college because I wanted to travel. When the local recruiter called and told me they had a position for a sports coach in Niger, I went. Teaching sports was something I knew I could do well and that had value for anyone. It conveys the message to the student that, "Look, there are things that you thought you couldn't do that you *can* do if somebody shows you how." I remember arriving at training and worrying that the other volunteers would think I was some dumb jock.

The biggest split in my group, though, was between the volunteers who lived in towns and those who lived in remote villages. The people assigned to the villages bragged about how tough they had it—no running water, walking ten kilometers to get to the nearest road. The ones who didn't brag were the nutrition education volunteers—who were out in the middle of nowhere. They couldn't get too cocky because it was damn hard to see babies die. But we used to joke about the differences in our assignments. At the end of training we put on a comedy show and did a skit about teaching starving babies how to play basketball.

My students were girls from the villages whose families sent them away to secondary school because they showed promise in the primary grades. It was their family's hope that they'd marry a functionaire [civil servant] who made some money.

The girls' physical education up to that point was limited to games like "duck-duck-goose." They'd never seen a bouncing ball before, but they had incredible balance and physical strength from carrying tubs of water on their heads. I designed a sort of remedial program which covered basic skills like throwing and catching and they just ate it up. The school didn't own any balls so I sent the girls out to scour the school grounds for rocks of a certain size and weight and we used them to learn how to throw. Since we had a lot of sand, I taught them the long jump and high jump, too.

I organized intramural basketball, and we played against another school in town. We didn't score a point all year, but the following year we killed them and I was real proud. It wasn't like an Olympic team was coming out of this, and I didn't have any illusions that I had saved any lives or made any great contribution to the country's movement toward modernity. But I felt I had exposed these girls to something new and maybe it helped them feel better about themselves. I think I probably had more impact on my houseboy. He learned how to repair bicycles working on my motorbike, and today, that's what he does for a living.

[McGehee visited Niger five years after completing her Peace Corps service. She located fifteen of her students at the national university. One of them, who was studying medicine, will be the first female doctor to have been trained in Niger. "Are you coming back to teach us basketball again?" they asked her. "We really miss playing."]

### Becky Raymond (Niger, 1978–81)

The clinic I worked in was staffed by a head nurse, three nurses, a midwife, and a few orderlies. We had no running water, electricity, or sanitation to speak of. I think the needles were boiled once a day.

I was responsible for the clinic's well-baby program. Every child under five was weighed once a month. I identified those kids who were severely malnourished and followed them more closely, weighing them once a week. I'd ask the mothers of these children to come back to the clinic the next day for a demonstration in which I would show them how to cook a nutritious porridge. But many mothers didn't come back. They knew this was for the benefit of their child, but they also saw it as more work to do.

The attitude towards children in Niger is survival of the fittest. Many infants are breast-fed until they start to walk. At that point, they receive solid food. Abrupt weaning can be difficult for children to tolerate and increases their risk for malnutrition. I hated what some of the mothers did to their kids. But at the same time, I realized it wasn't just them; it was their husbands, the culture, their living conditions, and their religion. The Muslim attitude *"Inshallah"*—"If God wills it"—prevailed. If God wants their child to live, he'll live. If God wants their child to die, he'll die. So they don't make a big effort. They can't afford to. These women also had terrific work loads. They're up before dawn getting water and chopping wood. Since their husbands give them very little money for anything besides food, they have to raise money on their own to buy clothes or medicine. I don't think I ever really got used to this way of life.

I got the mothers to come back for the nutrition demonstration by keeping the children's health cards. These cards detailed their prenatal care, the birth and the child's growth. They placed great value on these cards because they cherish anything that's written down, and these were probably the only records they had for their children.

I also visited their homes to cook with them and talk to the fathers about their children's diets. It was difficult to convince them that their children needed a varied diet because, as they would tell me, "We have eaten millet for generations and we survived." I usually went with the local midwives who helped me explain things to the parents. The midwives, in turn, helped me learn about traditional health practices.

The nutrition education volunteers felt we were addressing a more compelling need than volunteers in some other assignments. But we were also frustrated as hell because you can't change centuries-old traditions in two years or even in ten years. Our progress couldn't be measured like that of the English teachers.

I stayed in the Peace Corps for a third year because I wanted to get more accomplished and I wanted to start a nutrition education post in another part of the country. A year later, I went back to my first post to visit. When I had left there, I wasn't sure if some of the kids I had tried to help would survive. Some, in fact, did not make it, but it was the high point of my three years in Niger to see the others running around like normal little kids. You learn to accept small successes.

# Part Six

# The Reagan Years, 1981-89

# Introduction

When Ronald Reagan was elected in 1980, the Peace Corps was showing signs of renewed health. With White House support, the Peace Corps could finally step out of its doldrums, more able than ever, perhaps, to serve the developing world. Carolyn Payton's successor, Richard Celeste, a former lieutenant governor of Ohio, had worked hard to put the Peace Corps on the right track after the organization's rocky first two years of the Carter administration. Celeste reorganized the agency according to its new autonomous status granted by President Carter; he oversaw the revamping of recruitment and training; he boosted staff morale by discarding the Basic Human Needs mandate and trusting the overseas staff to "just tell us what programs will really work."

Following Reagan's victory, Celeste, a Democrat, headed back to Ohio, where he later became governor. Before his departure from the Peace Corps, he wrote the President-elect a three-page memo of carefully crafted suggestions that he hoped would sustain the agency's momentum. The Peace Corps, Celeste wrote, represented a "unique and important opportunity" for President Reagan's first one hundred days in office. Because the Corps' visibility had been so low for so many years, Celeste pointed out, the new president could easily "reclaim the image from Kennedy to Reagan, in keeping with your demonstrated appeal across party lines." The President's support of the organization, Celeste stated, would illustrate that keeping the peace requires not only a strong defense but compassion as well. The departing director also encouraged the President to cut the agency free of Action and to reestablish it as a nonprofit public corporation. Such a move would underscore the President's often stated belief, paraphrased by Celeste, in "the importance of involving individuals in activities which in the past have been too often handed over lock, stock, and barrel to the federal government."[1]

The new administration ignored Celeste's suggestions. Elected in a landslide, Ronald Reagan certainly didn't need the Peace Corps to enhance his prestige. The White House attitude toward the Corps was summed up succinctly by former director of the Office of Management and Budget, David Stockman. In his memoir, *The Triumph of Politics: How the Reagan Revolution Failed*, Stockman wrote that development-assistance programs did more harm than good, "turning third world countries into quagmires of self-imposed inefficiency." In President Reagan's first budget, fiscal year 1981, development-assistance programs were slated for a 45-percent cut, and "just for good measure," Stockman wrote, "the Peace Corps budget would be cut by 25 percent."[2]

In addition to the administration's aversion to the Peace Corps, another major obstacle preventing its comeback was lack of interest. In the 1980s, as record numbers of recent college graduates swarmed into M.B.A. programs, applications to the Peace Corps plummeted, reaching a low of 10,279 in 1987;* fewer volunteers served during the Reagan years—between 5,000 and 6,000 a year—than during any other administration except for Kennedy's, when the Peace Corps was newly established.

The Peace Corps persevered through the Reagan years, thanks to the aggressive leadership of a former Republican congressman's wife who had cochaired the 1980 Reagan-Bush campaign in Michigan. Loret Miller Ruppe steered the organization through the dangerous shoals of a hostile era. She strove to replace the negative image of the Corps, held by many in the conservative community, with "a new vision of the Peace Corps which supersedes any misperceptions of the long-haired hippie image of the Peace Corps of the 1960s," as she told the President's Bipartisan Commission on Central America in 1983. The volunteers of the 1980s, she said, were "older and better-trained, with a higher percentage highly skilled."[3] Packaging the Peace Corps as the alternative to 1980s selfishness, Ruppe told a conference of religious educators in 1987 that "volunteers demonstrate in remote villages and urban slums a very different vision of America. They show something better than 'Dallas,' 'Miami Vice,' and 'Dynasty.'"[4]

Loaded with charisma, Ruppe won the loyalty of both aisles of Congress, which appropriated funds significantly greater than those called for

---

*The Peace Corps maintains that this figure is the result of the organization's newly streamlined recruiting system.

in Stockman's annual budgets. Serving through both Reagan terms, she headed the organization longer than any other director, including Sargent Shriver.

At first, the Peace Corps staff was skeptical of Loret Ruppe, a wealthy housewife whose efforts in the Reagan-Bush campaign put her in line for an appointment. But her personal magnetism and abiding affection for the Corps soon won them over. Ruppe also understood Washington, and her eight-year leadership was distinguished by savvy maneuvering among often conflicting interests. While adroitly handling pressures from the New Right, Ruppe curried White House favor by positioning Peace Corps volunteers as supporting players in the President's foreign policy initiatives in Central America and the Caribbean. At the same time, she fought the administration tooth and nail in the halls of Congress. She made friends for the Peace Corps in the Republican community by adopting a probusiness philosophy and pushing projects in "small enterprise development," a favorite agency moniker.

"Loret was the most rational, most middle-of-the-road director since Shriver," says Jody Olsen, a country director in the Carter administration who stayed on at the Peace Corps till 1984. "She cared about the Peace Corps first and that was her only agenda." Ruppe was, in fact, a moderate Republican whose backing came from longtime friend Vice President George Bush. Her priority, as she stated frequently, was to "move the Peace Corps ahead." Essential to that goal was getting the agency's budget increased substantially. That necessitated building a favorable image of the Corps in the administration, the Congress, and the general public—a task for which Ruppe had great talent.

The New Right, however, had their own agenda, and Ruppe is credited with having appeased their desire to make over Peace Corps volunteers in Ronald Reagan's likeness. The chief irritant was the Peace Corps Advisory Council, a panel of twenty-nine White House appointees. The council strongly recommended that "more time and attention be given to the instruction of our volunteers on the philosophy, strategy, tactics, and menace of communism." They were particularly adamant that volunteer training include a thorough explanation of "the human repressions and economic failings of the communist system." The council also advised that the Peace Corps take special care to send overseas only those volunteers and staff who could be counted upon "to serve as effective representatives of American values and institutions."[5]

Ruppe placated the Advisory Council on both counts. For the first few years of her administration, the Peace Corps aggressively sought out retirees, because "they have the technical skills and the experience we need," said Thomas G. Moore, recruiting director at the time. "They also happen to be more mainstream, more traditional in their value system and conduct."[6] To satisfy the Advisory Council's concerns about volunteers' awareness of the evils of communism, Ruppe commissioned "Americans Abroad," a film in which the narrator cautions trainees, "Make no mistake—we are engaged in a worldwide struggle for control: an ideological confrontation."[7] Instructor Arthur Rodger recalls, "The trainees used to roar with laughter." The film was quickly and quietly shelved.

While Ruppe acquiesced to the council on certain issues, she won kudos from the Peace Corps community for her defiance of the administration on what was the most contentious issue surrounding the Peace Corps at that time. In 1981, a bill came before Congress that, if passed, would have finally severed the Peace Corps from Action. The White House opposed the bill. Ruppe lobbied hard for it. Her efforts provoked the Heritage Foundation, an influential conservative Washington think tank, to call Ruppe "an annoying thorn in Reagan's side" and state that the Peace Corps "still largely ignores the Reagan agenda."[8] Says Ruppe of her efforts, "It was a pretty big risk, but I felt protected by this armor of the Peace Corps being such a great organization. I was battling for what was right, and righteousness would protect me."

It was widely felt that the Peace Corps was seriously encumbered by the Action bureacracy, but Ruppe stuck her neck out for the bill for another reason. The White House had appointed as director of Action a former Army intelligence officer named Thomas Pauken. Pauken's background violated the Corps' prohibition against hiring anyone who had been employed by any government intelligence agency. The policy helps deflect charges that the organization's far-flung operations provide a cover for CIA activity. Pauken's association with the Peace Corps, Ruppe felt, could jeopardize its relations with host country governments. Congress rallied to her side and voted for separation.

On some occasions, in order to heighten the Peace Corps' exposure, Ruppe tailored programs to complement Reagan administration themes. The "Leadership for Peace" campaign, for instance, sought to attract material and financial support from the business and academic communities for Peace Corps projects. "Ten million people in more than sixty countries will once again know that America's corporate leaders and employees care," said one brochure. Despite its success, the campaign had its critics.[9] After Pfizer, The Gap, Safeway, and Coca-Cola signed up for various participation programs, one critic dubbed the Peace Corps "the Peace Corporation." In response to Exxon and Mobil's involvement, one former volunteer quipped, "That's like Kurt Waldheim doing public service announcements for Mother Teresa."

Ruppe also nurtured a "Small Enterprise Development" (SED) program, which echoed the Reagan administration's contention that the best way to address third world poverty was to stimulate local free enterprise. SED volunteers helped fledgling entrepreneurs by teaching them basic bookkeeping, sales techniques, inventory management, and, in some cases, assisting them in securing small loans.

Ruppe sought to enhance the Peace Corps' cachet by sending volunteers where their efforts would support delicate foreign policy interests. Soon after the United States invaded Grenada, volunteers were dispatched to the island with other forms of aid. Similarly, when the administration moved to stop the spread of communism in Central America decisively, the number of volunteers sent to the region rose dramatically. Many in the Peace Corps community claimed that Ruppe was "politicizing" the agency.

Ruppe defends her probusiness initiatives and sensitivity to foreign policy matters on pragmatic grounds. "When I came to the Peace Corps, I thought, 'My gosh, this is one of the best things our government is doing. Why is our budget still half of one B-one bomber?' Hopefully, some day, whoever makes these budget decisions will see that the work of the Peace Corps is the path we should be following. But the budget makers won't see this if we're not visible."

While many were disgruntled by the buildup in Central America, Ruppe won wide approval when she sought to revitalize the Peace Corps by embracing a potent and previously untapped resource: the alumni. Before Ruppe headed the organization, officials had only marginal involvement with returned volunteers, largely because the agency had lost touch with them, and until 1979, there was no formal alumni network to contact—with the exception of the radical Committee of Returned Volunteers, which from 1966 to 1971 claimed some two thousand members. The CRV, however, advanced the notion that the Corps was an instrument of American imperialism, and the agency had no desire for formal contact.

In 1979, eight years after the CRV disbanded, the less politically inclined National Council of Returned Peace Corps Volunteers was founded. Nevertheless, Ruppe got burned when she cosponsored a Peace Corps twentieth anniversary conference with the group in 1981. Among those invited to speak at the gathering at Howard University in Washington were Zimbabwe's Marxist president Robert Mugabe, Stephen Cardinal Kim Sou Hwan, archbishop of Seoul, and Senator Paul Tsongas (D-Mass., Ethiopia, 1962–64). Mugabe failed to appear, the cardinal accused

Washington of being interested in Korea solely for economic reasons, and Tsongas criticized President Reagan's opposition to SALT II and his gentle treatment of South Africa's apartheid policies. *Human Events*, the influential conservative weekly, summed up the conservative wrath when it called the conference an "anti-Reagan forum" and characterized the Peace Corps as "a dangerously anti-Reagan instrument [that] is likely to become an even more potent force for the left."[10]

For its twenty-fifth anniversary in 1986, the Peace Corps planned a low-key observance—a photo contest, the unveiling of a commemorative stamp, and a series of symposia on development—and, as a courtesy, the National Council and other alumni groups were invited to participate. But the former volunteers had more ambitious plans. They wanted to hold another conference in Washington and use it to launch a more active alumni movement, whose objective would be to fulfill the Peace Corps' third goal as stated in the Peace Corps Act: "To foster a better understanding of the world on the part of Americans," or, as the National Council printed on their T-shirts and tote bags, "Bringing the World Back Home."

Initially, Ruppe wanted to have nothing to do with another conference, but she changed her mind and cosponsored the event when it became clear that it was going to take place with or without the Peace Corps' involvement. In the five years since the Howard gathering, the National Council had evolved into a fairly sophisticated operation, and its officers had raised a significant amount of money from foundations, corporations, and individuals to mount a twenty-fifth anniversary conference. "I think Mrs. Ruppe also saw that among the alumni, there was considerable talent for creating positive publicity," says the National Council's president, Roger Landrum (Nigeria, 1961–63).

On an overcast September weekend in Washington in 1986, five thousand returned volunteers gathered on the Mall under a gigantic white tent that could have been held aloft by the emotional energy alone. Philippines President Corazon Aquino delivered the keynote address. Sargent Shriver recalled the Peace Corps' early days and spoke eloquently of the Corps' place in American history. Volunteers attended "country updates," embassy receptions, and panel discussions on development. On Sunday morning, they marched across Memorial Bridge and into Arlington National Cemetery carrying the flags of all ninety-four countries in which volunteers have served. A four-foot-high wreath with a ribbon saying "Thank You" was placed at Kennedy's grave, and a memorial service was held for the 199 volunteers who had died overseas.

Bill Moyers, who had left Vice President Lyndon Johnson's staff in 1961 to run the Peace Corps' public affairs office, told the gathering that the Corps was "a way of being in the world . . . that may yet save this fragmented and dispirited age."[11] Father Theodore Hesburgh, then president of Notre Dame University, said, "More than any other group, you have been the inspiration of this great nation."[12] That evening, Harry Belafonte hosted a gala performance at the Kennedy Center.

"For that weekend, it was perfectly fine to be idealistic," said a former volunteer, "perfectly fine to value commitment, to be moved to tears with stories of exemplary service. For that weekend, cynicism retreated or was converted."[13]

The White House rejected the suggestion that President Reagan host a Rose Garden reception for the volunteers who had served in 1961, many of whom had shaken hands with President Kennedy there. Instead, the administration honored the " '61ers" with a luncheon in a congressional office building. Vice President George Bush made brief remarks.

When Ruppe came to the podium in the big white tent on the Mall, she was blunt about the Peace Corps' predicament. "We are in the least liked, least supported, least respected account in the . . . budget of the United States: Foreign Assistance—and Peace Corps is listed in that account under the grandiose title: Miscellaneous One. . . . We are all in this together," Ruppe said, "and we must coordinate, to truly challenge the immense problems confronting our world. . . . You returned Peace Corps volunteers are called, you are chosen . . . you trod the path of peace once in a distant land. Now I must ask you to tread it again."[14] On the Monday after the conference, newspapers across the country ran editorials saluting the Peace Corps.

The conference spawned numerous local alumni organizations and country-of-service groups (Friends of Togo, Friends of Afghanistan, and others) and invigorated those already established. Flourishing today, many of them raise money for Peace Corps projects overseas, participate in community service activities, and visit local classrooms to talk about life in developing countries. In 1989, the National Council began an annual $150-a-plate founders' day dinner honoring President Kennedy's birthday. The first dinner, which made *The Washington Post* society page, was held at Washington's chic Willard Hotel with several Kennedys in attendance; it was hosted by Caroline Kennedy and Maria Shriver served as master of ceremonies. The council also commemorated the twenty-fifth anniversary of President Kennedy's assassination with "The Journals of Peace," twenty-four hours of continuous testimony by volunteers about their Peace Corps experience at the congressional Rotunda where Kennedy had lain in state. The ceremony made the network newscasts. Prominently affixed to all of these activities was the name of the Peace Corps—which by now was giving the alumni organizations wholehearted support, contracting with them to recruit, paying their postage costs, and assisting in the planning of other conferences. "Loret genuinely loves volunteers," says former National Council executive director Timothy Carroll (Nigeria, 1963–66). "She wasn't just using the alumni groups to merchandise the Peace Corps."

One of the more noteworthy alumni projects was a lobbying effort by the National Council and the Washington, D.C., alumni group to get Congress to mandate that the Peace Corps increase its ranks to ten thousand volunteers. They claimed that "a Peace Corps of less than 10,000 is a national embarrassment."[15] The ten-thousand-volunteer goal was incorporated into the 1986 foreign aid appropriations bill and adopted by the Corps as a rallying cry for funding increases. "It was a goal that people could buy into, like building a space station," says Tom Wilson, director of financial management at the agency in the early and mid-1980s. "Once it was decided that this was the objective, it was just a matter of how much we need to get there."

Ruppe seized on the ten-thousand-volunteer goal. "In 1967, when the world had three and a half billion people," says Ruppe, "and our country was one hundred ninety million people, we were able to have fifteen thousand development workers out there. In 1989, in a world of five and a half billion people and a U.S. population of two hundred sixty million, we can't figure out a way to have ten thousand development workers overseas? We're talking about making peace happen!"

But many within the agency were deeply skeptical of the goal of ten thousand. "Ruppe wanted to increase to ten thousand volunteers by 1992 but with no additional support," says Moira Crabill (Central African Republic, 1985–87), a desk assistant in the Peace Corps' Africa division. "There would have been no extra vehicles or additional administrative people. Volunteers' sites wouldn't have been checked before they arrived, and more of their assignments would have been poorly planned." The goal of ten thousand, says Jon Keeton, who was then director of the Asia region, revealed one of the organization's least admirable tendencies. "There was no significant consultation with the host countries, and for us to say that "in our wisdom, we have determined that you're going to have ten thousand volunteers—it's imperialistic and it's ugly. That number was manufactured for Washington consumption."

Some felt that the ten-thousand-volunteer goal indicated a superficial approach to development work. "The Peace Corps should be oriented toward accomplishing certain things," says Alan Silverstein, a former volunteer in Senegal who was a consultant to the agency during Ruppe's tenure. "Ten thousand doesn't mean anything unless you know what you are going to do with all of those people." Ruppe's critics say her infatuation with the goal of ten thousand was symptomatic of her tendency toward powerful rhetoric and little effective follow-through. "Loret was great on PR," says Linda Borst, former chief of operations for the Africa region, "and while she focused on the issue-of-the-week, she let her chief of staff run things— and he only wanted to hear good news."

Ruppe had no shortage of good ideas. But she was more skilled at promoting them than at making sure the nuts-and-bolts work got done. For example, in order to attract applicants with sophisticated skills, Ruppe arranged for a stint in the Peace Corps to be a part of various graduate school programs.* Officials at the first two universities to send students, Rutgers and Colorado State, however, say the Peace Corps paid little attention to their students' specialization when placing them overseas. "We had a young woman who majored in tropical agriculture, and the Peace Corps was about to send her to an arid country when we stepped in," recounts Bruce Tracy, associate director of Colorado State University's office of international programs. A student of hospital administration from Rutgers was assigned to a literacy program. "When other universities call me to ask how our Peace Corps program is going, I tell them that they aren't very good on the follow-through," says Jay Sigler, director of graduate programs in public policy at Rutgers. "You don't know who's in charge."

The farmer-to-farmer program was another well-intentioned but haphazardly executed attempt to provide developing countries with a greater level of expertise. The Peace Corps arranged with Volunteers in Overseas Cooperative Assistance (VOCA), a nonprofit technical assistance organization, to recruit retired farmers and agricultural experts to work with volunteers and nationals for a few weeks to a few months. But after the agreement was made, VOCA officer Charles Cox found that "Peace Corps' field staff didn't want another thing to be saddled with. They were worried these older folks were going to have sunstroke." Two of Cox's volunteers, experts in cocoa cultivation and dairy farming, were sent to Honduras and

---

*Universities that incorporated Peace Corps service into their graduate programs include Yale, Rutgers, Colorado State, Texas Woman's, University of the District of Columbia, Boston University, University of Alabama-Birmingham, and the University of South Carolina.

Cameroon respectively, only to find that the projects they were to work on were simply not viable. Cox also questions the value of short-term expert assistance. "The rice specialist we sent to Mali worked out very well, but we don't know what's left behind. The Peace Corps volunteer our expert worked with knows a lot more about rice, but she took that knowledge home with her. Maybe the VOCA expert's knowledge spreads like wildfire among the farmers in Africa, but we have our doubts."

## Chapter 11

☆═══

# The Caribbean Basin Initiative: "What Does a Sociologist Know About Business?"

In 1982, President Reagan announced that it was America's responsibility to go to the aid of her neighbors in the Caribbean whose economies had been devastated by the oil crises of the 1970s. In so doing, America was protecting the hemisphere from the encroaching "Soviet-Cuban-Nicaraguan Axis." Reagan's plan, the Caribbean Basin Initiative (CBI), offered duty-free exporting of Caribbean products to the United States and tax incentives for offshore investors looking to start or expand businesses in the region. The Peace Corps, eager to ingratiate itself with the skeptical Reagan administration and bolster its low visibility, fell in line, launching a new small-business program in the Caribbean in 1983 and even appropriating the CBI's name. Like Reagan's CBI but on the grass roots level, the Peace Corps' program hoped to boost economic activity in the region by advancing "microenterprise."

A few years later, Peace Corps director Loret Miller Ruppe boasted that the Corps' new Caribbean program was an "overwhelming success. . . . Some 6,000 jobs were created, boosting the average income of subsistence level farmers as much as 1000%." The Peace Corps, she said, was fulfilling the White House mandate to "show other countries that the road to economic progress lies through democracy, free markets, and human enterprise."[1] In reality, though, the Peace Corps' CBI wasn't the glowing success Ruppe claimed. Her extolling of the program was indicative of the agency's need to present a picture of a thriving organization to an unappreciative administration and a disinterested public.

Bill Gschwend, the Peace Corps official in charge of the program, could not confirm Ruppe's figures. "I'm not sure where those numbers came from," he says. "They probably counted everyone volunteers worked with in income-producing projects, not just the new program." Nevertheless, Gschwend says, the CBI did have many successes, citing volunteer Salvatore Castellitto (Dominican Republic, 1982–84), who worked with a women's ceramics cooperative, as one example. But Castellitto himself isn't so bullish about his efforts. "I'm surprised Bill would point to my project," he says. "The women gave only a few hours a day to it. I gave classes on quality control and the basics of design and tried to explain that they could express their identity through their work, but they were more interested in going to the United States or moving into the city and making more money." As it turned out, the Peace Corps' CBI was poorly conceived and ill suited for the region. In order to buttress its results with impressive facts and figures, Ruppe, apparently, quoted numbers borrowed from another program, Small Enterprise Development (SED).

From the start, the CBI was more of an adjunct to the SED program than a separate one with a distinct mandate. Both were directed at encouraging "agribusiness" among poor farmers and increasing the productivity of local artisans. The CBI enhanced the SED program by providing volunteers with extra training in business development and professional guidance from technical consultants.

But to Bill Gschwend, the CBI was the much more ambitious program. Gschwend felt that the Peace Corps could adapt the administration's emphasis on promoting exports for the small-scale farmers and artisans. By helping these people crack the export market, Gschwend says, the Peace Corps would "cut the little guy in on the CBI action." But volunteers and staff in the Caribbean soon learned that exporting was way beyond the capacity of the people with whom they worked.

"One person was experimenting with some farmers on making chocolate from cocoa beans," explains John Evans, deputy director of the Peace Corps' Honduras program in the mid-1980s. "By using a piece of their small landholdings to grow this new thing, they were making a real sacrifice and taking a significant risk because they needed every square inch to grow food for their families," he says. "Exporting wasn't as easy as it seemed," agrees a Peace Corps official in Costa Rica. "There were a lot of state and federal laws regulating it. To say what projects you could specifically tag to CBI—you got me. I don't think that anything came out of it. It seemed like a big, nebulous thing." Nevertheless, the Peace Corps' official record of its activities in the 1980s describes explicitly the outstanding achievements of "CBI volunteers" and "CBI projects."[2] It was evident to the business volunteers that the Peace Corps "jumped on CBI to be in harmony with the administration, but they didn't really understand what it was about," says Diane Bejarano (Dominican Republic, 1984–86). "They used it as a sort of a candy coating."

The increased emphasis on business baffled some Peace Corps staff in the Caribbean because host governments in the region had never expressed a strong interest in private enterprise projects. They counted on the Peace Corps to send teachers, health workers, and agricultural extension workers, in order to further the reach of their own programs or take the place of civil servants. "The governments of the eastern Caribbean were not clamoring for business volunteers," says Carol Ann Peese, who was a staff person there when CBI was announced. "They wanted to get professionals whom they couldn't afford to hire themselves." A Peace Corps official in St. Lucia explains why business assignments have never been a priority for the agency in general: "In much of the third world, people are concerned with just getting by each day. They don't plan for the future, which is the central concept behind business and the CBI program."

Some volunteers believe that poor planning doomed the CBI. Bill Weber, a retired insurance executive from Boston, arrived in the Dominican Republic only to find that his assignment—to coordinate the CBI activities of the Commerce Department and AID with those of the Peace Corps—had not been defined prior to his arrival. According to Weber, "The attitude was, 'Here, go see if you can make a job out of it.' That's how much thought went behind it." Peese recalls that "the business projects were hurriedly conceived. Washington was always pushing for results: 'How many volunteers are in the business program now?' they'd ask."

This lack of detailed planning has been attributed by some to the Corps' inexperience with the private sector. "The Peace Corps' business program was just a package of buzzwords, and they don't even know what *those* mean," says Bob Hyde (St. Lucia, 1986–88).

The Peace Corps' own institutional culture also precluded the program's success. To many volunteers and staff, promoting capitalism was anathema to the agency's mission. "They thought the business orientation wasn't idealistic enough," says Gschwend. "Some saw the Peace Corps as working in just health and education," adds Bruce Burton (Honduras, 1983–85). "They felt we shouldn't be associated with business and banks."

Martha Daniel, former associate director in the eastern Caribbean, contends that "some volunteers couldn't let go of itty-bitty projects. They liked a project to stay small to encourage creativity, but if a women's group had more than one weaving machine they could make enough goods to sell to the tourists."

Despite its many weaknesses, the Peace Corps' CBI was not a totally wasted effort. The additional training that it provided helped some volunteers make worthwhile contributions. Although Gschwend's vision of booming exports was never realized, in many cases volunteers were able to help the small-scale businessperson by arranging for technical assistance or facilitating bank loans. Richard Chavez (Dominican Republic, 1984–86) learned that sixty thousand pounds of turkey were imported from the United States every year at Christmas time and purchased at premium prices. He convinced a group of Dominicans—including small-scale farmers, schoolteachers, and uneducated laborers—to start a turkey farm. With the help of Chavez's congressman, restrictions on the shipment of fowl were waived and day-old poults from Minnesota were flown in. The Dominicans' initial loan, $10,000, was repaid in just a few years and the farm tripled its output, from 2,000 to 6,000 turkeys in three years. "I benefited from the CBI program," says Chavez, "in that I learned how to do a feasibility study and the CBI paid for two or three consultants to come work with me. But since we didn't export the turkeys, I guess it wasn't a true CBI project."

Perhaps the most serious repercussion of the Peace Corps' flirtation with the Reagan administration's initiative was its effect on volunteers. The Corps suffered a loss of faith as those involved recognized that the program was contrived first and foremost to fulfill the agency's needs in Washington, rather than those of the host countries. But for Ruppe, engineering the CBI was no less than a matter of survival. "I get irritated when people say we did CBI because of politics," she says. "If you're trying to figure out how to get the Reagan administration to really support the Peace Corps, wouldn't you look at programs that would make them feel positive about you? I had to talk about what Mr. Meese and Mr. Stockman were interested in. *The Wall Street Journal* wasn't going to write about digging wells."

## Bill Harris (St. Lucia, 1986–88)

(Harris was one of three volunteers, all mid-career marketing and management executives, who were sent to St. Lucia to advise the Ministry of Trade on exporting.)

An investigative team from the Peace Corps was supposed to come to St. Lucia and research the various constraints on exporting. Our assignments, at the St. Lucia Ministry of Trade, were then going to be determined based on their findings. But they never came down to do the research. There is interest on the island in exporting, but St. Lucia doesn't really have anything to export.

The three of us went to the Ministry of Trade every day at eight A.M. and sat there at these desks they had set up for us till four-thirty in the afternoon without anyone giving us so much as a "How are you doing?" I came from a situation in which I could hit a button and have six guys in my office in a second. Now I'm in a situation where the guy I report to won't even say hello to me. The officials at the ministry just wanted us to stay out of the way. They'd rather we didn't do anything and not cause any trouble.

After three months, I asked the Peace Corps for another job or a transfer to another island. They suggested that I go work with the St. Lucia Small Business Association, which, as it turned out, I really got to be a part of and enjoyed very much. We started a quarterly newsletter. I sold the ad space and edited it. I helped get a small grant from a foundation funded by the Rockefeller brothers to buy supplies. I helped plan the meetings where the members would holler about various taxes and restrictions and how something should be done. They didn't have enough momentum to stick with one thing long enough to really push it through, but I was still proud to be associated with them. At one of the meetings the president of the association said, "We have a Peace Corps man with us, and even though he doesn't look like one of us, he's one of us." It made me feel great.

I also went around looking for secondary projects in an effort to make a contribution. One project was teaching first aid to the officers of the police force who patrolled the waters. Another project was building a swing set for the school for the deaf.

There isn't much tangible evidence that I was there for two years, and I feel badly about that. I still think the Peace Corps is a super idea.

There are a lot of volunteers in St. Lucia who are doing good work. But introducing small enterprise development to the Caribbean turned out to be a bigger job than anyone thought it would be. If the Peace Corps had done its homework, we might have known where to start. But the Peace Corps hierarchy are all sociologists. What does a sociologist know about business?

## Bruce Burton (Honduras, 1983–85)

I saw a window of opportunity with CBI and I took advantage of it. I was a regional loan officer for a private development bank in Honduras and I happened to live down the street from some members of a fairly successful farmers' purchasing cooperative. They said to me one day, "We understand gringos eat a lot of vegetables, and we want to export something to the United States." We decided to try snow peas because we had heard about co-ops in Guatemala that were exporting snow peas to the U.S. and doing very well with it. Snow peas are a good product for this kind of development project, because growing them is labor-intensive and the only restrictions on exporting them to the U.S. relate to the kind of pesticides you use. Snow peas also have a high market value, so you could make a lot of money after subtracting your costs.

But there were tons of problems. This project could be a case study on the difficulties of setting up a business in the third world. It was successful though, because our peas were superb, the market was strong, and the twelve farmers involved were great. They each owned seventy-five to a hundred hectares of land and three of them owned trucks. If they were subsistence farmers we never would have gotten anywhere.

I put together a one-hundred-page feasibility study which we presented for financing to a variety of banks. We got a thirty-thousand-dollar loan from an office in the Honduras Ministry of Natural Resources that AID had set up. This money was going to go toward a refrigeration unit and to establish credit. But it took a year to actually receive the money, so we stored the peas in a cold storage unit in a nearby hospital.

The U.S. Department of Agriculture paid for two of the farmers and myself to go to Miami for a USDA conference for Latin American growers and American produce buyers. We connected with a broker there who would get our snow peas through U.S. customs and ship them to the wholesale markets around the country. We got a very competitive rate for flying the peas out on the national airline, although we once lost a load because too much gas had been put in the plane and it couldn't take off. So they dumped our peas onto the tarmac and they roasted. The following season, we had to rely on cargo flights because the farmers produced too much to send on passenger planes. But cargo flights run on very relaxed schedules in Honduras, and with produce, it's got to go or it's dead.

In our first year we exported thirty-five thousand pounds of peas and the farmers made very good money. But it doesn't surprise me that they're not exporting anymore. They had a professional manager come in after me but he didn't know the U.S. market, and our broker in the U.S. doesn't speak Spanish.

Exporting fresh produce from a third world environment is a real challenge. Critical factors like time and handling are things that these farmers never had to contend with before. It was incredibly gratifying to load our first shipment onto an airplane, watch it take off, and have the president of the co-op—whose reading and writing skills were at a sixth-grade level and whose grandfather had never seen a car or owned a pair of shoes— know that his peas were going to be eaten by Americans within the next week. The fact that they didn't continue to export snow peas isn't that important to me because the other benefits are much more relevant to them. This project put their co-op on the map. It got them into the government's model cooperative program, which offered them financing and the ability to diversify.

## Brian Hayes ( Jamaica, 1983–85 )

I was assigned to the National Development Foundation of Jamaica, which made small loans to people who didn't have anything to put up as collateral. The average loan was eight hundred to one thousand dollars. The director of the foundation would go on TV and say if you can't get a bank loan come to the foundation. Lines would form out the door. The receptionist would help them fill out the papers and I would go visit them to follow up.

One applicant I went to see was Avis Benda, a forty-five-year-old woman with four kids to support. She ran a six- by six-foot snack stand in the area of Kingston where there are a lot of garages and factories. She sold cold drinks, candy bars, and crackers to the men who worked there, and she knew she was sitting on a gold mine because she could get these guys' lunch trade. I made a three-hundred-dollar loan to buy chicken backs, chicken feet, canned milk, rice, and sugar so she could make boxed lunches. Mrs. Benda was barely literate but I didn't have to show her much; she knew how to price the lunches and how much she earned on each. Her daughter did the bookkeeping and she made all her payments.

Another woman I worked with, whom I called Miss Lilly, lived in a two-room hovel with her husband and three kids on a steep hill an hour outside of Kingston. They had no electricity and no indoor plumbing. She did beautiful embroidery on a treadle sewing machine which she sold to the best specialty stores in the city. Miss Lilly was going blind from working past daylight and wanted a loan so she could have the house wired for electricity and buy a new sewing machine. This would have doubled her output. I got letters of recommendation from the stores in Kingston she sold to and worked out some creative financing, but the foundation never made loans for construction work or anything they couldn't repossess. When I told her the loan didn't get approved, she didn't seem affected. It hurt me, though, because I liked her so much. I had dealt with a lot of jokers who just wanted to take the money and run. Miss Lilly was highly skilled and I knew she was serious.

I went down to Jamaica believing that America had the answers. But the U.S. government has a controlling interest in the IMF [International Monetary Fund] and they have a certain stake in keeping those countries down. They slash their wrists and send the Peace Corps to sew them up. I did the best I could. Because of the Peace Corps, Avis got help, but there were so many frustrations.

### Bill Weber (Dominican Republic, 1984–86)

During training, the country director got the idea that CBI might be something that I could participate in with the AID people. I'd be less than honest, though, if I said we ever really got it off the ground. We never produced anything that I would call successful. Because of CBI a lot of large-scale investments were made down there but the Peace Corps wasn't involved in them. It was not an area where we could contribute a hell of a lot. I had a lot of fun trying but it wasn't our ball game. Bill Gschwend is a dreamer, the eternal optimist. I think the Peace Corps has accomplished a great deal with Small Enterprise Development all over the world, and volunteers in the Dominican Republic have helped small businesses, but that had nothing to do with the CBI program. Volunteers worked with different groups that made fruit juices, raised turkeys, and grew pineapples. But we were never exporting bananas or beans or anything else.

In the beginning, I tried to see what the State Department was doing with CBI and spread the word that the Peace Corps wanted to be helpful. But you don't invite yourself into somebody else's ball game. I helped AID transfer the info on CBI to the various Dominican authorities and chambers of commerce. It seemed at that time that I was working more for AID and the embassy than for the Peace Corps. I made a lot of good friends with the AID people and the commercial attaché, and the Peace Corps was, overall, a great experience.

## Barcia Miller (Dominican Republic, 1984–86)

I was assigned to work with this government development agency that provided technical and financial assistance to small businesses. I got involved in one project when a man came into the agency with these very ugly ceramic ashtrays which he and his brother had been making in their backyard. He wanted to find out if the gift shops on the island could sell their ashtrays to the American tourists. I tried to explain to the brothers, Juan and Rudy, that the tourists like to buy things that are made of materials that are native to the Dominican Republic, like shells and coconuts. So they started bringing in ashtrays that were basically coconut shells cut in half. I introduced them to a volunteer who had majored in design and she helped them a lot.

In a little while, they were making some really cute things like wall hangings and coconut piggy banks in elephant, rhino, and dinosaur shapes. They made coconut earrings, in the shape of palm trees and fish. They even carved an American bald eagle out of a coconut.

I helped them figure out how to price the items and how to make sales presentations to shopkeepers. I went with them on these sales calls for three or four months. Then I said, "Okay, you guys, time for you to do it yourselves," and they did. I showed them some bookkeeping and how to factor in their costs when setting their prices.

They had this stuff all over their house so they got the idea to build a workshop. I thought it was a viable thing and went to work on getting them an AID loan which came through in about four to six months.

When I left the Dominican Republic, Juan and Rudy's workshop was completed and they were getting orders and upscaling their production. I felt great about it. Major social changes don't happen overnight. If you help a person create an opportunity which turns out to be successful, it then creates more jobs. Juan and Rudy started with just the two of them and have since expanded to about fifteen people. They call themselves Asociación de Artesanos Don Bosco, taking the name of the saint of handcrafts and artisan work. They sent me some newspaper clippings with pictures of them with the head of the Ministry of Tourism. They have their own letterhead and below their address they have their motto: *"Trabajo, honispidad, y dietoroyo"*—"Work, honesty, and development." They're now exporting to Puerto Rico.

## Diane Bejarano (Dominican Republic, 1984–86)

I majored in interior design and Spanish in college and was interested in working with exotic and unusual furnishings. I read a blurb in the American Society for Interior Designers newsletter about the Peace Corps looking for designers. I was somewhat of a joke to the other volunteers, who thought I'd be designing huts. They assumed I wouldn't last the two years.

The Peace Corps called my job "artisan's consultant." They didn't really know what that would entail. I spent the first three months traveling around the Dominican Republic to compile a report for the Peace Corps on the country's artisans and what was being made where. Then they assigned me to an association that made short-term loans to small businesses and gave technical assistance. One of their clients was a jeweler and I worked with him figuring out better ways to display his pieces. He had been just setting things up in the window with no real arrangement to attract shoppers. I also did research on growing bamboo on the island so that the local furniture makers wouldn't have to import it from the Philippines.

Another business volunteer, Barcia Miller, asked me to meet these two brothers, Juan and Rudy, who were making ashtrays and candy dishes out of coconut shells and carving sharks out of cow horn. They wanted to sell these items to the souvenir shops, but the things were really hideous. I suggested different things to do to craft the shells like carving, sanding, and shellacking. We got some money from the Peace Corps to buy tools like knives and sandpaper. They had been using knives with no handles. They eventually made some very nice things and didn't need me anymore.

I also worked with a company in Santo Domingo that made jewelry from cow horn. They'd cut out a circle and call it an earring. I suggested different shapes and sizes and that they maintain a certain level of quality. But shortcuts are old habits for them. I think they may have improved their quality to keep me happy. It was a question of how much work are they willing to put in. In the United States we put in a lot of work and just hope the product sells. They're less willing to put in the time.

I also worked with an association of rocking-chair craftsmen. A set of rockers is a customary wedding gift in the Dominican Republic. The craftsmen support their families picking coffee and try to earn additional income selling the chairs. They made inferior-quality rockers so customers would eventually come back to buy another. I thought that because of the dwindling supplies of local wood, they should make better-quality chairs and I invited industrial arts students from the University of Santo

Domingo to come and give a course in refinishing. I could have given the course myself, but the craftsmen wouldn't have shown up because I'm female. After working with them a while, they did start to take more care in how they handled completed chairs and some were shellacking better and using better woods. But they never were able to improve the overall quality of the chairs or standardize the size.

The American Society of Interior Designers paid for me to go to trade shows in Chicago and Los Angeles where I set up booths displaying handcrafts from the Dominican Republic. I took potholders, chairs, dolls, cowhorn jewelry, coconut ashtrays, picture frames, and papier-mâché masks. The objective was to open communication between American designers and Dominican artisans.

But through a course offered by AID, I learned that artisan groups needed a lot of inventory that was of high quality in order to export to the United States. A few could have done it, but most couldn't have produced the necessary quantity *and* maintained quality. They'd be overwhelmed. CBI was twisted around by Peace Corps and was painted to be a more exciting deal than it was.

I thought the rocker craftsmen could have improved the quality of their chairs just enough to sell to tourists. But then, three months before I left, the government confiscated their equipment because of the island's severe deforestation problem. That was hard to take, but I didn't feel like a failure because it was out of my control. I also knew that I was not able to solve all their problems.

In addition to working with different artisans, I did a lot of public relations for the Peace Corps. When designers came to the island, I used to meet with them and give them tours. I took Loret Ruppe on a shopping spree.

# Chapter 12

☆===

# "Sex Is Scary Here": The Peace Corps Confronts AIDS

Peace Corps volunteers have often had to contend with malaria, venereal disease, diarrhea, and other maladies when they failed to take precautions. Those diseases can be extremely uncomfortable, but at least they are curable. For volunteers in the 1980s and those currently serving, disregarding certain precautions became a dangerous and sometimes fatal risk. The presence of AIDS has been reported in well over half of the seventy-six countries in which volunteers are serving. In those areas of the world, the virus is spreading through the general population and the prevalent means of transmission is heterosexual contact. While the number of volunteers who have tested positive for HIV antibodies may seem relatively small—24 as of January 1991—the rapid spread of AIDS prompted the Peace Corps to initiate a series of policies to educate volunteers, protect the agency's relations with host countries, and prevent medical liabilities.

Dick Wall, country director in Zaire from 1984 to 1988, was perhaps the first Peace Corps official to grasp the seriousness of the AIDS epidemic and its potential impact on the organization. In March of 1984, Wall had dinner at the Kinshasa home of Bill Pruitt, his predecessor as country director. The other guests included Dr. John Moran, the Peace Corps medical officer in Zaire, and two epidemiologists from the Centers for Disease Control. Wall learned that evening that the CDC researchers had found thirty-seven cases of AIDS in two Kinshasa hospitals. The researchers wanted to discuss ways in which volunteers might assist them, and, in the course of the evening, they inquired as to how the Peace Corps was dealing with AIDS. "At that time, AIDS didn't seem to be common enough to be a real threat to us," says Dr. Moran. "The volunteers had heard about AIDS," says Dick Wall, "but it was something somewhere else, in New York or San Francisco. I realized that evening that if AIDS was an issue for Zaire, it was very likely an issue for the volunteers who were working there."

Indeed, in 1984, nine countries in East and Central Africa—later known as the AIDS belt—reported cases of AIDS to the World Health Organization. Six of those countries hosted Peace Corps volunteers. The Corps also had volunteers in eight other countries—in the Caribbean, Central America, and East Asia—that were reporting cases by that time.

The Peace Corps' initial steps in addressing AIDS were sporadic and uncertain. "There were some strange moments," says Martha Bennett (Zaire, 1984–87), who remembers receiving a letter from a staff member cautioning her about her romantic involvement with a Zairian man. "The letter never addressed the AIDS question, just whether I was being objective about the relationship. He hoped I'd forget him and go on with my life." Susan Eisendrath (Tanzania, 1983–86) says that she and her fellow volunteers learned more about AIDS "through word of mouth and reading *Newsweek* than from the Peace Corps. It was appalling. They didn't send us any information on AIDS until it was already an epidemic. We didn't even get condoms."

Some volunteers think that the Peace Corps' slow action on AIDS was related to the Reagan administration's delayed response to the epidemic. "Reagan didn't mention AIDS publicly until 1987," points out Brian Cole (Central African Republic, 1985–87). "He considered it an issue for gays, IV drug users, and Haitians. When you start testing volunteers, you're admitting they might be at risk. That's a heavy thing to say about the nice boys and girls of the Peace Corps." Dr. Theresa H. van der Vlught, director of Peace Corps medical services in Washington, counters that the Peace Corps responded to AIDS as scientific data became available.

Matters of diplomacy also affected the Peace Corps' response to the AIDS crisis. In the early and mid-1980s, many host country governments denied or minimized the extent of the disease's proliferation in order to protect tourism and foreign investment. Under these circumstances, the Peace Corps has had to exercise some discretion or risk offending its hosts. "We couldn't make a formal announcement about our AIDS policies," says Dr. Ken Bernard, the Corps' epidemiologist, "because host governments weren't admitting that AIDS existed in their populations. But we did provide some AIDS education in a less formal way." Dr. Moran, for example, says he incorporated information about AIDS into his talks to trainees about venereal disease and birth control. "I told them it was fatal, how it's spread, and that they should avoid contact with those who they thought might have sexually transmitted diseases, and that if they did have sex, they should use condoms."

Some volunteers think the Peace Corps gave short shrift to the whole issue. "We got a couple of information sheets on how AIDS is transmitted and prevented," says Susan Eisendrath. "They were factual and perfunctory, the sort of leaflets they'd drop from a plane. They weren't really in touch with what volunteers were doing. They didn't state, for example, that if you're in contact with prostitutes you should use condoms and get tested." Mike Tidwell (Zaire, 1985–87) recalls, "We were briefed on the risk of AIDS during training but there was no follow-up. You get out there and you melt into a different world. A lot of men didn't seem to take AIDS very seriously. They slept with whores repeatedly."

During her visit to Zaire in the summer of 1985, Peace Corps director Loret Ruppe was told of the gravity of the AIDS situation there by the American ambassador. When she returned to Washington, she instructed medical director van der Vlught and the Corps' general counsel to begin working with the State Department and the National Institutes of Health on a testing policy.

In November 1985, for the first time, a Peace Corps volunteer showed symptoms of HIV infection and tested positive for HIV antibodies. Shortly thereafter, Bill Pruitt, the former country director in Zaire and a hemophiliac, was diagnosed with AIDS.

In 1986, AIDS education was made a mandatory part of the training curriculum and as of November of that year, all accepted applicants received a two-page notice describing AIDS, its quick spread throughout the world, and how it could be prevented through safe sex and cautious medical procedures. The notice cautioned volunteers to "avoid all practices that result in penetration of skin surfaces (such as tattoos, ear piercing, blood brotherhood ceremonies, or other incisions of the skin during traditional ceremonial or healing practices)." In 1987, the Peace Corps announced its mandatory testing policy: Proof of seronegative status for HIV antibodies was now a prerequisite for final acceptance, and volunteers completing their service were required to be tested.

Such AIDS testing policies are widely criticized as discriminatory. The Peace Corps, though, had no other choice. Certain vaccines (measles, mumps, rubella, and yellow fever) may not protect a volunteer who is HIV-positive, and multiple concurrent immunizations, a common Peace Corps medical practice, could adversely affect the course of the HIV infection. In the third world, it would be virtually impossible for the Peace Corps to provide adequate medical attention for volunteers who have AIDS or are HIV-positive. In Africa, they would face an especially dangerous threat from a new strain of malaria that is resistant to conventional treatments. The strain is particularly lethal to the HIV-positive individual and may aggravate the infection. According to the agency's policy statement, testing is also necessary to safeguard United States-host country relations, which could be strained if it was discovered that a volunteer had infected a national.

By 1988 volunteers were deluged with information on AIDS. Condoms were included in every volunteers' medical kit and set out in candy dishes in Peace Corps offices around the world. But as Dick Wall says, "Volunteers are human beings. No matter how much you push them, they will internalize the information and alter their behavior accordingly only when they are ready."

"We got a letter from Peace Corps headquarters in Washington which described the dangers of AIDS and listed the high-risk groups," recalls Brian Cole. "It also cautioned us against sharing razors. This shook people up, but a lot of volunteers dealt with it by making a joke about how we *always* share razors."

Some volunteers dealt with AIDS by abstaining from sex, but their will power usually doesn't last, says Antonia Makowsky, who was on staff in Zaire in 1986–87. "Once they were settled in, most volunteers became sexually active with nationals or other volunteers. The majority were pretty careful, I think. But not all. I remember one woman telling me, 'Oh God, I just sucked up more SIDA the other night' " [using the French acronym for AIDS common in francophone Africa].

Whether they learned about it by word of mouth or from Peace Corps mailings, AIDS, to some, was too remote a possibility to require serious attention. "It seemed like you could get away with it," says a volunteer who tested positive shortly after coming home. "The risk wasn't stopping people."

After the Peace Corps had its AIDS policy in place, the agency began offering to send volunteers to help host country governments with their AIDS education programs. But the stigma of the disease makes those governments wary of accepting the assistance. Until 1987, it was widely believed in the West that AIDS originated in Africa. Inviting Americans who are not health professionals to preach safe sex reinforces the age-old notion of the white man's burden. "They would take the Peace Corps' attention to AIDS as an insult," says Sonia Walker (Zaire, 1984–86).

## Martha Bennett (Zaire, 1984–87)

My fiancé is a Zaire national who is a friend of a friend of one of the training instructors. He dropped out of law school to run the family-owned sand quarry after his father died. We didn't talk explicitly about AIDS. It crossed my mind but the more time we spent together the less it occurred to me. We were good friends before we became involved and really trusted each other. We're very much in love and if he has AIDS, it's a risk I'm willing to take.

## Carol Moore (Central African Republic, 1985–87)*

When I went into the Peace Corps, there was a lot of attention on Africa as the birthplace of AIDS. The night before I left, I seriously considered whether I really wanted to go. When I got to the Central African Republic, there was a volunteer who was going home with AIDS. For some reason, this didn't inhibit us. AIDS might have tempered our enthusiasm but many of us got into the cultural promiscuity. There are beliefs that if a man goes for a month without having sex his penis will fall off, and if a woman doesn't have sex for a month she'll get sick. My neighbors used to offer to send their son over to sleep with me. Morals broke down there. Volunteers had affairs with married men and some had several partners. They carried on as if there were no AIDS.

I didn't have any Central African boyfriends but I got involved with someone from the French volunteer organization and with another Peace Corps volunteer. Both had had relationships with Central African women. But since one was French and the other American, I figured neither of them could possibly have it, so we didn't use condoms. I admit there was some racism going on.

The Peace Corps practically shoves condoms down your throat. But twenty-two-year-olds think they're invincible and they don't like condoms because they interrupt the mood. Central Africans don't like the way they feel. Two of my friends never used condoms and they both came home

---

*The volunteer's name has been changed to protect her privacy.

with herpes. A lot of volunteers get chlamydia and other sexually transmitted diseases. They get them a few times and occasionally they have more than one at a time.

When I got home, I couldn't look at my dad because he would say how glad he was that I came home in one piece and meanwhile I was waiting to get the results back from my AIDS test. I wouldn't want to be a Peace Corps volunteer in the Central African Republic now. A woman in my group tested positive when she finished her two years.

### Brian Cole (Central African Republic, 1985–87)

A teacher in my school had a clotting disorder and had gotten transfusions. I think he died of AIDS. The gym teacher began wasting away and a Peace Corps training instructor died of it. A friend of a volunteer, a Central African woman, was also wasting away but I never learned if she had AIDS.

I had a Muslim girlfriend who was more reserved than other women. She didn't sleep around, so I assumed she wasn't carrying HIV. But I always used a condom. My students told me that using a condom is like saying to a woman you think she's a prostitute. I told my girlfriend, "I don't think you are. I just wouldn't want you to catch anything from me." She accepted that.

### Terry Rey (Zaire, 1986–88)

When I first got to Zaire, I wrote my parents that I had seen a lot of AIDS patients in the hospitals and that celibacy was going to be my means of avoiding it. At the time I really believed that. But there's a fascination with African women. They're very strong and very beautiful. It was very easy for me to fall in love, and before I knew it I was seriously involved.

I met her in the market where she worked. She was a merchant. She sold whatever she bought the week before: usually salt, beer, corn. She's absolutely beautiful—five feet ten inches, arms as large as mine, beautiful skin tone and high cheekbones. She's twenty or twenty-five and has two children. When she and her husband split up, she started selling in the market to survive and was successful at it. She had an eighth-grade education from a poor school system. Most people in Zaire speak two or three languages. She knows seven: French, four local dialects, and two other African languages. She lived in the village about a kilometer away from me. We just got talking and had a few beers together. She's very strong and very spiritual and we hit it off. I was swept away with passion. AIDS was the farthest thing from my mind.

A few days later, I got a memo about AIDS from the Peace Corps office in Kinshasa. It had a picture of the grim reaper on it and I just fell apart. I thought for sure I was going to become infected. Before I became sexually active, I had diarrhea and lost a lot of weight and yet once I became sexually active I thought, "Shit, I lost five pounds this week— I'm fading." [In Central Africa early signs of AIDS include rapid weight loss and chronic diarrhea.] I thought, "I've only slept with this woman about four times and three times I used condoms so I'm not at that great a risk. I'm okay, so quit now." I told her I couldn't continue our relationship because of my fears. But I was genuinely in love with her and she was very comforting. She said, "You have nothing to worry about with me because I haven't been with many men." I believed her because she's a mother and her husband hadn't left her that long ago.

We started living together. She stopped working in the market and took care of me. I was eating better and was very content. But AIDS never really left my mind. Every day I thought about the possibility of becoming infected. There was a period when I drank a lot and took Valium to mellow myself out. I thought about using condoms but in a long-standing relationship are you going to use them every time? And she found them offensive. She would say to me, "You think I have some disease?"

After I got home, I received the results of my AIDS test by mail. I was dancing around the living room and my family asked if I had just won the lottery. I said, "No, I'm going to live, though."

## Hank Dungan (Gabon, 1988–90)

(The following is from a letter to the author that was written in December 1988.*)

During training, there was practically endless discussion about AIDS; we heard about condoms, safe sex, statistics on Africans with AIDS, demonstrations of how to use a condom (condom on a broomstick that is). Also, relations between staff and trainees were strictly forbidden on the grounds of "professionalism," but later I found out that the year before, a particularly popular (African) male instructor had died of AIDS. Sex is scary here. . . . The fact that women here are extremely willing doesn't help either.

---

*Hank Dungan is a pseudonym for a volunteer who requested that he remain anonymous.

(Hank Dungan wrote another letter to the author in March 1989, a part of which follows.)

To be my lover would doubtlessly raise a Gabonese woman's social standing as well as her income. . . . It's a strange thing to know that virtually any young unattached woman that speaks to me is probably playing her cards to try to get into bed with me. Three days after I arrived here, a woman who works in the school where I teach asked me when I was going to come to her house to make love to her. We'd hardly spoken for more than ten minutes up to that point. At first I thought she was kidding, just trying to get some sort of reaction out of me. But it's clear she wasn't. . . . There's one volunteer I know who's gone nuts. He admits to making love to nine different Gabonese "women." His partners are mostly under twenty; the youngest was fourteen. . . . He's sort of a geek, probably wasn't very popular in high school or college.

## Alice Kraft (Central Africa, 1984–87)*

My site was quite remote and the roads were terrible. It took one or two days to go a hundred kilometers. I worked within a thirty-mile radius of my village, demonstrating to farmers how to build and maintain wells in their fields.

At the end of my first year, I had a relationship with the son of a family I knew who lived in a nearby town. I hadn't thought about sex since I'd been there but something reawoke when we met. He was a couple of years younger than me and was studying business in the capital. We got to be friends and planned to meet in the city when I went on vacation. He used condoms on his own initiative. I was offended to think that he thought he might catch something from me. But I think he was more concerned about preventing a pregnancy than about AIDS. I wasn't worried about getting pregnant because I knew my cycle.

AIDS didn't concern me or the other volunteers at that time. We thought about it more later on when we began getting information from the local people, magazines from home, and from the Peace Corps. As far as I know, though, most volunteers didn't change their habits regarding sex. I suppose I just didn't want to deal with the fact that a lot of people around

---

*Alice Kraft is a pseudonym for a volunteer who tested positive for HIV antibodies ten months after she left Africa. She agreed to be interviewed for this book in hopes that her experience might help current and future volunteers understand the need for caution.

me might be carrying the AIDS virus. Yet we were all well aware that receiving a transfusion outside of the Peace Corps medical auspices was a virtual death sentence.

While I was waiting for the results of the two blood tests, I admitted to myself that I could have become infected.* I was terrified thinking about what I would tell my parents, that I'd be going home as a pariah. After I found out my first test was negative, I figured, "I can judge." But a negative test isn't necessarily the final word. The Peace Corps didn't tell us that it could take months after infection for it to show up on a test. When we went for our tests, we weren't asked when we last had intercourse. That's where I screwed up. You can't know as much as you think you know.

At the end of my third year, I got to be friends with another man in the area. We had talked about AIDS, which he blamed on Europeans. I figured that if he's talking about it, he must be careful about who he goes to bed with. I also felt safe because it wasn't like I had picked him up in a bar.

When I finished my Peace Corps service, I traveled to another African country to catch a plane home. But I met some friends and ended up staying about six weeks. I was introduced to William, a national, at a party in the capital and we became very close. He was a lawyer and less influenced by tradition in how he related to women than the other two men I had been involved with in Africa. I didn't think I was a risk to him or that he was a risk to me.

When I came home from Africa, I enrolled in a graduate program for agriculture. I wanted to get my master's and to go back to East Africa to live and work. William came to visit about eight months after I got home. During his stay here he discovered he had swollen lymph nodes. The doctor recommended that he get an AIDS test when he got home and told me that I should be concerned about AIDS also. When he said all this, I thought, "You racist bastard."

I wasn't worried about myself because I had tested negative when I left the Peace Corps and I figured that once you test negative you're fine. But soon after William left I got very sick for about a week. I was running a fever, my joints felt very stiff, and I developed a painful rash on my face and chest. A friend of mine, who is knowledgeable about AIDS, said

---

*As is the Peace Corps' policy, Kraft had an AIDS test performed when she completed her two-year stint. Kraft decided to extend her service for another year and, in compliance with agency policy, she had another AIDS test performed when she finished her third year and left the Corps.

these were the symptoms of seroconversion. I went for a test and it came back positive.

Now I'm in an odd culture in my own hometown. It's like life in Africa when I first got there. I'm a freak, a little strange. My friends are fine about it but I haven't told my parents. I feel shut out of any relationships with men, but the most painful thing is that I cannot have children for fear of passing the virus and condemning the child to a very early death. And I don't know about going back to Africa because the necessary treatment might not be available there if I got sick. I feel perfectly fine but I'm worried about everything.*

The Peace Corps gave us material on AIDS. I got enough info to know I was taking a chance. But at the same time, I wasn't doing anything more risky than other volunteers.

---

*Kraft recently completed her master's degree in agriculture. She is in good health and is looking for a job that will take her back to Africa.

*Chapter 13*

☆===

# *Honduras: The Peace Corps as Smile Button*

A Peace Corps volunteer waiting on line at an ice cream stand in Tegucigalpa, Honduras, strikes up a conversation with the man in front of him who looks like a local but speaks English without an accent. The man explains that he's training Contras with a contingent of Hispanic-American Green Berets and they occasionally accompany them on incursions into Nicaragua. "If any of us get killed or captured in combat, it will be assumed that we're Contras, not Americans." Another volunteer introduces herself to an American soldier at a dance in the capital and asks him what he does in Honduras. "I'm teaching a bunch of brown-skinned monkeys how to kill and loving every minute of it."

Such reminders of United States military activities in Honduras were a part of Peace Corps volunteers' daily life there in the mid to late 1980s. "Jets roared overhead and helicopters and transport planes flew back and forth all the time. You got used to it," remembers Harold Neidinger (Honduras, 1987–89).

What was harder for many volunteers to get used to was the pervasive sense that their presence was somehow a part of the Reagan administration's master plan to stop Communist encroachment in Central America. In June 1985, a planeload of trainees increased the size of the Peace Corps program in Honduras by 50 percent, from 200 to 300. The ranks continued to swell, sometimes hitting 400—making the contingent the largest in the world—at the same time that America's proxy war against

Nicaragua, staged primarily from Honduras, intensified. While the Peace Corps claims to operate detached from foreign policy decisions, many volunteers took it for granted that they had been dispatched to Honduras by Washington strategists to serve as "the smile button" on the lapel of United States foreign policy. "The Reagan Administration considers taxpayers' money well spent if they just act like nice North Americans, helping people in little ways so that the militarization of Honduras, which is visible and intrusive, doesn't look so bad," wrote Lisa Swenarski (Honduras, 1984–86).[1] To many volunteers, it was unsettling to think that the Peace Corps had subordinated its humanitarian goals to the administration's foreign policy needs.* "Politics came into it more than anyone wants to admit," says another volunteer, "It makes you wonder if we were doing good for the wrong cause."

Though many volunteers believed that Washington strategists were behind the Honduras expansion, it was Peace Corps director Loret Ruppe who actually urged policy advisers to implement the program. Anxious for opportunities to prove the Peace Corps' worth to the administration, Ruppe carefully monitored White House policies toward host countries. In 1983, when President Reagan convened a blue-ribbon advisory panel, the National Bipartisan Commission on Central America, headed by Henry Kissinger, Ruppe went into action and declared before the commission that the Peace Corps could make a significant contribution. (The Reagan administration already knew it wanted to use military means to unseat the Sandinista government, but Congress and the public were reluctant. The White House gambled that a high-profile bipartisan advisory group would support its plan.)

"We had to prove ourselves somehow," says Ruppe, of her determination to have the Peace Corps included in the commission's recommendations. "I heard about the Kissinger Commission and I thought, 'How can we get into this thing? Maybe we can get some money from them.' If they are talking about a ten- or twenty-year plan for developing the economy, quality of life, and stability of Central America, then the work of the Peace Corps must be represented."

In her testimony before the Kissinger Commission, Ruppe claimed that the Peace Corps was

---

*This was not a new accusation. In 1969, a volunteer serving in the Philippines wrote that the Peace Corps "deflects criticism from the more distasteful elements of the American presence— the military, business and embassy communities. The youthful idealism and activity of the volunteers are an effective counterbalance to the offensive displays of whoring and drinking of soldiers on R & R."[2]

uniquely qualified to serve as an . . . important component of overall U.S. policy toward the region. . . . At a time when the Cubans have moved massively into the public diplomacy area of Central America, we should not overlook our Peace Corps volunteers . . . the lasting friendships, understanding, and respect created by the Peace Corps volunteers, not only with the people but also with their country's leaders, is of paramount importance to our long-term foreign policy objectives.[3]

Both Ruppe and President Reagan got their wishes. The commission report stated that it was in "our own national interest" to send substantial military aid to the Contras and America's allies in the region.[4] The commission also counseled massive amounts of economic and humanitarian aid, and in this portion of their report, they recommended a substantially larger Peace Corps presence in the region.* Congress adopted the recommendations and gave the Peace Corps extra funds to augment its operations in Central America. By 1987, the Corps' program in Guatemala was the fourth largest (219 volunteers) of its sixty-two programs around the world. Costa Rica was the ninth largest. Tiny Belize (population 200,000) hosted the world's highest concentration of volunteers: 1 for every 1,385 citizens. In Honduras, a country the size of Ohio with 4.5 million people, the Peace Corps contingent swelled to 400. "A joke went around," recalls Janet Coffey (Honduras, 1986–87), "that every Honduran family has a mother, a father, six kids, and a Peace Corps volunteer."

By pursuing the Kissinger Commission, Ruppe got volunteers into a position where their work was noticed. But the prize was not without a price. The crowding of volunteers into Central America—and Peace Corps officials' lack of candor about it—cost the trust and affection of many volunteers and alumni.

Peace Corps officials in Washington routinely sidestepped accusations from the Peace Corps community that they were violating the apolitical spirit of the Corps by catering to the immediate foreign policy needs of the Reagan administration. "We provide technical assistance and do not dictate priorities," said Luis Del Rio, director of the inter-America region in the mid-1980s.[5]

In Honduras, as volunteers watched U.S. Army helicopters carry tanks through the sky toward the Nicaraguan border, Peace Corps country director Peter Stevens was also evasive. "When a question came up about the Peace Corps and U.S. policy, he'd just ignore it," says Christine Just

*The commission called for as many as thirty-six hundred volunteers to teach and train local teachers in remedial literacy and primary, secondary, and technical education.

(Honduras, 1986–88). "It was like, 'You're the private and I'm the general, and you only need to know what I tell you,' " according to one volunteer who asked not to be named.*

Stevens gave the smile-button theorists added credibility by discouraging controversy. Volunteers who wished to make public their criticism of President Reagan's Central America policy say that Stevens made it clear that such an action would jeopardize their standing in the organization. Though the Peace Corps manual states clearly the agency's policy on political expression, Stevens's implementation of this policy created an atmosphere of oppression. One volunteer wrote an essay condemning United States interference in Central America and in accordance with the Peace Corps manual, he showed it to Stevens before mailing it off to his hometown newspaper. "Stevens asked me not to send it," he relates. "It was clear to me that life would be difficult if I did." Stevens says he does not recall the incident and that "I'm not vindictive towards volunteers."

Whether or not Stevens discouraged volunteers from exercising their First Amendment rights, Loret Ruppe maintains that any controversy surrounding the Corps could be very damaging: "You can't speak out until you're big enough to withstand the down side of speaking out because you're going to make people angry. In the late 1960s, the Peace Corps almost went under because of volunteers who protested the war in Vietnam. In trying to move the Peace Corps forward, you don't need any bad public awareness or controversy."

Not every volunteer was compelled to speak out. Indeed, while the experiences of most were in some way affected by the United States military presence, their reactions to the situation covered the spectrum. "Volunteers talked about how they sometimes felt like pawns," says Paul Ingle (Honduras, 1986–88). "I didn't agree with U.S. policy toward Nicaragua, but I thought I was doing something positive so I overlooked it. When you're working one-on-one with the people, the politics are behind you." Some volunteers were proud to make a contribution to America's effort in the region. "They spoke of it like they were in Nam," says Christine Just, "and 'We're going to teach these people.' "

Still others had no opinion at all. "I didn't know much about the politics so I couldn't say much," says Brian Smith (Honduras, 1986–88). "I just did my job and the GIs did theirs." Adds volunteer Lisa Johnston (Honduras, 1984–86), "It was like living in California: You know about the earthquakes but you don't worry till something happens."

---

*Stevens, who describes himself as "an up-front, frank person," says, "I avoided no questions."

Through the mid-1980s there had been frequent demonstrations by Hondurans calling for the removal of American military personnel, the Contras, and the United States ambassador. By 1988, the anger found expression in sporadic violence. In April, two thousand students rioted at the American embassy in Tegucigalpa. Five people were killed when Honduran security forces tried to quell the melee.* Offices were looted and twenty-five embassy vehicles were set ablaze. Volunteers in the capital were ordered to stay in "safe houses" (the homes of U.S. government personnel) for the week following the riot.

"We went out in a jeep to try to find two of our friends who weren't accounted for," recalls Nancy Finkle (Honduras, 1986–88). "We drove down one street and there were the demonstrators half a block from us. When they saw us they yelled, *'Gringas. Vamanos.'* About half a dozen started running toward us. We screamed and turned around fast. There were reports that day of Swedes and Germans who had been mistaken for Americans and got beaten up."

Before the month was out, a U.S. Army convoy was ambushed with rifle fire. While no one was hurt in this incident, in July five American soldiers were injured in a grenade and rifle attack in the city of San Pedro Sula. An underground leftist group, the Chinchoneros Movement, claimed responsibility for the assault. In September, an American businessman living in Tegucigalpa was killed by a gunman while jogging around his neighborhood. Another leftist group, the Morazonista Patriotic Front, claimed responsibility.

The same month, a Peace Corps trainee, Matthew Sherman, twenty-two, of Minster, Ohio, was shot in the head and killed instantly by a night watchman at the Peace Corps training facility. He and a fellow trainee were mistaken for intruders when they entered the grounds through a break in the fence that was used frequently by many trainees as a shortcut. A State Department investigation determined within days that the shooting had no political motivation. A volunteer offers one possible explanation: "The guard was scared for himself because of increased tension between America and Honduras. It was his responsibility to protect this American installation. When Matt and his friend came through the fence, he must have assumed the worst. It was a combination of factors that made it happen."

---

*Students from both the Left and Right protested the United States' disregard for Honduran sovereignty. Days earlier, suspected drug trafficker Juan Ramon Matta Ballesteros had been captured by law-enforcement officers and taken to the United States despite the fact that Honduras and the United States had no extradition treaty.

Just two months after Sherman's death, violence struck the Peace Corps again. At 3:50 in the morning on December 19, a sophisticated explosive planted in a door frame destroyed Peter Stevens's office and blew out the building's windows and those of the adjacent building.

"After that, you wondered when you went to the Peace Corps office if a bomb is going to go off or if someone's going to drive by with an automatic weapon and take a few potshots," says Brian Smith. "The bombing sparked a lot of talk," adds John Gavin (Honduras, 1987–89). "Volunteers wanted to know what would prompt the Peace Corps to pull out of Honduras. When one of us is killed? Matt's death was considered an accident. I don't know if anyone asked. It's a touchy question and volunteers might not want to bring it up." Then, in 1990, a volunteer was gang-raped and robbed by four members of the Honduran military.

The Peace Corps responded to the violence against Americans and the bombing in several ways: Volunteers were cautioned against congregating publicly in groups of more than four or five; they were asked not to go to bars or restaurants frequented by other Americans, and not to stay out late; the night watchmen at the Peace Corps office and training site were replaced by professional security guards; and volunteer postings were phased out in the capital and San Pedro Sula, where anti-American sentiment was the most intense.

One volunteer says he occasionally heard "Yankee trash, go home!" and similar endearments yelled from passing cars, and some volunteers have been spit upon and told, *"Vayase de aquí con la SIDA"* ("Get out of here with your AIDS").[6] In towns along the northern coast, from which the United Fruit Company withdrew its operations, leaving thousands unemployed, men mutter on the street, "I'm going to kill you." One volunteer says, "I didn't want to make a big deal out of it. You didn't take it seriously."

In addition to sporadic hostility and political ambiguity, some volunteers in Honduras had to contend with what they considered to be misguided assignments, particularly those in the literacy program. The emphasis on literacy originated with the Kissinger Commission, which had been impressed by the accomplishments of Cuban literacy programs in Nicaragua. In embracing the commission's interest in literacy, director Ruppe's testimony before the commission put the challenge squarely in the context of anticommunism. The Peace Corps, she said, would consider "engaging ourselves more actively in literacy programs. . . . This certainly would be an area where Cuba and its socialist doctrine would exist in direct competition with the United States. . . . Education helps make a free man, free to choose among political systems, free to choose his own way."[7]

When the commission recommended a large Peace Corps for Central America, a team of former volunteers, Peace Corps staff, and AID personnel were sent to Honduras to determine in what areas of assignment additional volunteers should be programmed. The team concluded that the Honduras program should enlarge its literacy sector, despite certain circumstances that would probably compromise such an effort. "Literacy volunteers didn't make much sense for Honduras," says Susan Caparosa, a staff person in the early 1980s, "because literacy is not a priority for the Honduran government. The priority is that a few at the top get richer." Former deputy country director John Evans points out that "Cuba sends teachers whether they want to go or not, and Cuban literacy instructors already speak Spanish. In addition, the Nicaraguan government really wanted to boost literacy. Honduras doesn't have the political will to do this."

The so-called literacy brigade faced serious difficulties from the start. Volunteers were assigned to the Honduran government's literacy program, Plan Alfa, which amounted to little more than a goodwill gesture by Honduran President Roberto Suazo Cordova toward the campesinos. The role of the volunteers was that of liaisons between Plan Alfa's regional supervisors and the actual classes that were taught by those local people who were literate. Volunteers conducted teacher-training workshops for the instructors and visited the classes periodically to provide additional support. Mismanaged and inadequately funded, Plan Alfa was all but forgotten when Suazo left office in 1986. "We weren't necessarily placed to fill a need," says former literacy volunteer Lexie Vaughn (Honduras, 1985–87). "We were just placed. But that's the way of the world, not just the Peace Corps. I would be cynical about it if I had a fairy tale notion of the Peace Corps as a noble mission to help the poor."

### Virginia Pace (Honduras, 1984–86)

On paper the literacy program was stunning and our group couldn't wait to get to Honduras. But the Peace Corps had jumped on the Kissinger Commission bandwagon and Plan Alfa was on its way into the grave before we even got there. The beans and corn which the Honduran instructors received as payment were either rotting or full of worms. When word got out in one town that the paymaster was arriving on the coming Saturday to pay the instructors, people came in from the mountains and slept on the streets for three days waiting for him. But he never arrived. The following year, the administrators of Plan Alfa, who worked in the capital, couldn't understand why we were unable to recruit local teachers to participate.

No attention was given to the fact that supplies had to be transported to rural communities by muleback. Some of the villages we were supposed to visit were four to six hours off the main road, accessible only by these muddy mountain trails. You couldn't even get to them three or four months out of the year. Some volunteers found themselves sleeping on the floors of roach-infested huts. We had no idea it would be like this.

When I told the Peace Corps staff that Plan Alfa was falling apart, they just said, "Stick with it. It's going to get better." I thought they were being dishonest. They made me feel like, "Where is your loyalty to your country?"

## Peter Buckey (Honduras, 1985–87)

When the limitations of Plan Alfa became clear, volunteers just had to go out with what they had and not wait for things to improve.

There's not much tradition of education in Honduras and all of a sudden we're saying to the campesinos that they should give up an hour a day five days a week for this. The first year there might be ten to twenty-five people in a class. Then it got down to two to eight people. The men between twenty and thirty years old dropped out first. They were tired from working in the fields all day. Most of those who came to the classes did so because the teacher was their friend or because I had asked them to come. A fewer number came because they felt that they needed to learn how to read and write.

A lot of volunteers dropped out because it was so arduous. It would be ninety-five degrees and you're sweating all over, the sun was going down so you're squinting at the blackboard and the mosquitoes are attacking your ankles. Some Hondurans have learning disabilities or night blindness because of malnourishment so the lessons progress very slowly. Volunteers had visions of working with hundreds of teachers and having a noticeable impact but that was naive. I would say I helped twenty teachers who felt they really made strides, and one hundred people, mostly kids and young women, who got the rudiments of literacy.

## Brian Smith (Honduras, 1986–88)

I was assigned to a remote village called San Isidro. You get off a bus and walk twenty-four miles up into the mountains. I taught farmers about weed control, planting densities, spacing their rows, soil conservation, and contour planting. I tried to show the farmers the value of soil sampling and how to measure their yields. I got money from the Peace Corps to take about twenty farmers on a field trip to an area where World Neighbors [a Christian development-assistance organization] had been working for about five years. The people there used to be desperately poor but World Neighbors helped them turn it around. I took my guys into the fields and had the farmers explain what it was like before and after they learned about new methods. This really paid off because they were hearing about new ways of doing things from people who were once in their same situation. Some Peace Corps officials were hesitant to put money out for this trip. If you stay at your site and build an irrigation system, they can see it. But the farmers went home really encouraged. Some even stopped slashing and burning. I almost hugged them.

Sometimes I went to this lake that had some hotels on it to get me a hamburger and shoot some pool—take a reality check. GIs went there too on R and R. They were friendly guys. Sometimes they'd take me out on the lake in a motorboat. Some thought I was weird because I was in the Peace Corps. But others seemed to admire me for it. A few said they couldn't tell me what they were doing in Honduras.

I heard about volunteers who quit because they didn't like being window dressing for the Army. I didn't care about that. Maybe we were, on the big scale, but I was down there on the small scale and I felt good about what I was doing. The people in my village were glad I was there. Even when the embassy was under siege, this older lady said, "If there's ever any trouble, you stay with me and everything will be okay."

There's a lot of military activity along the borders with Nicaragua, Guatemala, and El Salvador, and there are a lot of listening stations all over. Every now and then a mortar shell got lobbed into one or some automatic-weapon fire shoots out from the bushes. But that stuff didn't affect me much. The majority of people are very pro-American because they see all the money coming down. There is a handful of radicals who are displeased with American involvement so they incite a riot or throw a bomb into a disco or pizza place frequented by Americans.

I got shot at once in 1988. I was playing pool at a hotel with some American sailors and we went out around midnight to buy some beers. On our way back to the hotel, someone fired a few rounds at us. One of the guys pulled out his gun but he didn't shoot because the whole place would have blown up. We got up against a building and a few more shots whizzed by before they stopped. Hondurans shoot because they're macho and they want to show they're tough. We shouldn't have been out that late anyway. The Peace Corps never found out about it.

Three other volunteers had some trouble. They were in a bar and a Honduran guy asked one of them to dance. When she said she didn't want to, he got kind of rough. He threw her down on the floor and shot a couple bullets around her head. They carry pretty good-sized egos down there.

I found out through the grapevine that Matt Sherman had been shot. I met him once and we had a bite to eat. After the riot at the embassy the guards at the training camp were told to be tighter with security. The camp had some thefts around that time. People had been coming through the fence and stealing chairs. That doesn't justify shooting someone before warning them. It was a strange time. Everyone was saying, "Wow, you know, this is getting real."

## Ron Holcomb (Honduras, 1986)

The Peace Corps was something my wife, Kathy McCann, and I both wanted to do for as long as we can remember. We had been married a few years and we were at a point in our careers where we were ready for a change. We didn't have any children yet so it seemed like the ideal time to go.

When we were offered positions in Honduras, we were a bit skeptical. From reading the papers and watching the TV news, we knew that Honduras was being used for the Contras. But we went anyway because as volunteers we saw ourselves as separate from what was going on in the news. We were going at Honduras's invitation and answering a particular need.

We first got concerned at the orientation in Miami. We envisioned we'd be in a group of twenty to twenty-five going down to Honduras, but there were more than a hundred of us. It was one of the largest training groups they'd sent to Honduras. Someone asked a staff person why so many were going to Honduras. The answer was, "Well, because of the Kissinger report," and there wasn't a lot of elaboration on that. We tried not to let this bother us because we figured we'd find out more when we got there.

One of the training instructors loaned me a copy of the Kissinger report, which stated that the Peace Corps should send volunteers who are fluent in Spanish. But in our group there was only a handful, five at the most, who were advanced or really fluent in Spanish. The rest had some Spanish in high school or were starting from scratch.*

While we were in training [spring 1986], Nicaragua supposedly invaded Honduras. This was right before a vote in Congress on aid to the Contras. We could see U.S. Army planes flying toward the Nicaraguan border. We asked the staff, "What is the United States really doing in Honduras?" They told us, "We're not here for military purposes."

We were very uncomfortable about the kinds of answers we got to what we thought were very legitimate questions. Too much information was readily available to just ignore these issues or blow them off. It was an insult to our intelligence.

Kathy was assigned to a mental health facility in San Pedro Sula. When she met with the director, he said he thought she might organize women's groups for talking, sewing, or whatever the women wanted it to be. Then he told her, "Well, I didn't really want you here." I was assigned to a government-run day center for newspaper boys who don't go to school. The idea was to start some workshops and sports programs. The Honduran fellow who ran the center was doing fine. I felt uncomfortable being assigned to a facility that I felt was up and running on its own.

It's difficult for the Peace Corps to place married couples, and I was open to taking an assignment that wasn't related to my background in environmental issues. But the philosophy of the Peace Corps is that you bring a skill that you try to pass on to the local people. It would have been great if they could put a volunteer in there who had a well-defined skill, like carpentry, that they could teach.

It was hard to deal with not having specific jobs, and not being really needed or wanted. The Peace Corps staff was trying to paint a picture of "You're here because the country needs you" or "You were requested." But it was pretty clear we really weren't. I guess we were more the idealistic types; we quit careers to do this and we wanted to contribute in a meaningful way.

We weighed all this information and came to the conclusion that we wouldn't be able to ignore our being representatives of the U.S. government, which had no business meddling in Honduras's internal affairs. The Peace Corps appeared to be a piece of the puzzle and even though it may have been a very small piece, we didn't want to have anything to do with it.

---

*"Spanish speakers were not really required," says Peter Stevens. "We instructed the trainees in Spanish to the point at which they could be effective. If they could not achieve that level of competence they would not be sworn in as volunteers."

Resigning from the Peace Corps was probably one of the more difficult decisions we've ever had to make. [Holcomb and his wife left the Honduras program a few days before completion of the twelve-week training period.] We left our jobs at home and invested a lot of time and energy into doing this. We also had invested a certain amount of time in Honduras and felt an affinity for the people. So we looked around for jobs on our own and found out about this bilingual school there that needed teachers so we applied. We felt we could contribute a lot more as private citizens than as Peace Corps volunteers.

## Nancy Finkle (Honduras, 1986–88)

My village wasn't far from the Rio Coco area where the Contras were running around. There wasn't any danger though, because there were no roads leading in that direction. But some kids once came across a live grenade in the street and blew themselves up. From time to time we would see these convoys on the highway outside the town that were headed to the CIA base at Catacamas. You could always spot the Contra vehicles because they were the only cars that didn't have license plates.

The Hondurans we worked with could distinguish between volunteers and other Americans. We rode mules, took buses, or walked, just like they did, as opposed to riding in cars or coming down from the sky in helicopters. But one Honduran I met at a dance said to me, "I'm not going to tell you my name because you're going to write it down in a little book. You're just here for the CIA." He eventually believed me when I told him I had nothing to do with the CIA, but he couldn't believe that none of the volunteers were working for the CIA.

Some of us felt that we were a sugarcoating on the less pleasant things our government was doing in Honduras. But there was very little we could do about that. I just concentrated on my daily work and tried not to think about the larger picture. I was there to do what one person can do. I tried to help people focus their energies on their own lives and not waste a lot of time being indignant about what the United States was doing there. "Deal with your own life," I told them. "Make your kids better able to face up to the challenges that will come along, because the United States isn't leaving your country any time soon, and the only way you can play a role in your economic and political future is through education and sound health practices."

One of my Honduran friends was a student leader and was politically inclined. He kept it hush-hush though and didn't even tell his family. He said that if he went blabbing about it, he wouldn't last very long. He and his buddies went inner-tubing down the Guayape River and they floated by the CIA base at Aguacate. They were removed from the water and held for three days without food. It was obvious that he had been through something that he didn't want to talk about. He said they had shocked him and that it was white men, not Hondurans, that did that to him. He had some weird scars in his armpits. It was humiliating to me that this kind of stuff goes on by American hands. It was real hard on my conscience.

## Mary Shoemaker (Honduras, 1982–86)

I wrote a letter to my congresswoman after having spent a few days in a village about five miles from my site. The only way to get there was by mule or on foot. During my time there the helicopters were circling overhead. The contrast and irony was too much. I also felt that the news coming out of Honduras had little to do with the reality of the situation. People had almost no understanding of why we were hearing bombs going off at night just a few miles away. I felt it was important that people other than my family and friends at home had an inkling of the life of the people in this country that was suddenly so much in the media.

(The following is from Shoemaker's letter to Congresswoman Patricia Schroeder [D-Colo.].)

Dear Representative Schroeder:

I am a Peace Corps volunteer working in Honduras. I have been here two and a half years now. . . . Maybe some of my day to day experiences could help you direct our Central American policy.

Today I visited a two-teacher school house. . . . There are 125 students, grades one to six, registered in the school. One teacher has first and second, the other has three through six.

Today only about 80 kids showed up because it is the planting season and the kids must help in the fields so the family can eat. Even with one third of the students missing there were not enough benches for all the kids to sit down.

This school is different from many because there were a few books visible in the classroom. Usually there are no books. . . . They were hoping for another teacher this year, but with 20,000 unemployed teachers and thousands more graduating each year, Honduras can afford to hire only 100 to 200 new teachers a year for the whole country. . . .

For the cost of one helicopter flight those kids could have new desks.

Of course, that many desks wouldn't fit in the existing building. For the cost of one day in Tegucigalpa for one U.S. soldier you have half a month's pay for a teacher.

The amazing thing is how hard the kids try. Most of the kids today had rubber flip-flops on. In many schools they are barefoot. Few have more than one change of clothing. Some have just the clothes on their backs.

I'm not trying to tell you a sob story. In many ways it is not sad because although the people are poor, hungry, etc., they always have the goodness, the richness of human spirit to offer food, drink, and rest to visitors. Sometimes it shames me. . . .

Honduras needs jobs, education, jobs, health care, jobs, fairer distribution of land; not military "aid." . . . Sometimes I think if all of us, me included, would pull out and let them alone, they would do much better. . . . It makes me sad, ashamed, and angry to see how the U.S. manipulates Honduras. . . . Please do what you can to change our policy here in Central America. Thank you.

I wrote the letter and forgot about it. Pat Schroeder read the letter into the Congressional Record and a few weeks later, when I was in Tegucigalpa, I was confronted by a livid, totally out of control, purple-with-rage Peter Stevens. It scared me. I thought he might physically attack me. He was so out of it with anger! Anyway, it took a while to unravel what it was that I had done. I kept telling him that it was my right to write my representatives and that I would continue to do so. He threatened to kick me out of the Peace Corps, but he knew that I would make life hell for him if he did. So we went round and round with me continually walking away from him because I was scared of his ranting and raging. I kept trying to explain that I was not mixing in the internal affairs of Honduras. You see, there was no separation between U.S. policy and Honduran sovereignty in Peter Stevens's mind. To so many people, Honduras did not belong to the Hondurans. It was a strategic site from which to harass Nicaragua. To me, this was a crashing bit of reality.

So I was banished to my village. It became impossible for me to get Peace Corps vehicles to deliver books to the fifty literacy sites within my area. It was impossible to do any of the kinds of work which involved signatures and the nod of approval from the Peace Corps office.

☆

[Stevens says he thought Shoemaker's letter to Pat Schroeder was "very good. I didn't object to it." He adds that "I have no recollection of talking to her about it, and I have never been purple with rage." Regarding permission to use vehicles, Stevens says, "vehicles were not provided to volunteers. The fact that she didn't get to use one had no relation to her letter. I deny that permission was refused for her projects. I'm more mature than that. I'm not vindictive."]

## Lisa Johnston (Honduras, 1984–86)

I was living near Danlí, a town fifteen miles from the Nicaraguan border. Townspeople used to point out the Contras to me just as general information. I told them not to tell me because I thought it was better not to know. That might sound like sticking your head in the sand but I wasn't there to address the Contra issue and it didn't affect my work at all.

Every now and then the Sandinistas would lob something over about fifteen or twenty miles away. The closest they ever got to my village was five miles. They didn't hit anything, except an occasional cow. The explosions sounded like thunder and for the longest time I couldn't understand why it didn't rain after I heard it.

In November 1985, a teacher at the local high school told me that a Honduran military official had spoken to him about closing the town during elections. [Outbursts of violence around election times are common in Latin America.] I told a Peace Corps staff person about this and said I wanted to leave my site for that week. He called the embassy about it and the embassy decided two days later that my area was not safe at all and I was given a day's notice to move out. I wondered what they knew that they weren't telling me. I know it sucks but they have to do it. They weren't going to take risks of an international incident.

I had gotten an eighteen-hundred-dollar loan for the local school to start a chicken project and the students were going to sell the eggs. The first eggs were laid the day I moved out.

# Chapter 14

☆⹀

# *The African Food System Initiative: "They Used to Do a Thousand Hectares of Rice Here"*

Over the course of its thirty-year history the Peace Corps has taken several different tacks in fulfilling its objective of providing skilled manpower. In the 1960s, more than half of the volunteers were teaching; in the early 1970s, older, more experienced volunteers were placed in more technically sophisticated jobs such as civil engineering and parks management. In the early 1980s, the Corps championed small-enterprise development. In 1986, the organization turned its attention to the critical food shortages in drought-stricken Africa. Over the next four years, nine hundred volunteers, were placed in seven countries under a program called the African Food System Initiative (AFSI). In 1989, I went to Mali to see the first AFSI program in operation. The following is my report.

Volunteer Jack Brooks walked me out from his cement-block house on the outer edge of Fonfana, a village in the scrubby, flat expanse of southern Mali, to a grayish-brown plain that he said was once a thriving rice field. I struggled to keep pace as we trudged across the empty land in blinding sunlight and one-hundred-degree heat. Fine lines of brown dust formed in the crook of my arms and a light, gritty powder collected on my front teeth. Dead stalks crunched under our feet, and the hot dry wind blew the leaves against my ankles. "They used to do a thousand hectares of rice here," Brooks said. "Now, because there's less rain, they're down to about one hundred."

We were in the middle of the devastating African drought that America followed through graphic pictures in *Time* and *Newsweek*, and that inspired the pop song "We Are the World." The people in Brooks's village weren't emaciated like those who stared sadly from the covers of magazines, but at certain times of the year, they may not have had enough food to eat every day.

One of Jack's neighbors made us a bowl of *toh* and some sauce made out of leaves for lunch. A spongy, almost flavorless dough made of pounded millet, toh, I learned, is the Malian staple, because millet is the only crop that farmers can grow in any quantity from soil that is quickly turning to desert. Pieces of toh are dipped into a sauce made from leaves or groundnuts, one of the Malian people's few sources of protein. In another village, volunteer Laura George and I were served a delicacy for our supper, chicken and rice. On top of a mound of rice in a tin bowl were what I took to be the chicken's wings. It was, in fact, the whole chicken. Already one of the ten poorest countries in the world, Mali was hit hard by the drought. Few Malians live beyond the age of thirty-eight and for every ten babies born, two die before their first birthday.

I had expected to find Jack Brooks toting around a hand-held computer reviving the desert with cutting-edge biotechnology. But in fact, he and the other AFSI volunteers were digging wells and planting rice, just as their predecessors did some three decades ago. What made the AFSI new was the Peace Corps' decision to formalize procedures that had been in use sporadically for several years. The backbone of the AFSI is the team approach, wherein volunteers with complementary skills are posted in small groups to address drought-associated problems. To ensure a lasting impact, each team is maintained for a period of ten years. As members finish their service, they are replaced by new volunteers whose skills reflect the changing needs of the area. The AFSI plan also calls for the Peace Corps to integrate the volunteers' work with development activities of the host government and humanitarian organizations such as CARE and Save the Children.

In Mali, the AFSI program was tackling three drought-related problems that inhibit food production. Brooks, a water resources volunteer, was showing the rice farmers of Fonfana some simple irrigation techniques to restore some of the rice yield lost to the drought. But making more efficient use of scarce water was only a first step. After Brooks completed his irrigation work, he planned to ask his two AFSI colleagues—one of whom was trained in forestry and the other in agriculture—to lend their expertise. The forestry volunteer would show the farmers how "live-fencing" around the rice field would help prevent wind erosion, and the agriculture volunteer could assist the farmers in starting a vegetable garden beside the rice field to take advantage of the moistened soil. When Brooks and his AFSI team members finished their Peace Corps service, they would be replaced by a new team that would bring the skills necessary to pick up where Brooks's team left off.

Volunteers in Mali praised the AFSI. (One AFSI grouping referred to themselves as "the dream team.") "It gives us a feeling of continuity," said Julie Mann (Mali, 1987–89). "It used to be that the Peace Corps just put people out there and told them, 'Do what you can.' With AFSI, we document our projects so they can be followed up on. You don't feel like you're just doing two years and leaving everything you did to just fall apart and disappear." Country director Hilary Whittaker was also very enthusiastic about the AFSI. "I think we've got a tiger by the tail," she insisted over coffee after dinner one night in her comfortable ranch house in Bamako, Mali's capital. "I see AFSI as an opportunity to plug up those gaps that I think the Peace Corps has been facing for twenty years."

The AFSI approach was certainly logical. In fact, some volunteers said that the Peace Corps was merely pasting on a fancy title to common-sense practices. "There was no revolution," admits George Scharfenburger, a veteran of Peace Corps operations in Africa and the chief architect of the AFSI. "Much of the concept was already in the Peace Corps' programming manual, but we didn't have the time or the resources to carry it out."

While the AFSI made a lot of sense, it was not necessarily easy to implement successfully, as it requires a thorough understanding of local conditions and continual monitoring of volunteers' progress—the Peace Corps' chronic weak spots. But Scharfenburger felt that the AFSI was important enough to the agency's prestige to guarantee that it would receive the resources and support it needed.

Unfortunately, while the AFSI has made possible some encouraging successes, many in the agency believe that it has disappointed expectations. The Peace Corps maxim, "You can't program from Washington," aptly explains the discrepancy between the blueprint and its realization in Mali. "Part of the AFSI was to let Hilary run with her vision," says Carroll Bouchard, former regional director for Africa. "She scrapped the original program and did her own thing. But it was too visionary and not practical enough." Also jeopardizing the AFSI's success was the Peace Corps' failure to sustain the necessary support after the initial burst of excitement. "The Peace Corps goes through these theme fads and AFSI is one of them," says Malcolm Versel, a development consultant and former volunteer who inspected the AFSI program in Mali with a team of evaluators in 1987. "The average life span of these things is six months to two years. They get bored in Washington and start to think about some new little jingle."

Indeed, the AFSI is vulnerable to criticism as a gimmick to exploit congressional and public interest in the African famine. "We had to fight for every dollar," says former Peace Corps budget director Tom Wilson, recalling the crippling budget cuts by the Reagan White House. When the famine in Ethiopia began making the news in 1984, Wilson saw an opportunity. "Congress likes to see something sexy. I thought we could package together what we were already doing in Africa with some new stuff and ride some of the concern about the drought. When some congressman says, 'I saw all these pictures of starving people on TV last night. What are you doing about it?' we can say we have this new program."

But according to Wilson, the AFSI was created not only to impress Congress, but as a legitimate way to strengthen the Peace Corps' agricultural efforts in Africa. "One of the things that was decided early on was that we would organize this program very well before we sent any volunteers," he said.

Considerable time and energy *were* invested in the AFSI. The Peace Corps hired a battery of consultants and solicited help from the Agency for International Development, the Department of Agriculture, and numerous private development organizations. Assessment teams and program designers traveled to Africa and consulted with host governments. When, after two years of planning, the program was ready to be unveiled, the Peace Corps sent Scharfenburger around the country promoting it.

Meanwhile, in Mali, the first indication that the AFSI faced trouble was the sudden departure of some of the program's staff members shortly before the first contingent of AFSI trainees was due to arrive. It was suggested that this group be postponed or that its size be reduced. But Hilary Whittaker declined the offers and welcomed the first AFSI group of thirty-four people on schedule. Thereafter, Whittaker expanded the AFSI program rapidly, resulting in confusion. "It's been a scattered effort," said Tom Elam, associate director for monitoring and evaluation in Mali. "We've been here for about three years but nobody is quite sure what's going on with the AFSI program."

When a team of consultants went to Mali to evaluate the AFSI in

1987, almost two years after its start-up, they found "a number of areas where the program can be strengthened."[1] More candidly, one of the evaluators says, "AFSI was fudged." Adds Malcolm Versel, one of the consultants, "They just put bodies out there and did not necessarily put any time into selecting sites. Hilary grabbed the easiest rung on the ladder, the team. There were just these clubs of volunteers out there. They weren't tied in with the food systems at all."

Whittaker acknowledges that the first AFSI volunteers were dispatched to their posts somewhat haphazardly. "The staff went out and programmed whatever they could find," she says. Whittaker also decided to place teams in areas of the country that were not designated by AFSI planners. But this, she feels, was not necessarily harmful. "We're finding out which areas work and which ones don't and for what reason."

"There's been frustration about the program in Mali because there's been a lot of deviation from the original design," says John Zarafonetis, the former AFSI coordinator in Washington. Former regional director Bouchard says that Whittaker "chose to convert all the volunteers in Mali, including those in standard teaching assignments, to AFSI volunteers." The evaluation team also found that volunteers' activities weren't sufficiently integrated with those of the host government or private development organizations.

The staff in Mali were especially concerned about the rapid increase in volunteers. "The program is getting so big so fast that we're just trying to figure out, 'Gee, where can I put fourteen new people?' " says Tom Elam. "It's planning by the seat of your pants, which is very typical Peace Corps management."

And so, when I set out from Whittaker's house in Bamako to tour Mali's southern region, I found that the gaps she said the AFSI had plugged were still open. "Finding sites should be more important than before," says Billy Fanjoy (Mali, 1988–90), "but the staff doesn't have the time to do it. The Peace Corps should also try to figure out what other development agencies are doing and where we can play a part, but they just don't have the time for this." The AFSI's goal of continuity was thwarted as Mali accepted more volunteers and their level of language and technical proficiency decreased. This, in turn, prohibited volunteers from picking up where their predecessors left off.

The uneven capabilities have been noted by Malian officials. "I'm very satisfied with volunteers' achievements, but their stay is quite short," said Allamir Maiga, governor of Sikasso. "Their replacements can't work on the same level. If you start to build a bridge you should finish it." Karim Sacko, an official in the Ministry of the Interior, said he's received reports that volunteers' work was appreciated but he added, "Some organizations send young people to make friends but when someone is sent to do a job, it's important that the job gets done."

Defending the AFSI, John Zarafonetis says the Mali experience was "an aberration." Whereas Hilary Whittaker's planning led to an unwieldy program, he explained, other countries started their AFSI programs less aggressively. The Peace Corps' operation in Niger, for instance, began the AFSI in 1987 with only fourteen volunteers and, four years later, has only about twenty-seven. When Corps officials realized that conditions in Guinea were not suitable for the AFSI, they scrapped plans rather than proceeding for the sake of public relations.

A year after my trip to Mali, an agriculture specialist at Peace Corps headquarters told me that the AFSI was in a "maintain mode." Carroll Bouchard says that special funds for the AFSI had "dried up" and the AFSI coordinator's position had been eliminated. Whether the Peace Corps executes the AFSI agenda to the letter is ultimately of little consequence, Scharfenburger says. "I knew that there was a fairly high likelihood that the Peace Corps would not be able to keep up this kind of sustained effort over the long term," he says. "If it doesn't survive as it was brought forth from the womb, the important thing is that it has an overall positive effect. Comparing the reality to the concept is less important than looking at the reality and seeing how positive it is compared to what went on before the AFSI."

### Billy Fanjoy (Mali, 1988–90)

The Peace Corps used to come into a village and construct these fairly complicated wells that required these big expensive metal forms to make. Volunteers tried to teach the villagers how to build these wells but that wasn't as important as the finished product. My predecessor, John, taught the villagers how to build a Dutch brick well. This kind of well is dug by hand and they can make the bricks themselves from an inexpensive mold which they can buy in the town near here. My job here, as I see it, is to make sure that after two years they can do everything themselves. I should work myself out of a job.

A problem I've run into, though, is that while the villagers have learned the Dutch brick well technology, they have a labor mentality. They need the *toubob*, the white guy, to lead them. One farmer I'm working with can't figure out the logistics of building a well and he doesn't have the confidence that he can learn how to do it. For years and years volunteers have been out here reading the metric tape for him. It's not hard to get them to follow you out to the garden to teach them how to build a new pump. The problem is stopping yourself from leading too much and doing the work.

I'm trying not to repeat the work of the previous volunteer, but rather pick up where he left off. I worked with my predecessor in showing this mason how to build the Dutch brick well. When the mason came to me about building an adjoining cistern, I sent him to a guy who had learned about cisterns from my predecessor. The mason built the cistern himself and I stayed out of the picture. The cistern would have turned out better if I helped him because I worked with cement for years when I had my own landscaping and construction business. But if I were involved, the mason still wouldn't have the confidence that he could build the cistern by himself. I purposely left the village the day he was finishing it just so he couldn't ask me any questions.

After the mason finished his cistern, he and I then went to the Catholic mission and bought the cheapest hand pump you can buy in Mali. The mission trained him on how to set it up. Once we got it working, I asked another volunteer to come get him started on banana trees. He also wants to do mangoes and oranges. He used to grow only onions, which he does well with, but he could do well with other crops and improve his diet.

I'm trying to give some permanence to the Dutch brick wells by setting up rotating funds for this village and another village in the area. This way, the Peace Corps will no longer be funding the construction of wells directly but rather funding a fund that the villagers can borrow from and repay over time. To get the funds going, I asked for help from two other volunteers—a math teacher and a SED [small-enterprise development] volunteer—who aren't even in AFSI. I would have called on them even if we hadn't been told in training that we should collaborate with each other. The SED volunteer helped me put together the credit program and the math teacher showed the villagers, in Bambara [tribal language], how to do the arithmetic they'll need in order to run it. The math teacher also taught them how to read a metric tape.

To make the Peace Corps better, I would go with the AFSI thing. If you didn't have AFSI, it would be the old Peace Corps. You'd sit in your village and you'd come out having a great idea of what the culture is all about but you might not have gotten that much done. The villagers here know that I know how to build a well or a dam and that I have friends who know about trees, gardens, loan programs, and math.

I keep in touch with my Malian homolog [a host government employee who is assigned to work with volunteers] but he's not interested in the Peace Corps. People from the other development organizations don't take us seriously either. We don't have any training in development, we're here for only two years, and they know it's going to take us a year and a half to just figure out what's going on. So I could understand why they aren't particularly interested in me. My homolog has been through three volunteers already.

## Jim Kmetz (Mali, 1988–90)

The previous volunteer in my site was building rice dams so it was just assumed that the volunteer who replaced him would continue. [By building a dam in a seasonal river bed, farmers can irrigate the adjacent fields for paddy rice.] Right now there's a rice dam craze. It's almost like keeping-up-with the-Joneses. I wonder if building these dams is really the best project. The Malians have misconceptions of what the rice dam will do. The chief in one village thought he was going to step outside his hut and see this beautiful lake of water. All it's going to do is inundate a couple of hectares for rice, and maybe they can do some gardening alongside it.

I have some problems with the rice dams from a health standpoint. It's a common practice here when they're out working in the rice fields to urinate in the riverbed. Snails, which breed in standing water, will then ingest the urine and excrete microorganisms that cause schistosomiasis.* I'm going to have a hard time teaching these people to change their habits.

The Peace Corps is wholeheartedly in favor of these rice dams. I've had some trouble getting my supervisor to understand that they could cause problems. Some people argue that all we're doing with the dams is bringing the water level back to where it was ten years ago. That reasoning doesn't make any sense to me. We're going back to the good old days when they had schisto in their seasonal riverbed. We can't pretend it will never be a problem. If there's a potential for schisto, we have to approach it seriously.

The volunteer here before me, who was so successful with the rice dams, tried to teach the villagers about health issues but we're not going to change habits they've had for years in ten sessions or twenty. I've told the villagers that the rice dam could be a health hazard, but they don't make decisions based on health. Because I can't defend the dam one hundred percent, I'm not going to attach my name to it. I'm still going to

---

*Prevalent in developing countries, schistosomiasis kills about 800,000 people a year.

help them build it, but I'm not going to arrange the funding through AID. The dam will be financed by the Malian government. It's going to be their baby.

## Julia Earl (Mali, 1987–90)

We're having a lot of success with AFSI in terms of collaboration among the volunteers. It happens naturally when people want help from each other. But I've found that working with the Malian government has not been as successful. As a forestry volunteer, I'm working for the Malian government's Bureau of Water and Forests which subscribes to development by authority. They order and threaten villages to plant trees. I won't do that.

At a monthly meeting of all the bureau agents, my supervisor said in front of everyone that what I was doing was not work. I answered back that it was work. "Are you telling *me*," he said, screaming and yelling, "someone who's worked for the bureau for more than twenty years, what is work and what is not work?" Then he said to the whole room, "Maybe she thinks she's better than us. She's an American. Maybe she thinks she knows more about forestry than we do." I was ready to cry.

During that time I didn't get much help from my Peace Corps supervisor. The staff is really strained and they just have too much responsibility to help us as much as we would like. But by working with this man, I knew that his technique is to humiliate people. I just decided I wasn't going to let him get the better of me. It was a matter of hanging on to a belief that I know inside is right.

I know that I don't want to be the white person who explains a problem to the villagers and then tells them the solution. I think they should realize the problems and arrive at the solutions themselves. I'm trying to encourage this kind of thinking by practicing animation. [Animation is a community development technique whereby group discussion is used to guide villagers toward defining the problem, its causes, and possible remedies.] When I pose questions to help them recognize the problem of deforestation, they often say, "Allah brought the drought and Allah plants the trees. Human beings can't do it." I don't try to argue with them. I say, "You're right. Allah has willed this drought." But then I ask them, "What do we women have to do to prepare a meal?" They explain how they have to walk miles into the bush to collect wood. "That's hard work, isn't it?" I ask. Then, when I ask, "Why are there less trees today?" and they say, "Because of Allah," I show them pictures of a woman carrying wood, a man pulling a donkey cart full of wood, and someone cooking over a fire. This gradually brings out the idea that people are also responsible for deforestation, not Allah alone. When I ask, "Is there something we can do about this?" the people in one village may say, "No, there isn't. We're too old. It's not for us to change the ways of Allah." In another village they may say, "Yes, we can plant trees."

Setting up the meetings in order to arrange these discussions takes a lot of work. I might have had a meeting set up with the village chief but when I get there I learn that he's gone out to collect termites to feed to his chickens. That's the way it is here. So I'll hang out with his wives for a couple of hours just talking and joking. I tell them that I'll come back tomorrow. It may be a few months after I've begun visiting a village that I'll actually hold discussions about planting trees.

The women in one village decided that they wanted to plant nere trees. This is one of my favorite projects because nere is an indigenous species that is disappearing. The nere also grows these pods which contain a powder that's high in protein. The women use the powder in cooking. In other villages, several farmers are planting cashew trees. We chose cashews because we heard about a cashew-processing plant in the Ivory Coast that would buy the nuts.

In another village, the women were very receptive to the animation. They said they wanted to plant nere and baobab trees. A couple of days later, I met with the men of the village to discuss trees. They gave me all the classic lines: "Allah has willed the drought;" "There's nothing we simple humans can do;" "All the young men have left the village." I thought maybe I could use the women as a motivating factor. "You know, the women are going to plant trees," I told them. The chief said "No, the women can't plant trees." When I asked one of the women about this she said, "We're too old." I said, "Oh, come on. We can start slowly." Then another woman said, "We don't work with *dabas*" [*dabas* are small all-purpose farming tools]. That's malarkey. These women work in the field like mad. "Then I can teach you," I said. The woman took my hand and felt my palms and asked me, "Where are the hard spots? You don't work with *dabas*. You can't show us how."

My rapport with this village has gradually gotten better just by hanging out there, doing things with the women, and paying my respects to the chief. When I came by one day, the women were singing and dancing and playing drums. The chief's mother had died and they were celebrating the fact that all her hard work has come to an end. I stayed the whole day and night to participate in the funeral. They danced all around the village carrying her corpse and then they made a mad procession weaving through the millet fields and into a sacred forest. Women aren't allowed to enter a sacred forest, and as a white person, I certainly wouldn't be allowed. But they let me go with them.

The following day, an old man on a bicycle came to my house. The chief sent him to thank me for taking part in his mother's funeral. This doesn't mean I'm going to change their feelings about planting trees but now I have more hope.

Last year when my supervisor was screaming at me, I wondered, "What am I doing here? Am I having a positive impact?" How seriously can any of us expect to reverse the spreading of the desert in Mali? If you think about those things too much, you get completely discouraged.

# Part Seven

☆

# The Bush Years, 1989–92

# Introduction

In 1989, recently appointed Peace Corps director Paul Coverdell had a new phone system installed at the agency's headquarters in Washington. It was a prophetic decision because a lot of important people were about to dial his number. A confluence of events around the world was suddenly making the Peace Corps extremely popular. Following their break from Moscow, Poland and Hungary asked the Peace Corps for teachers and business advisers. When President Denis Sassou-Nguesso of the Congo and President Yoweri Museveni of Uganda began relaxing their socialist policies, they invited the Corps as part of their initial efforts toward warmer relations with the United States. When Namibia achieved its independence from South Africa in 1988, the Corps readied a program for the new country. Operations in Nicaragua and Panama were resumed when friendly governments came to power, and when Laos showed sufficient cooperation with the United States' drug interdiction efforts, Congress lifted its proscription against American assistance and the Corps opened discussions with Laotian officials.

The brisk expansion was precipitated by these political changes and by two highly significant invitations—from Pakistan and China—which bestowed renewed prestige on the Corps. From the late 1960s until 1988, when the invitations were announced, the organization was "entering small countries and leaving the major countries right and left," explains Jon Keeton, director of international research and development.* "The invi-

---

*The following is a list of prominent countries and the years in which the Peace Corps withdrew: Pakistan, 1967; Turkey, 1970; Nigeria, 1971; India, 1976; Brazil, 1980; and South Korea, 1981.

tations from China and Pakistan show that our goals have validity, that it's not politically embarrassing to have the Peace Corps because it's not only for the poorest of the poor or the microstates." The attention focused on the invitation from China in particular—it made front pages of several major papers—also may have prompted the recent windfall of invitations. "Countries realized there are good feelings here about the Peace Corps," says Keeton, "and at a time when the United States isn't being very generous with foreign aid, they know that the administration and Congress will be happy that they invited us."

But regardless of the diplomatic underpinings, how the Peace Corps responds to the flurry of interest will determine the agency's future. Paul Coverdell could not afford to put anyone on hold, especially since the organization was known to be deficient in many areas. In May 1990, the General Accounting Office released an extensive report on the Corps which detailed numerous weaknesses. A large number of volunteers' assignments were made by "guesstimate" and lacked specific tasks or objectives. Some assignments made little contribution to development, benefited wealthy landowners, or took employment away from qualified nationals. The report also noted that one out of three volunteers drops out early.[1] A few months later, another report, by the House Committee on Government Operations, criticized the Corps' failure to meet host government requests for skilled volunteers and its "largely ineffectual" mechanisms for evaluating its programs.[2]

As the Peace Corps marches forward, planting new flags across the globe, the unflattering revelations have placed the agency at a crossroads. Throughout the 1980s, director Loret Ruppe worked hard to dismantle the Corps' reputation as a haven for hippies and draft dodgers, and to rebuild its image as one that Democrats and Republicans both could love. Despite chronic weaknesses, one official says, "the Peace Corps was becoming apple pie again." As the organization enters a new era, Paul Coverdell, Ruppe's successor, shows little desire to rely on good public relations and claims to be intent on addressing the Corps' problems. "We have a responsibility to certify that we're doing the best we can with our resources," he says. "If you're saying you're doing something, then do it. Go for the real."

According to some, Coverdell is a welcome change. "He may not be good on the public relations like Loret Ruppe, but he's a solid manager," says Linda Borst, former chief of operations for the Africa region. "He wants to know if the fisheries program really increases the amount of protein in the African diet and augments the farmers' income." Adds Jon Keeton, "We've been in some countries for twenty-five years and Coverdell has come back from his visits to these places wondering why we're still there and if we're being taken for granted. Loret wouldn't have asked those questions."

At the same time, many are suspicious of Coverdell. Though he professes to feel strongly about the painstaking and costly task of monitoring and evaluating the Corps' work overseas—"it's terribly important that we measure our impact"—many on staff, who asked not to be identified, say that Coverdell is actually cutting back on such qualitative measures. "After these new posts are established," says one staff person, "the program is left to operate on a bare-bones budget." She also points to the elimination of two programming specialists as evidence of Coverdell's disinterest in the Corps' contribution to development. The laid-off employees, a fisheries expert and an agriculture expert, oversaw the work of a large portion of volunteers. (About 5 percent of the volunteers are in fisheries assignments, and 20 percent are in agriculture assignments.)

Coverdell maintains that the Peace Corps can expand *and* improve operations if two newly instituted programming and budget systems are strictly observed. "There's a tendency among some people here to exempt expansion and really concentrate on the programming," Coverdell says. "But then the organization would become so stale and ingrown that it would be highly detrimental. And new country entries is part of the Peace Corps' mission of the pursuit of peace." As the Peace Corps universe grows larger, and does so in compliance with the new systems, Coverdell insists that volunteer enrollment can increase from the present level of six thousand to a "maximum peace strength" that he sets at twelve thousand.

His critics contend that the new management systems will not necessarily solve the agency's problems. "He just wants to build a monument to himself that looks functional, like he's done something," says one desk officer, "but these new systems were forced on all the countries at once without enough preparation and planning. There was no chance to find the kinks and work them out." Another employee adds, "You can't just put together these new manuals, mail them out, and expect the overseas staff to comply. There has to be support and follow-up, but it just isn't happening."

"It seems a lot of money is going toward plane tickets to Atlanta instead," says one department head, who speculates that Coverdell, a Georgia state senator and chairman of the Southern Steering Committee for George Bush's 1988 campaign, is trying to make a name for himself in order to strengthen his own standing for a U.S. Senate campaign.

Reaching Coverdell's "maximum peace strength" of twelve thousand volunteers would be possible if the Peace Corps could place that many "generalists"—the vast majority of the applicant pool. The "generalists," however, lack the technical skills that make up a large share of the requests the Corps receives from host countries. "We have more generalist applicants than we can place," says one official. The Corps is trying to have it both ways. Volunteers with special skills are being sought through direct mail campaigns, technical colleges, and by linking up with graduate programs to offer credit and scholarship money for Peace Corps service. Jim Scanlon, director of recruitment, is hopeful that the Peace Corps will beef up its technical training, thereby making it possible to place more generalists.

But training is a sore subject at the Peace Corps. Expenditures have been "squeezed" in recent years, according to a report by regional director Jerry Leach.[3] In 1988, for instance, training periods for assignments in francophone Africa, where volunteers must be proficient in French and a local language, were shaved from fifteen to twelve weeks. Carroll Bouchard, former regional director for Africa, says he would certainly have liked to see the three weeks' training restored, but at the same time, he cautions, "The Peace Corps should not allow itself to think that it is more of a development agency than it was intended to be. We shouldn't try to compete with the volunteer organizations from Germany or Japan, for instance, which offer more sophisticated assistance. Our strength, as foreign leaders see it, is the blending of the three original objectives"—to meet the needs of developing countries for trained manpower; to promote a better understanding of the American people on the part of peoples served; and to promote a better understanding of other peoples by the American people.

# Chapter 15

☆

# *China: "Road to Nowhere"*

In April 1989, the Peace Corps invited thirty-two carefully selected applicants to Harpers Ferry, West Virginia, for a week-long retreat during which officials observed them carefully in a series of exercises designed to test their emotional maturity, social skills, and adaptability to new situations. "It was like being a lab mouse," says Ron Hamelin. "The constant assessment was nerve-wracking. They even studied us at meals." Years earlier, this rigorous screening exercise had been deemed too unnerving and too expensive and was abandoned. But the Peace Corps revived it in order to select the very best candidates for what was to be its most sensitive program, China I.

When the People's Republic of China invited the Peace Corps, it was hailed as a significant step on the road to improved Sino-American relations, and a successful China program would demonstrate that the Peace Corps was a dynamic organization capable of responding quickly to the ever changing geopolitical climate. The Corps had to be sure that the volunteers of China I were exemplary. Like thousands before them, these volunteers would be teaching English at universities and teachers colleges, but they would be serving in the Peace Corps' most difficult post.

"Psychologically and physically, China would be the most demanding," said Kathleen Corey, programming and training officer for the China program. "Volunteers would have to be able to withstand more scrutiny than in most countries." The people of China had for years been told by their government that Peace Corps volunteers were really spies for the CIA, and China's tradition of shunning Western influence would further isolate them. The volunteers would also be walking point for the Peace Corps in a bona fide superpower, and it rested upon them to maintain this latest link in the gradually strengthening of ties between the two nations. "Everyone kept stressing how important this program was for U.S.-China relations," recalls trainee Lisa Smoker, "and how our behavior could affect the whole program." In addition to these factors, volunteers would have to negotiate many physical hardships. Sichuan Province, where they would be located, "is gray, bleak, and can get quite cold," says Kathleen Corey. "The classrooms are not heated. The teachers frequently wear heavy coats and gloves with the fingers cut out so they can hold the chalk. The pollution is so bad that your skin gets grimy, and there is terrible overcrowding. Families of five or six people are crowded into very small four-room flats in these massive concrete block buildings."

Of the thirty-two applicants who went to Harpers Ferry, twenty-three were chosen to train for China, and they were an impressive lot. Most were in their twenties or early thirties. One trainee, Bill Campbell, was a retired history professor and university provost, and a number of others had degrees in East Asian studies. Some had lived in China and had some knowledge of at least one of the Chinese dialects. A few had master's degrees in teaching English as a foreign language and had taught professionally.

To prepare the twenty-three trainees for the challenge, the Peace Corps conducted a special training course at American University in Washington. In addition to the Corps' regular trainers, eleven Chinese instructors were hired to teach Mandarin Chinese and Chinese history. Tai chi classes were held three mornings a week, and to acclimate the trainees to the Chinese bureaucracy, they and staff related to one another according to their assigned roles in the dan wei, or Chinese work unit. To learn about China informally and practice their Mandarin outside of class, the trainees were paired with Chinese nationals living in the Washington area. Trainees were also coached in public speaking to prepare them for the one-hour lectures on life in America that were to be a part of their assignments. "It was clear they spent a lot of money on this program," says one trainee.

"You are the handclasp between us," said Peace Corps director Paul Coverdell in a toast at a special ceremony marking the beginning of the training period. "You are the symbol of relations between two nations and their commitment to peace."[1]

Four days after Coverdell made his toast, the Chinese Army used lethal force against prodemocracy demonstrators in Beijing's Tienanmen Square, killing hundreds. To express the United States' disdain of the brutality, the administration and Congress imposed a series of relatively mild economic sanctions against the Chinese government. The Peace Corps though, was considered an educational program, and it was decided with little debate that the trainees should go to China as planned.

In the weeks after the Tienanmen Square incident, the trainees became increasingly distraught over the events taking place in China and less enthusiastic about the Peace Corps. While officials assured them that the program would go forward, many of the trainees suspected that it would not. "I thought the odds were against it," says trainee Mary Lynn Moore. "We would not be welcome after the sanctions, and I don't think the Chinese leaders would want us at their universities making contact with students who might have been involved in the demonstrations.*

"The Peace Corps didn't want any of us to quit, though, because if it did go through, it would be very important that the Peace Corps deliver the agreed-upon number of volunteers," she adds. "The Chinese are very serious about upholding agreements. We felt the Peace Corps was our cheering squad, that they weren't being straightforward." Not all the trainees thought the staff was misrepresenting the situation. "They had put so much time and effort into it that they didn't want to believe that there was a possibility we might not go," says Colleen Broderick.

In fact, trainees continually received mixed signals from the Peace Corps. During the weeks following the Tienanmen Square incident, the trainees' schedule for one day included an enthusiastic talk about the educational system in China by a Chinese embassy official, and a meeting with Peace Corps recruiters who told them about programs in other countries.

As their situation grew increasingly ambiguous, the trainees' enthusiasm dissipated. "It was difficult to continue training and concentrate," says Catherine Dunn. "I felt frustrated because I was emotionally involved in an experience I didn't think I was going to have." The anxiety was such that some trainees experienced sleeplessness and nightmares.[2] According to trainee Jackie Bruhn, "People were sick, losing weight, gaining weight, and developing rashes. Some started smoking." One of the instructors noted that the group had broken into rival cliques.[3]

The trainees were especially troubled by the latest manifestation of a concern that volunteers had wrestled with for years: By going ahead with the China program so soon after the Tienanmen Square massacre, some felt, the Peace Corps—and by extension, they themselves—would be lending

---

* Indeed, shortly after the Tienanmen Square massacre, the Chinese government expelled two Americans, a teacher and a student, who were suspected of having ties with prodemocracy demonstrators.

legitimacy to the ruthless Deng regime. Others maintained that the Peace Corps is a people-to-people program that should deploy its volunteers to serve where there is need, regardless of the sort of government in power or Washington's relations with it. "It was a burning issue," says Kathleen Corey. "The trainees did a lot of soul searching. Some of them felt that relations between the United States and China had become so tenuous that the Peace Corps, in a minute way, could make inroads in rebuilding a relationship. Others questioned whether they could serve in a country that was capable of the brutality at Tienanmen Square. We encouraged them to address their feelings about this."

But according to trainees, the Peace Corps avoided addressing the political ramifications of the China program. At one meeting, Mary Lynn Moore recalls, "Jon Keeton said, 'If you feel like you're a political pawn, tell me right now.' This was direct intimidation. We *did* feel like pawns, but it was like he was daring us to admit it. Everyone stayed silent." Keeton says it was more likely that he asked the group if they felt they were "being used" in some way. "I wanted them to express themselves," explains Keeton, "but the rigors of the program, specifically the selection exercise in West Virginia, fostered a sense of paranoia which is reflected in that trainee's recollection."

Two of the trainees resigned from the program as a protest against the Chinese government's brutality. "Dave Moore [no relation to Mary Lynn Moore] and I were the personification of the Peace Corps volunteer who *does* consider the moral aspects on the job," says Jon Simon, who, with Moore, switched to the Corps' program in Nepal. "We served as the conscience of the group." An agency official close to the program says that Simon resigned because the Tienanmen Square massacre reminded him of the Holocaust and that Moore preferred to serve in Nepal because it would offer him the opportunity to pursue his interest in Eastern religions.

The rest of the trainees stuck with the program, inspired by their Chinese instructors, who told them that the demonstrators in Tienanmen Square would not want them to quit. Nevertheless, they continued to wrestle with the ethical questions. "It took up all our time, even when we tried to get smashed and forget it all," says George Durgerian.

Peace Corps officials maintained that the organization functions apart from geopolitics, and that volunteers should not withdraw as a means of expressing opposition to the United States or a host government. "Our volunteers represented the values of change and democracy with a small *d*," says Jon Keeton. "They were examples of what so many people in China wanted. If they had the confidence that they were quietly and apolitically making those changes, it would indicate tremendous political maturity on their part."

Therein lies the paradox of the Peace Corps' China program. Despite all the ceremonies and speeches honoring China I as a momentous step in furthering human contact, the program was contingent on political realities. The invitation from the Chinese government was extended not as a desire to make a breakthrough for brotherhood, since approximately ten thousand Americans have taught in China under private auspices since the restoration of diplomatic relations in 1978. China's invitation to the Peace Corps was, rather, a well-timed friendly gesture toward Washington.

In 1983, the Reagan administration had relaxed restrictions on high-technology exports to China. On the eve of President Reagan's reelection in 1984, Chinese officials told the American ambassador's staff in Beijing that they would be pleased to welcome the Peace Corps. "The Chinese invited us to improve relations with the United States," allows Jon Keeton, "and because they needed English teachers. They were not interested in the Peace Corps' cross-cultural goals or international understanding."

The invitation was, indeed, a measured one. When Corps officials proposed an initial contingent of forty volunteers, the Chinese said they would accept no more than twenty and the arrangement, which was documented by an exchange of letters rather than the usual formal agreement, was to be considered a "pilot." The Chinese insisted that the Peace Corps call its operations by another name, since for several years the Chinese government had accused the Peace Corps of operating as a front for the CIA. (The Chinese approved the name U.S.–China Friendship volunteers.) The Chinese also stipulated that the Peace Corps send no staff personnel. "They wanted to supervise the volunteers themselves," says Keeton. "A country director wouldn't fit into their dan wei," adds former China desk officer Chuck Howell. The Chinese compromised, allowing one administrator, who would be called a team leader, to accompany the group.

Another Peace Corps practice that was set aside concerned volunteers' living arrangements. Traditionally, volunteers find modest accommodations among host country nationals, a custom that maximizes cultural exchange. Chinese custom, however, dictates that foreign nationals live somewhat removed from daily life. Accordingly, the Chinese planned on placing volunteers in apartment complexes specially reserved and furnished for foreign students and faculty. Some of the apartments were appointed a little too comfortably for the Peace Corps ethic of living on the same level as their host country peers. At one campus, the apartments had been outfitted with pink silk bedspreads and window curtains. "We thought it was too nice," says Chuck Howell, "but it wasn't something we thought we could negotiate."

All these details, however, weren't even addressed until 1988, four years after China's initial invitation. "Four years is really nothing," says David Scotton, Peace Corps chief of staff during the Reagan administration. "In terms of Chinese time, it was very fast. They speak in terms of hundreds of years."[4] It is more likely that the Chinese delayed the Peace Corps when relations with the United States temporarily chilled. China was selling Silkworm missiles to Iran, and in retaliation the Reagan administration tightened exports of high-technology products. When China ceased the missile sale in 1988, Washington lifted the export restrictions and China's foreign minister, Wu Xueqian, stated publicly that his country would now welcome the Peace Corps.

In June 1989, three weeks after the Tienanmen Square massacre, politics intervened again, just weeks before the trainees were to arrive in Sichuan Province. Washington had announced its sanctions against China, albeit mild ones, and the United States embassy in Beijing was providing asylum to Chinese dissident Fang Lizhi. The Chinese Education Association for International Exchange, the government agency sponsoring China I, informed the American embassy that it was "inconvenient for them to receive the U.S.–China Friendship Volunteers."[5] The trainees were reassigned to other programs.

China's decision was "the logical next step in the changing relations between the two nations," says Lisa Smoker. "As Congress began canceling economic agreements and offering visa extensions, the Chinese felt compelled to meet cancellation with cancellation."

### George Durgerian (Thailand, 1989–91)

When my roommate told me what happened at Tienanmen Square, I thought it was a joke until I saw our Chinese instructors glued to the TV with stricken looks—many had family living within a couple of miles of Tienanmen Square. I knew instantly we wouldn't be going to China, then kicked myself for being such a selfish bastard.

### Lisa Smoker (Tunisia, 1989–91)

On the morning of June fourth we met our exchange partners who were Chinese nationals working and living in the D.C. area. We practiced our

Chinese with them, asked them about China, and helped them with their English. We were eating lunch when one of the other trainees told me she'd heard a report on the radio about violence in Beijing. We didn't share the info with our guests. By that evening everyone was watching the news.

That was both a great day and a terribly sad day. On the one hand, we were seeing the brutality of the Chinese forces, and on the other hand, we were meeting Chinese nationals who were enthusiastic, friendly, and supportive. In addition, that evening was one of my favorite times of the training. Six of us trainees and four of the language teachers stayed up late playing Pictionary, communicating as best we could, using dictionaries to translate.

## Mary Lynn Moore (Botswana, 1989–90)

After our meeting with our Chinese partners that Saturday, we all went to lunch. After I finished, I was walking away from the table and another trainee came up and said, "They're firing on the students in Tienanmen Square." I think the shock was accentuated by my just having had lunch with these two Chinese men. I looked back at my partner and wondered if he had family in Beijing. I didn't have the heart to say anything to him.

After I walked him to the corner, I headed across the campus and ran into two other trainees. "Well, this is it," we said. "What are you going to do now?" We expected the program would be called off the next day but we didn't hear a word from the Peace Corps till Monday.

Saturday evening I went with another trainee to the instructors' dorm to offer our sympathy. They didn't seem wrecked. They took it philosophically. To see how they were bearing up and being cheerful made it more poignant. I never saw them break down. They were like rocks.

I went to church that Sunday and talked to a few people after the service. They seemed not very well informed and sort of callous about it.

## Janelle Cavanaugh (Thailand, 1989–91)

During classes everything was very professional. But there were many evenings of tears in the dorms as we all watched the TV news. Some trainees would go for walks with an instructor just to be a friend and listen. I don't think I would have cried or felt such pain in my heart for the Chinese people if it weren't for the new relationships established with the instructors.

## David Moore (Nepal, 1989–91)

At the time training started, the world was witnessing dramatic changes in China; the government was showing tolerance, patience, and a willingness to listen and negotiate. We were euphoric because we were going to participate in, witness, and experience that development and cultivation of the human spirit firsthand. But euphoria is a temporary estrangement from reality. By June tenth I had the habit of singing the Talking Heads song "Road to Nowhere." It become our unofficial theme song.

## Colleen Broderick (Costa Rica, 1990–92)

The weeks between the crackdown and the postponement were like a roller coaster. I have never lived so closely to a political event and been so affected by it. I asked myself, "Is it morally correct to go and serve as a volunteer in a nation that kills the very students whom I am going to teach?" I also thought that maybe this is what should be done to help the students who had suffered so much. In all of this was the consideration of the Peace Corps as an apolitical organization.

## Lisa Smoker

When I was trying to decide what I should do, I asked each of the Chinese instructors their opinion. All of them expressed a desire to continue the program. They did not support their government's actions but they still identified with their nation. Therefore, they believed it possible for us to be U.S. citizens but not necessarily share the views of our government. They were willing to adopt the approach of working within the system to alter it. With this information presented to me, I decided to stick with it.

## Susan Wyllie (Costa Rica, 1990–92)

It was very stressful, yet also inspiring, to have instructors who were still one hundred percent dedicated to teaching while their family and friends in Beijing could not be located for weeks after Tienanmen Square. It pushed me twice as hard to prepare to go to China and dedicate myself to China and the Chinese for at least the next two years of my life. I still know I will be in China someday, and not as a tourist. I hope to continue language studies in graduate school after the Peace Corps and then go to China professionally.

## Jon Simon (Nepal, 1989–91)

What amazed me was the learned helplessness that overcame the trainees. Two people in particular denied that a massacre had taken place. While watching the news one night, one of them exclaimed, "That's not true!"

I'll never forget the moment they said on the news that twenty-six people were dead. I thought, "Well anything can happen in an ouster." Then I heard that five hundred people were killed. I was appalled and I decided someone had to show some sort of dissatisfaction. I resigned less than a week later and transferred to the Nepal program. Everyone told me what I was doing was wrong. I caused a little uproar.

I am proud of my country and government. When protestors march in Washington, we don't mow them down. I think it is our responsibility to maintain that standard of excellence. I am amazed that ten percent of the trainees (Dave and I) resigned for moral reasons. Hell, we were still in the eighties, but Michael Milken had not triumphed.

## Mary Lynn Moore

We were all very committed to the program and Jon's leaving gave us a sense of being abandoned. People felt bad he wasn't sticking it out. It made some of us think, "Am I just going with the crowd rather than doing what's right?" Some didn't see the moral or political side of it at all. They were more pragmatic. They wanted to go to China and they weren't going to back down.

I considered leaving, but I was caught up in the program and in events. One person isn't going to make a difference, but you felt that by going, you were in some small way making the statement that Tienanmen Square doesn't change anything about how the U.S. treats China. Because there were so few sanctions, we felt that sending the Peace Corps was part of Bush's gentle treatment of the Deng regime. If he had even used harsher language, I would have felt it was okay to go.

I stayed with the program out of a sense of commitment and obligation. But I dreaded going to China and finding tension and fear. People might be afraid to interact with me. I'd be more isolated. Commentators were saying another cultural revolution was coming. But to learn Chinese and get experience would be more of a benefit for my career than going to someplace obscure.

## David Moore

I try to practice my values. This has the tendency to make those who are less intent rather uncomfortable. I simply could not accept the Chinese government's execution of peaceful protestors. One man with nothing stopped the movement of tanks. When I heard that man had been executed, I wept. I snapped. A part of me died with him. I still cry when I think about it. On June sixteenth, discouraged and saddened, I called the Peace Corps placement office and moved over to the Nepal program.

I'm sure the Peace Corps had reasons for wanting the China program to go. I could no longer accept the personal implications inherent in continuing. It was my perception that if I went it would mean condoning and accepting the violence as a legitimate means to solve problems. I think the Peace Corps should have made the decision to cancel the program then and there.

## Tim Perkins* (Sri Lanka, 1989–91)

There was a faction within the Peace Corps administration that wanted us to go to China no matter what. So everything they told us was said to make us believe we were going. One member of the staff would come to see us and would actually cry. I think it was his career he was worried about. He didn't want us to get discouraged and leave.

## George Durgerian

I think the Peace Corps would have landed us in the middle of a war zone. They wouldn't want to blow this public relations dream come true. As much as I despised this mind-set, I would have gone because I wasn't going to China to support the government, but to teach.

☆

On the afternoon of Friday, June 23, the trainees were asked to report to the dorm lobby after the last class of the day for a meeting. "We always dreaded these meetings," says Mary Lynn Moore. "They usually just said the same things over and over, speechifying the party line: 'We're pretty

---

*Name and country of service have been changed at the volunteer's request.

sure you're going.' " When they all gathered, Jon Keeton read aloud a letter received at the U.S. embassy in Beijing from the Chinese Education Association for International Exchange, which stated briefly that it would be "inconvenient" to receive the volunteers in August as planned. "People shook their heads and said, 'I knew it,' " recalls Mary Lynn Moore. Others tried to hold back tears and some hugged. "Keeton cried too," said one trainee, "but he cried the first time he ever spoke to us. He tends to get overwrought by his speeches." Keeton recalls that afternoon: "I was beside myself. I so much wanted this to happen. They're not used to seeing a middle-aged bureaucrat be so emotionally honest. We were trying to achieve very idealistic people-to-people goals. It was an historic event and we worked very hard on it."

### Jacqueline Bruhn (Botswana, 1989–91)

The U.S. government, not the Chinese, should have canceled the program. I thought that by sending us, the Peace Corps was supporting the regime that killed peaceful demonstrators. The U.S. did not cancel because of global politics, and the Peace Corps feared that if we canceled, we would not be invited again. This made me feel like the U.S. had wimped out, but it was still sad because I wanted to go. It was hard to be sad, though, because looking at the larger picture, the cancellation meant nothing compared to the tragedy which the Tienanmen Square massacre was for others.

### David Moore

(Moore resigned from China I five days before the program was postponed but stayed on at American University while finalizing plans to join the Peace Corps in Nepal.)

Hearing the letter was an emotionally draining experience. I think there would have been more honor in the program had the Peace Corps postponed or canceled it. As it was, the Chinese simply postponed it and a very empty feeling was all that remained.

We had been planning a party for that evening to release some of the tension and it turned into a very loud and disruptive wake. The next day many folks were hung over by the stress and alcohol.

I was definitely saddened for my friends and colleagues because they still tried to have faith in the program. They suffered when that faith was taken from them. But I think some of them were relieved because they no longer had to make a decision.

☆

To bring the program to an end, a "funeral" was organized at the American University chapel. Trainees, instructors, and Peace Corps officials sat in a circle for three hours and read poems, sang, or said a few words about how they felt. "It was great to be able to cry with everyone openly and honestly," says Jackie Bruhn. "If the Chinese officials could see you in tears," Jon Keeton told the trainees, "the decision would be reversed because you're showing you're above politics. You're committed and mature."

### Susan Wyllie

What I remember most vividly is the encouragement given by our Chinese instructors to go on and succeed in the Peace Corps, and not be angry with the Chinese government, but rather to pursue our dreams of China someday in the future.

### George Durgerian

The Peace Corps offered me a choice of about ten programs. I took Thailand because it left soonest—I had to get this whole deal out of my mind and get on with what I had joined the Peace Corps for. I emerged from the China training with a much changed view of the Peace Corps, a view that now considers the Peace Corps as a rather benevolent, but ineffective bureaucratic beast, that, at least in Thailand, tries to keep itself alive in a country with little or no need for the majority of its volunteers.

### Lisa Smoker

Sometimes the Peace Corps in Tunisia seems like a big fraternity and I'm not into that. I guess I expected more professionalism. For China, we were being trained seriously for serious positions. Here, as in many host countries, training was like summer camp, and the adjustment was difficult to make.

My first year here was spent teaching at the language institute. Next year I will be in the university teaching history, culture, and language. I think the students have seen an American who is interested in their success, but I have stressed that what is important in my classroom is effort and having fun. I'm not going to yell at every mistake or try to humiliate them into learning. I think I've contributed if you look at it in terms of sharing of who I am and my understanding of language learning. Just yesterday I received a note from a student that said, "I am very joyful for spending this school year with you, because you were very nice and kind and understanding with us and helped us like class." When you're a teacher you can't ask for much, except a thank-you. And a thank-you to me means I've succeeded in sharing and facilitating.

## Ron Hamelin (Tunisia, 1989–90)

I had no choice but to stay in the Peace Corps. I had given up my teaching job, sold my car, et cetera. I had nothing else. I taught university-level English, U.S. history, composition, and comprehension. Sometimes I felt that I was free labor. There were other Americans and British people teaching with me. They got four times my salary and did the same thing. However, I was the only Arabic speaker and the only one with extensive contact with the Tunisians outside of class.

Before the trainees for China arrived in Tunisia, the Peace Corps administrators there had built us up as the cream of the crop. When we got there, the other trainees called us "the Chinese Americans," or "the yellow people."

## Jon Simon

I love it here. The Peace Corps office in Nepal is the best in the world. They leave us a free hand in the field, which is what makes the Peace Corps so great. In my first year, I taught English and in my second year, I am training Nepalese teachers. I think this assignment is worthwhile. I have built new desks and blackboards and am installing a water system at my school.

## Colleen Broderick

I had studied Spanish and Latin American history so I felt most qualified to serve in a Spanish-speaking country. I heard many things about how beautiful Costa Rica is and how peaceful and democratic the country is. It has proved to be one of the best decisions I have made to come here.

## David Moore

Some may ask, "Well, since the Peace Corps did not share your views by canceling the program, do you think it's right to serve in the Peace Corps?" My answer to this is, "While we do not live in a perfect world, that doesn't mean we should not strive to make it a better world." The irony is that I chose to go to Nepal, where prodemocracy-related violence is my karma again.* It causes me to wonder if I made the right decision. But I'm an idealist.

---

*In February 1990, at least fifty prodemocracy demonstrators in Nepal were shot or beaten to death by police.

# Chapter 16

# *Eastern Europe: "121 Points of Light"*

On the morning of June 15, 1990, 121 Peace Corps trainees filed into rows of folding chairs in the White House Rose Garden. The last time trainees were welcomed to this garden was in 1961, when John F. Kennedy shook hands with the first few hundred volunteers before they left for Africa and South America. Twenty-nine years later, President George Bush commended his guests as they were about to "take leave of these shores" for Poland and Hungary, and inaugurate the Peace Corps' first programs in Eastern Europe. "Bar and I visited famine-stricken regions of Africa and we saw the quiet heroism of volunteers providing relief," the President told the gathering. "In Eastern Europe there's a different kind of hunger and craving than we saw in Africa, but the need is real—for democracy and free enterprise."

The President emphasized that the trainees, who would be teaching English, are "investing their birthright in the people of Eastern Europe." Peace Corps director Paul Coverdell then took the podium and reminded the President that in his inaugural address he had asked Americans to help him make a gentler world. "These one hundred twenty-one people answered your call," said Coverdell. They are "the best America has to offer and this is a historic mission of profound proportions." President Bush then asked the volunteers to rise for well-deserved applause.

The trainees were excited to be at the White House, but many were unsure of the President's comments. "I thought Bush's speech was very paternalistic," says one of them. "His comment that 'we Americans will teach them the wonderful language of English and the way to use freedoms—which you were given as birthrights' is a very egocentric sense of entitlement." Some trainees were skeptical about the appropriateness of the Peace Corps for Eastern Europe. "When we arrived in Washington," says Elizabeth Jones (Hungary, 1990–92), "we were constantly referred to as one hundred twenty-one points of light. But many of us were doubting the need for volunteers in Central Europe.* The Peace Corps treated the issue almost like a coach would conduct a pep talk."

While the volunteers were downplaying the significance of the event, and Coverdell and President Bush were, perhaps, overplaying it, the Eastern Europe initiative has provoked some of the most heated debates within the Peace Corps community in recent years. One argument, a perennial, is over the Corps' relationship to foreign policy. By sending volunteers to Poland and Hungary, critics say the director has aligned the Corps too closely with the President's foreign policy needs. "The White House is interested in promoting a relationship with Poland and Hungary," says one official who requested anonymity, "and Coverdell is a Bush supporter so he jumps on Bush's bandwagon." Staff members were particularly disturbed by the director's quote in *Parade* magazine: "The Peace Corps has to keep abreast of changing American foreign policy in order to remain vital," he said. "Agencies that don't keep up simply wither and die."[1] According to Kurt Tjossem (Poland, 1990–92), it is generally acknowledged by the volunteers that there are politics involved in the program. "During training, the Peace Corps skirted the issue," he says. "But everyone knows that part of the reason we are over here is that we are pawns used by President Bush to 'beat the Germans' to Eastern Europe."

But to others, the political implications are dwarfed by the program's lofty purpose. "Our name is *Peace* Corps and we're celebrating *peace* in Central Europe," says Jon Keeton, director for international research and development. "We can play a useful role in bringing people and nations together again in a key part of the world. People here say that Paul Coverdell is politicizing the Peace Corps, but you don't hear that in Poland or Hungary. There's just this joy that they can have contact with people who represent values that they want in their new democracy."

Nevertheless, some observers still question whether the Peace Corps should serve countries that are not nearly as desperate as others. "The

---

*The Peace Corps uses "Central Europe," rather than "Eastern Europe," as is preferred by leaders of the region. "Eastern Europe connotes their former status as a part of the Soviet bloc," says Peace Corps regional director Jerry Leach.

short term needs arising from Communist mismanagement . . . hardly equal those of countries where development, and the Peace Corp's contribution to it, may be the only alternative to death by starvation or disease," wrote former Corps official, Edward Patrick Healy, in a letter to *The Washington Post.*[2] "Foreign assistance programs from Western Europe and Japan are swarming into Eastern Europe," says a returned volunteer. "This means there's less need for the Peace Corps to be there. Meanwhile, what agencies are going to be paying attention to Chad?"

The initiative has also been attacked by those who feel that Eastern Europe is not sufficiently exotic to provide the "Peace Corps adventure." "Living in rural Hungary is like living in rural Ohio," says former regional director Frank Mankiewicz. "They're very Westernized." Indeed, the Peace Corps informed trainees that American Express cards are welcome in the big hotels in Budapest. They can also buy Adidas sneakers there, eat at McDonald's, and purchase Estée Lauder cosmetics. In their free time, they can attend the ballet and stroll past beautiful cathedrals. In Polish cities, volunteers can enjoy an elegant tea in a velvet-upholstered salon overlooking a centuries-old cobblestone square. "There was a joke during our training," says Jennifer Olsen (Poland, 1990–92). "This isn't the Peace Corps; this is Club Med."

Sargent Shriver defended the Eastern Europe initiative by pointing out that "the original intention [of the Peace Corps] was not only to deal with economic poverty. It was also seen as a way of demonstrating to people with no knowledge of this country or of a free society . . . what kind of people this society produces."[3] Supporters of the Eastern Europe programs also point out that according to the Peace Corps Act, the only location in which the agency is prohibited from operating is the United States. Skeptical officials note, however, that since it was amended in 1978, the act has provided guidance with respect to need. Following the declaration of the Corps' first goal, "to meet the needs of developing countries for trained manpower," the amendment inserted the phrase, "particularly in meeting the basic needs of those living in the poorest areas of such countries."[4]

Most of the volunteers in Eastern Europe are teaching English in teacher training institutes or high-school-level polytechnics.* The concentration on English instruction, some think, fails to address the needs of newly unemployed industrial workers who were hit the hardest by the economic

---

*A small number of volunteers in Poland, Hungary, and Czechoslovakia are business advisers. The volunteers in Romania, a much smaller program, are working in orphanages, and the program in Bulgaria consists of business advisers and agricultural extension volunteers.

turmoil. "If there's anything Poland needs right now it's more food, not more English," says a former volunteer. "Increasing the number of English-speaking Poles will be more of a help to American businesses setting up shop in Warsaw." Kurt Tjossem says his students seem to be from families "at the mid-level." Dorothy Weller (Poland, 1990–92) says her students' parents are mostly teachers who "moonlight to make ends meet." Jennifer Olsen says her students seem to be of the "intelligentsia, or high economic status."

English instruction, according to Peace Corps elder statesmen Warren Wiggins and Sargent Shriver, is out of sync with the needs of Eastern Europe. "The Peace Corps is playing it safe," says Wiggins. "Volunteers should be addressing the same issues that Poland is addressing. They need to develop political parties and get the private sector in gear. They should send accountants, labor union people, and political organizers to help develop the democratic process." Shriver agrees that English is not a critical need. "Hungarians seem to learn languages faster than any people on earth. They need to speak three languages just to go fifty miles, so teaching English in Hungary is not a particularly important contribution."[5]

Peace Corps officials maintain that English instruction will have a far-reaching impact. "Poland has opened its doors to the west and speakers of English will serve as the bridge," states one internal report. "Economists, politicians, business people, engineers, and scientists will all need fluent English to help Poland move toward economic and political freedom."[6] To that end, the report also notes, volunteers working in the schools can encourage the formation of student governments and introduce the next generation to the democratic process.[7] Felix Lapinski (Poland, 1990–92) believes that it is this aspect, not the relative comfort, that makes the Poland program unique. "The Ministry of Education has asked us to open the minds of its young people to democratic ideas. We're teaching a course in U.S. life and institutions, and how each volunteer handles this may have important long-term effects."

In addition to helping them mine the treasures of democracy, some volunteers have their own ideas about how they can contribute. "Maybe I could teach aerobics and tell people how to keep cholesterol down to prevent heart disease," says one volunteer. "Just sharing the information I collect living in America can be helpful." Elizabeth Jones says the pollution in the city of Zalaegerszeg is so awful—"I'm afraid to exercise outdoors!"—that she would be interested in helping to start "some sort of Environmental Protection Agency." Felix Lapinski is interested in establishing exchange programs between Polish and Polish-American churches.

While the Peace Corps has great hopes for the Eastern Europe program, some officials are openly concerned about the accompanying risks of such a high-profile undertaking. "English is going to change students' lives and they aren't going to take it lightly if their teacher doesn't have control of the grammar," says Jon Keeton. "Reporters and congressional junkets will be descending on Central Europe," he adds, "and news of volunteers who are struggling at the blackboard could have serious repercussions in the American media and in the Peace Corps' budgeting process. I told country directors that they should put some superstar volunteers close to the capital cities." At her site just two months, volunteer Jennifer Olsen says, "Polish education is quite rigorous and I have a feeling that the Peace Corps' standards may be lower than Polish standards as far as teachers go." Kurt Tjossem adds that most of his students "take English lessons outside of school and their grasp is above their grade level."

"The Peace Corps can gain a lot from being in Eastern Europe," comments one staffer who asked not to be identified, "because we'll be working at a more sophisticated level so sloppy programming and poor training will become apparent very quickly. There's a real chance for us to bomb if we operate there as we've operated in some other countries."

## *Felix Lapinski (Poland, 1990–92)*

When my wife retired, we were going to travel, do volunteer work, and take courses. I've done a lot of volunteer work at the Smithsonian. I also organized a neighborhood watch and I had a victory garden in the park. But then my wife died about a year ago and doing those things alone would be just occupying myself and not giving enough of myself.

My parents were born in Poland. My grandmother came over first, entering the United States through Ellis Island. When she had raised enough money cleaning Pullman cars, she sent for my mother and her sisters. My father left Poland to avoid conscription into the czar's army. My parents used to tell me about the religious celebrations in Poland and the foods they prepared. They made the same foods at home and we kept the same celebrations, particularly at Christmas. I'm dedicated to my assignment because of the heritage my parents gave me and I want to give something back.

I'm in the city of Katowice, which is in an area that is a major producer of coal, iron, and steel. There's a haze of light gray pollution and coal dust is everywhere. During training we heard horror stories about the extremely bad air in Katowice. For instance, one shouldn't eat the vegetables because of the contaminated soil. I use a water filter and I boil all my drinking water. I also buy powdered milk instead of fresh. Many volunteers have voiced their concern privately that two of the older volunteers were assigned to Katowice where the "climate" isn't so good. [Lapinski is sixty-eight. The other volunteer assigned to Katowice is seventy-two. Because of a chronic cough caused by the pollution, this volunteer has been reassigned to Warsaw.] But personally, I feel that a Peace Corps volunteer should go wherever sent.*

I teach at a newly established teachers' training college. The college is fraught with problems. One class is held in a computer room and we have to sit and teach around them. Another problem is that the department of English is actually at Sosnowiec, a town a half mile away. That's where our library, copy machine, and typewriter are. The former Communist party headquarters in Katowice has been given to the university and they are currently renovating it. This will eventually allow the whole English department to move to Sosnowiec. The building there has two stories, a gym, toilets, and places to hang up coats, but other than benches in the hall for students to sit on between classes, there is no place to go. There are no pencil sharpeners, no water fountains or coolers. The Poles seem to believe drinking cool water is bad for your health. Since the teaching staff of nine are mixed—six Poles, one Britain, and two Americans—it's hard to establish a special American stamp to the English teaching. But we will do what we can with whatever we have.

The general expression of the people is glum, tired, and weary. The uncertainty of the future and how they are going to get out of this economic mess is most worrisome and shows up in their faces. There is no question about the fall in the standard of living. Prices are so high in comparison to wages and salaries that people are not able to buy very much so they do without. A new store opened up here, a Polish-Belgian partnership, called Supermarket. Prices are astronomical. It resembles an American supermarket and there are lots of customers. But most of them come just to look.

---

*According to Jean Zukowski/Faust, associate Peace Corps director in Poland, the Corps was not going to send any volunteers to Katowice unless they *wanted* to go. "The two volunteers who took assignments there desired a rich cultural environment," she says. "Katowice has theaters and a symphony orchestra. One of them has relatives there. Before she left training, she dismissed the heavy pollution. 'I'm from Detroit!' she told me."

## Jennifer Olsen (Poland, 1990–92)

I applied to the Peace Corps after I graduated from college. While waiting to find out if I was accepted, I went to live and work in England for a few months. During that time, I went to Germany with a friend and we drove to Berlin and then around East Germany and East Berlin. I would have thought previously that Eastern Europe was the same as Western Europe, which is much like America. But we noticed that all the buildings looked the same and there were no signs. In East Berlin we saw a lot of graffiti and sheets strung up saying, "Happy Revolution," "Don't Leave Our Country," and "Things Are Getting Better." That was exciting. When I heard that the Peace Corps was going to be sending volunteers to Eastern Europe, I was thrilled, and I wrote to them saying that I wanted to be considered for that program.

At the completion of training though, I had my doubts. The training was quite bad. It focused on "communicative teaching," which means using games and role plays to make students use the language in realistic situations. This approach is good but that's not all that there is to teaching. We spent a lot of time playing these communicative games when it would have been more appropriate to just describe the games and then talk about how to integrate them into other aspects of teaching.

One of the directors told me that they would not send anybody to Katowice, the most polluted city in Poland. But two of the oldest volunteers have been assigned there. A lot of people said, "This is how the Peace Corps is—everybody hates the training and hates the bureaucracy, but they love the country and the people. When they go off to their site, the Peace Corps disappears and they have a great time." I think that that is just not right. If I had begun thinking clearly earlier, I probably would not be in the Peace Corps right now. But I felt too involved in the country and the people I'd met and too committed to helping, to make going back to the U.S. an option.

I'm in Rzeszów, in the southeast part of Poland. The town is surrounded by farms. I teach English to high school students who are concentrating in math and physics. They are extremely interested in learning English. They all say English is the international language. Many people have asked for private lessons—students, teachers, and my landlady.

The television is dominated by American shows. *Dynasty* is the newest and the most popular. I've been asked, "Do you have a swimming pool and why not? Do you have a psychiatrist and doesn't everyone in the

U.S. have one? How many rooms are in your house? You eat lots of vegetables in the U.S., don't you?

I visited Auschwitz. I came at it from a sort of Jewish perspective and was a bit put off by the fact that all the focus was placed on the Poles that were killed and tortured. I suppose that's to be expected in Poland, and of course many races were targeted by Hitler. I argued about this with the two Poles who took me. I told them that in the U.S. we learned that it was primarily Jews who were killed. After talking a bit, we all shrugged our shoulders and said there was no answer really, but that there had been anti-Semitism in Poland before the war. Poles have little tolerance or understanding of different ethnic groups: "Black people are very dirty, aren't they? The Jews in the U.S. are probably very rich. . . ." Of course, some people I've spoken to are quite well-informed about minorities and race relations in the U.S. and I've had some great conversations about these problems.

All through training and here at my site, the best part of the experience has been the Poles. They are very warm and friendly, interesting, and interested people.

### Elizabeth Jones (Hungary, 1990–92)

I had always associated the Peace Corps with helping people with food and water. Now we're in a civilized country to teach English. I understand both needs and I'm thrilled to death to be a part of this, but sometimes I'm bothered by the amount of attention we're getting. I must have been interviewed ten times since I've been here and the photographers have been nonstop. Film crews have been lurking about as well. Meanwhile, there are so many volunteers in really tough situations all around the world.

I'm in southwest Hungary about an hour from both the Austrian and Yugoslavian borders. The area around the town is hilly and surrounded by forests and fields of sunflowers. It's absolutely spectacular. I have bicycled along the foothills of the Alps. My apartment is beautiful. I have a bedroom with a little dressing area, a large living room with colorful rugs and drapes, and a balcony. I'm so comfortable—right down to the sheets and towels. So here I sit watching British MTV and eating ice cream. Am I in the Peace Corps or on an all-expense-paid, two-year vacation? I can't help but think that all this money could go to someone a bit more desperate.

The school where I teach is a hundred years old and absolutely gorgeous! Tape recorders, overhead projectors, tapes, books, a TV, and VCR are all readily available. I'm only limited on my use of the copy machine. My classes vary from six to twenty-two students, ages fifteen to nineteen. The students are totally dedicated. I'm the one who is struggling to keep up with them. They have told me that they think English sounds more beautiful than any other language, even French.

My students are very eager to learn and I have absolutely no discipline problems. They stand when I enter the room and when I walk down the hall they all move aside so that I can walk first. It's as if I were parting the Red Sea. They see me coming and they say, *"Kezet csokolom,"* which means "I kiss your hands" and is the ultimate in Hungarian politeness. They're so formal though, it's almost a problem. I need for them to relax a bit so we can talk. I don't want to just drill and lecture. They love to hear about the stupid mistakes I make adjusting to their culture. After I tell one of my "disaster stories" and they finish laughing, they are much more comfortable and willing to explain what I did wrong. This starts the conversation rolling.

They are extremely interested in American music. They want to understand the lyrics to rock songs so I've written out more lyrics to songs than you can imagine. From New Kids on the Block to M. C. Hammer to Poison to the sound track from *Hair.* All the T-shirts are printed in English—"I'm the Boss," and sadly, "Where's the Acid Party?" The stores have some American products like Aquafresh, Juicy Fruit, and Levi's. But they certainly crave more.

Generally, most families seem much poorer here than at home. During training I lived with a family of four. All of them would sleep in one room so that I could have the only other room to myself. The rest of their flat was a tiny kitchen and bath. But they did have a nice TV, a VCR, and a telephone, which is rare in Hungary.

In the Peace Corps world my experience is unique because I am living in the lap of luxury. I love the work that I'm doing, but there is a smidgen of disappointment that I'm not having the typical Peace Corps experience. The pollution, though, is absolutely awful. You wouldn't believe the amounts of exhaust that belch forth from cars and buses. I can't stand to breathe when I'm in the center of town. I hope to incorporate some environmental issues and campaigns in my work which, hopefully, will make my stay a bit more Peace Corps-ish.

## Dorothy Weller (Poland, 1990–92)

After the Hungarian uprising in 1956, I was involved in helping to resettle some of those who immigrated to California. When I heard about the

Peace Corps going to Eastern Europe I thought, "Why not?" There are a lot of twenty-three-year-olds [Weller is seventy-two] and I'm impressed with the intelligence, idealism, and education level of the group.

I'm teaching in a town about ten or fifteen miles from the Baltic. It's surrounded on other sides by forests. I requested a small town, not too polluted, and not too difficult to get to Switzerland from. I am in a "residence hotel" for employees at the college and their families, and am the only American. I have a nice apartment, but it's a fourth-floor walk-up. This has caused me knee problems. It is also lonely and I have no access to a phone. I have tea with the other language teachers, but they don't speak my language, nor I theirs. Shopping for groceries can be a time-consuming pain, but the Poles think it is a great improvement over last year. If you want to buy three things you might have to go to six stores, and not adjacent either.

I am in a teacher training program for twenty-year-old college students. They're eager, responsive, funny, and charming. We have just moved into reconditioned quarters on the fifth floor of an office building. The rooms are freshly painted but too small, and furnished with new, but mostly unmovable furniture. This is traditional in Polish schools, but not flexible enough for modern teaching styles.

There's no library and few supplies, but we are getting a photocopy machine. The lack of books and teaching materials is a problem. I have the same students sixteen hours a week and I have only one book per student. Any other teaching materials I want to use I must create myself, so I've been working long hours at home. The students are great people and they deserve better. So do I.

Two trainees did not swear in because they were disenchanted with the Peace Corps' performance. The Peace Corps is a typical bureaucracy with typical bureaucrats. There's a belief among the volunteers that opening up a program here was a heavyweight job given to a lightweight crew bent on empire building for themselves, and little regard for the volunteers. There have been broken promises and misleading information.* They didn't know what to do with people older and more experienced than themselves and who also needed a more flexible learning style. However,

---

*"Volunteers tend to be a critical bunch, and with the complications of setting up a new program, our shortcomings come into focus," says associate director Zukowski/Faust. "Most of the staff has been with the Peace Corps for years, but the culture and language were new to all of us. We also had a hard time getting our office phones working, and we had no budget and no vehicles. I don't think the volunteers understand how difficult our job really is."

I enjoyed the younger volunteers, and found some of them very friendly, talented, and helpful.

## Nili Abrahamson (Poland, 1990)

I applied to the Peace Corps for the chance to go to Central Europe. I didn't join as an idealist, but I turned out to be the worst kind of idealist. I thought the program should be conducted professionally and efficiently but it wasn't.

The Peace Corps rushed too quickly to fill George Bush's promise. The program was slapped together and there was a shabbiness about it. I had the impression they rushed just to get warm bodies. Too many of the trainees had wanted to go to Africa or Latin America. Some were supposed to go to other places and were yanked out at the last minute to go to Poland. Twenty of the sixty who came to Poland had just graduated from college with no teaching experience and they had majored in subjects unrelated to English. Some of the older volunteers had no teaching experience either. Some people caught on, and some didn't.

The Peace Corps said we'd be great teachers when we were done with training, but many were *not* prepared. How could you claim you're sending all these "points of light" and "the brightest and best"? I thought maybe this was all in my mind, but a lot of Poles who hosted trainees were really turned off by what seemed to be this giant, glitzy, empty advertisement for how wonderful the United States is. One Polish woman who took one of the practicum classes we gave said that she could pick out grammar and spelling mistakes the trainees were making on the blackboard.*

Some Poles have told me that it doesn't matter if the volunteers aren't good teachers. "What we need is Americans to serve as examples of other ways of living," they say, because under communism there was only one way. If you did something different you were suspected of having ties to the West. So everyone became the same. "Forget the quality," they told me. "Just let us have contact with the West that we haven't had."

The Peace Corps didn't seem to be the organization that it said it was. They kept telling us how important we were, and how "the volunteers and staff are one," and "we're working together to build this new program."

---

* "It's common for new teachers to make a lot of errors their first few times at the blackboard," says Zukowski/Faust. "Some of the trainees got very nervous and just turned into jelly. But those problems cleared up by the end of training."

When I told the staff that I didn't know if I was going to stay, they didn't seem to care.

When the other trainees heard I wasn't swearing in, they came up to me and said, "Oh, Nili, I hear you're not one of us anymore." That comes from the mild brainwashing they did. There was a real stigma about "early termination"—"ET." It was like wearing scarlet letters. Some said they admired my decision. "You're the hero of the day," one woman said to me.

I decided to stay in Poland and I got a job teaching at the Institute for Applied Linguistics at the University of Warsaw. It's basically an institute for translators. I'm teaching conversation and writing, and I do some tutoring. I live in one of these horrible block buildings.

# Conclusion

☆════

Perhaps now more than at any other time since its founding, the Peace Corps has a chance to really make a difference. Interest in volunteerism is growing among America's public and its policy makers, and the collapse of communism has spurred world leaders to envision a new world order characterized by international cooperation. Though the turmoil in the Mideast and in the Soviet Union may have tempered initial optimistic projections, the Peace Corps' mission—its limitations and its possibilities—should nevertheless be reconsidered in the context of such historical changes.

When and if a new world order emerges, the Peace Corps could well become the United States' lead scout. Soviet President Mikhail Gorbachev has already put forth a notion that suggests such a new role for the Corps. Before the UN General Assembly in 1988, he announced, "We support the proposal to create under the auspices of the United Nations a voluntary international Peace Corps to assist in the revival of Afghanistan." [1]

In a new era of international cooperation, could Peace Corps volunteers and volunteers of other nations consolidate their efforts? "An internationalized structure," says Harris Wofford, one of the Peace Corps' founders, "would be a true venture in peace."

Internationalized volunteer service is probably the most idealistic outgrowth of the Peace Corps' founding, and the idea has been entertained several times over the past three decades. In his first report on the Peace Corps, written in early 1961, Sargent Shriver said, "We should hope that our citizens will find themselves working alongside citizens of the host country and also volunteers from other lands."[2] In 1962, the Corps played a leading role in the founding of the International Secretariat for Volunteer Service (ISVS). A consortium of forty-one countries, the ISVS advocated and assisted in the establishment of numerous national volunteer programs around the world. In 1963, the Peace Corps Act was amended to add Title III, which mandated the agency to encourage other countries to organize volunteer programs. And in 1969, President Nixon asked Peace Corps director Joseph Blatchford to explore the possibility of a joint volunteer program with Arab nations. Nixon also endorsed the proposal for a United Nations volunteer program, which was established in 1971.

Unfortunately, most of these initiatives have fizzled. The ISVS disbanded in 1976; Blatchford held only preliminary discussions with officials in Libya and Lebanon; and Title III has been all but forgotten. The UN's volunteer program, however, is still functioning. It sponsors 2,000 professional development workers in 110 countries.

It is doubtful that any alterations that dilute the agency's identity as an *American* program would be favorably received by policy makers. "Peace Corps volunteers have worked with volunteers from other countries informally on occasion," says regional director Jerry Leach, "when their projects naturally suggested a collaboration. But countries want their volunteer programs to have their own distinct identity." Adds Wofford, "In listing their reasons for supporting the Peace Corps, I'm sure Congress would put the PR contribution and the education of Americans first. An international structure would diminish those priorities." Indeed, current Peace Corps director Paul Coverdell takes considerable pride in the Corps' American identity. "The Peace Corps will be an important element of [the United States'] communications to the rest of the world," Coverdell said in a recent speech. "After all, no one can define America to other nations better than an American."[3]

But there is good reason to think that the Peace Corps *could* collaborate with volunteer programs of other countries and still maintain, and possibly enhance, its own identity. A recent report by the Overseas Development Council (ODC) suggests that in light of world events, it would behoove the Peace Corps to downplay the donor-recipient approach and pursue an active collaboration with volunteer programs of other nations. The formation of so-called "partnerships for peace" would symbolize the United States' commitment to international cooperation.[4]

The ODC report lists several examples of such collaboration already under way. The volunteer organizations of Norway and Finland, for instance, are working with a counterpart agency in Brazil to establish a joint health program for Mozambique; the World University Service of Canada has collaborated with the Sarvodaya Shramadana Movement in Sri Lanka and the Malaysian Red Crescent Society.

The ODC report also advises that the Peace Corps take note of the fact that the volunteer programs in some host countries, some of which are almost as old as the Peace Corps, have grown increasingly influential, and these organizations are insisting that they "figure more prominently in the thinking of donors. These groups contend that foreign donors too often fall into the trap of promoting 'neo-colonialism.' "[5]

Active relationships with other volunteer programs would further the Corps' development objectives by exposing its volunteers and staff to a wider range of methods and approaches. And cross-cultural exposure would be multiplied. The ODC report further notes that sponsorship arrangements with other volunteer organizations could facilitate the Peace Corps' entrance into countries that might otherwise be precluded by political considerations.

The Corps, they advise, should also be sensitive to the concerns of host country officials or "gatekeepers," who are likely to choose from any number of foreign assistance programs the ones that address not only the pressing needs of their people, but also their own needs for lawyers, accountants, and economists, for example.[6]

The Peace Corps' best first step may well be to call for a reconstituted ISVS in order to foster collaboration among national volunteer programs. This would reaffirm the Corps' stature as a leading advocate for peaceful change and demonstrate the United States' commitment to addressing world problems through cooperative, rather than competitive, actions.

The new ISVS, and the Peace Corps' support of it, could have more than symbolic relevance. With the fall of communism, the skills and energies of thousands of people could be redirected from security needs to neglected domestic works and overseas development projects. Programs established for this purpose (and financed by the World Bank, perhaps) would not only accomplish vital work, but also retrain participants in valuable skills. This idea is also applicable to those countries teeming with educated young people who are shut out of a limited job market.

This is by no means a new idea. During the Great Depression, President Roosevelt put thousands of jobless Americans to work constructing parks, building schools and hospitals, and running literacy drives. National service programs in Indonesia, Costa Rica, Thailand, Malaysia, and Kenya, have been organized specifically to harness the energies of young people and provide them with valuable training in construction, forestry, agriculture, and teaching.*

In an era of internationalism and global economics, it is incumbent upon Congress to fund the Peace Corps so that it may pursue more aggressively one of its often neglected founding goals—"to promote a better understanding of other peoples by [the American public]." In 1961, there was a consensus that Americans needed to know more about the conditions in the rest of the world in order to better understand their leaders' foreign policy. Today, America's provincialism is well documented,† and it may ultimately cripple the country's ability to participate in international trade. With experience in over one hundred countries, the Peace Corps and its 130,000 alumni comprise a vast, largely untapped repository of practical knowledge.

Director Coverdell has addressed this responsibility by inaugurating the World Wise program, in which volunteers exchange letters with elementary school classes. Over sixteen hundred classrooms in all fifty states are participating. But a more aggressive approach could serve the Corps' development objectives and make the volunteer experience accessible to a more representative cross-section of Americans.

Many Peace Corps observers have suggested that the agency establish "home bases" or affiliates in American communities and religious and educational institutions interested in broadening their international perspective.⁷ Such connections, which might include weekly discussion groups, guest speaker programs, and advisory exchanges, could be the catalyst for creative expansion of the Corps' activities. One Peace Corps alumni group, Returned Peace Corps Volunteers for Global Awareness, has established this kind of home-base relationship with 140 inner-city schools around the country. Founded in 1986, the privately funded group works with teachers on curriculum development and sponsors an annual essay contest. The winners and their teachers then travel overseas to spend a few weeks with Peace Corps volunteers at their assignments.

---

*For a thorough study of national volunteer organizations, see Irene Pinkau, *Service for Development: An Evaluation of Development Services and Their Cooperative Relationships (Volume I)*. (Dayton, Ohio: Charles F. Kettering Foundation, 1978)

†For example, many public schools do not require students to study geography or foreign languages. In a 1988 Gallup study of citizens between the ages of 18 and 24 in nine industrialized countries, Americans scored the poorest in a quiz identifying 16 geographic locations on a world map.

Along similar lines, the Peace Corps should consider reviving two previously abandoned programs. The first is a "reverse Peace Corps" in which volunteers from other countries work in the United States in Peace Corps-like assignments. In 1965, the State Department sponsored such a program, Volunteers to America, which brought 104 foreign nationals to work in the United States; the program was terminated in 1967. With the support of other institutions, the Peace Corps could reactivate it. From 1969 to 1976, the Peace Corps sent families overseas in an effort to provide host countries with volunteers who possessed greater technical capabilities, and to present a more accurate cross-section of the American people. Its high cost and myriad logistical complications contributed to its demise. But corporate sponsorship could give this program new life, while broadening the companies' international scope.

If the Peace Corps is going to undertake such an ambitious agenda, the agency must first improve its operations, which, after thirty years, continue to frustrate its good intentions. Poor programming and an overriding concern for size inhibit the organization from providing the most effective assistance possible. Some argue that by concentrating on technical assistance, the Corps would forfeit its goals of cross-cultural exchange. But it seems clear that the volunteers' ability to share useful skills and knowledge is the foundation upon which the cross-cultural goals can truly be reached.

Each Peace Corps director in turn has pledged to reform operations in order to maximize development and cross-cultural objectives. But the comments of today's volunteers, who arrive at their sites with no clearly defined job waiting and no one even expecting them, are depressingly reminiscent of their predecessors' recollections of being "parachuted in" with only a vaguely defined assignment. As former Deputy Director Warren Wiggins says, "A volunteer sitting around without a job is not going to do a very good job of furthering human understanding."

The Peace Corps is instituting a new, comprehensive methodology for planning volunteers' assignments and evaluating their progress. Called simply the Programming and Training System, the procedures, outlined in a 233-page manual, have been favorably received throughout the agency, and their implementation could result in vastly more effective operations. Unfortunately, the ratio of volunteers to staff—in some countries, forty-five to one—and insufficient staff training leaves little time available for cracking the book. For this reason, it is critical that the Corps balance the quality it hopes to offer with the number of volunteers it desires to maintain. Achieving this balance necessitates that the organization set a standard by which it can guide its efforts. The volunteers should embody that standard. As David Levine, head of programming during the Carter administration, says, "If we take the volunteer seriously, we can deliver seriously."

The outlook *is* positive. At the beginning of its fourth decade, the Peace Corps has, in fact, begun to apply some of these lessons. The African Food System Initiative, begun in 1986, strengthens the Corps' efforts in agriculture through a long-term team strategy. The associate-volunteer program, begun in 1987, collaborates with universities and professional associations to send experts to work with volunteers and nationals for periods ranging from a few weeks to one year. By definition, these programs emphasize the value of the individual volunteer, and the success of the programs depends on planning that is geared to small numbers. Further, the Peace Corps is beginning most of its new country programs with contingents of no more than thirty, and some are half that number. In order for meticulous planning to be effective in the field, however, applicants must be held to rigorous standards for technical proficiency and language aptitude.

The result may be a smaller Peace Corps, but its volunteers will be well placed, fully able to share valuable skills and to establish a level of intimacy where cultures can truly cross. They will be serving the needs of others and serving their country with distinction.

# Epilogue

# A Forecast

Exciting times have engaged the Peace Corps since the hardcover edition of this book was published in July 1991. Breathtaking expansion, increasing demands for highly skilled volunteers, and a quick succession of Peace Corps directors are challenging the organization as never before.

## The Former Soviet Union

After the final dissolution of the Soviet Union in 1991, requests for volunteers poured in from Estonia, Latvia, Lithuania, Russia, and Ukraine. The Peace Corps moved quickly, and by the end of 1992, 224 volunteers had been placed in these states, where they are working as English instructors and small business advisors.

These new programs have inspired considerable positive emotion in the Peace Corps community. "This is about replacing suspicion and hostility between two countries with peace and understanding," says Peace Corps staff member Chris Davis. "This mission really validates our name."

Excitement over the Corps' invitation from the states of the former Soviet Union can be attributed to the success of the programs in Poland and Hungary, which were much criticized when they were initiated in 1990. Many in the Peace Corps community felt strongly that volunteers did not belong in Europe, where conditions are not as dire as in other countries served by the organization. Poland now hosts one of the Corps' largest contingents, and the percentage of volunteers serving there who have asked to extend their two-year tour is now higher than in any other country.

"Former volunteers are realizing that the Peace Corps can't stay exactly as it was in the sixties," says Charles F. Dambach, executive director of the National Council of Returned Peace Corps Volunteers. "A lot of us went overseas twenty-five years ago singing, 'the times they are a changin',' but now, we've got to prevent ourselves from becoming calcified old farts."

Concerns have also been laid to rest that volunteers' accommodations in Eastern Europe and the states of the former Soviet Union would be too comfortable for the Peace Corps tradition of spartan living. "These places are no cakewalks," says Regional Director for Africa Jack Hogan. Conditions in the former Soviet Union will be especially difficult, says Jon Keeton, former director of international research and development. "The irony of serving in Russia is that you can attend a wonderful opera, look at magnificent architecture, but not find much food or medicine," he says. "It's likely that some volunteers will go through the winters with little or no heat." Keeton adds that volunteers in Russia, unlike their colleagues in Eastern Europe, may also encounter some resentment. "In the former Soviet Union, the Peace Corps presence is an indication of their nation's defeat in the Cold War. Volunteers will get through their two years if they genuinely feel that they're part of history and that they're getting to witness the most important event of this century."

Despite unique difficulties presented by the states of the former Soviet Union, the Peace Corps is planning rapid expansion there. By the end of 1993, a total of 630 volunteers will be at work in Estonia, Latvia, Lithuania, Russia, Ukraine, Armenia, and Uzbekistan. Another 250 volunteers will be sent to five of the Central Asian republics (Kirghizia, Moldova, Turkmenistan, Byelorussia, and Kazakhstan).

## China

Volunteers are finally heading to China, four years after the Chinese government canceled the original contingent ("China One") in reaction to U.S. sanctions against China following the Tienanmen Square massacre. China's renewed interest in the Peace Corps can be attributed to "some changes in leadership and further economic reform," says Acting Director Barbara Zartman. "The Bush administration would tell you the program came about through subtle diplomatic measures, but the simple fact is that the Chinese are so eager for English teachers and this is one way to get them."

The eighteen volunteers of "China Two" will teach English at the same universities in Sichuan province that had been designated for China One. Like the earlier program, China Two volunteers will live in housing reserved for foreign faculty, rather than among their Chinese peers, as is Peace Corps custom. Peace Corps staff will also once again be referred to by the Chinese government as "volunteer leaders." The Chinese government has, however, relaxed its position on how the Peace Corps identifies itself. The Peace Corps is now free to use its name, rather than the previously stipulated "US–China Friendship Volunteers."

## The Right Volunteers

The Peace Corps' greatest challenge at present is finding qualified volunteers. The tight job market and the publicity generated by the Corps' entrance into the former Soviet Union have created a surge in applications. But host countries' increasing demands for highly skilled volunteers are forcing the Peace Corps to turn away applicants who would have been suitable just a few years ago. "We're discouraging the B.A. generalist," says Tom White of the Peace Corps' Recruiting Department.

Host countries, particularly those in Eastern Europe, are requesting English instructors who have masters' degrees. The former Soviet republics are asking for people with M.B.A.'s and substantial business experience. "We're reevaluating how we use the word *volunteer*," says Tom White. "Applicants are aghast that we can't send them overseas. 'Since when do *volunteers* have to *qualify*?' "

## The Clinton Administration

The Peace Corps community anticipates that President Clinton will embrace the Peace Corps as an enduring and popular model for national service. They hope he will demonstrate his professed commitment to service by appointing a former volunteer as director. "It's about time that the job go to someone who really appreciates the Peace Corps' mission and understands life in the developing world," says Charles F. Dambach.

A former volunteer at the helm would be especially invigorating after the unsteady leadership during the Bush administration. In July 1991, after serving just over two years as director, Paul Coverdell, a former chairman of the Southern Steering Committee for George Bush's 1988 campaign, announced his intentions to leave the Peace Corps and return to Georgia to run for the United States Senate. Peace Corps staff members weren't surprised: In January 1991, the *Washington Post* reported that in the 17 months since his appointment, 26 of his 45 domestic trips on agency business were to Georgia. In November 1992, Coverdell unseated democratic Senator Wyche Fowler, Jr., in a runoff. (One of Coverdell's least popular initiatives, changing the organization's name to United States Peace Corps, is being gradually phased out. Stationery and press releases now read Peace Corps of the United States, but the last four words are in faint, minute type.)

To succeed Coverdell, the White House appointed Elaine L. Chao, who was then deputy secretary of transportation and former chairperson of Asian-Americans for Bush/Quayle in the 1988 presidential campaign. In August 1991, ten months after her Senate confirmation, Chao resigned as Peace Corps director to head up the United Way of America.

If a former volunteer is not named Peace Corps director, it is doubtful that the organization will suffer much for it. In its thirty-two year history the Peace Corps has weathered far more serious reversals. The essential spirit manages to prevail despite politics and bureaucratic fumbling. "We've said for years," laughs Jon Keeton, "that the volunteers do pretty well in spite of us."

# Notes

## Introduction

1. Ira Mothner, "JFK's Legacy: The Peace Corps," *Look* (June 14, 1966), p. 34.

2. For a detailed account of these proposals, see Gerard T. Rice, *The Bold Experiment: JFK's Peace Corps* (South Bend, Ind.: University of Notre Dame Press, 1987).

3. Henry S. Reuss, "A Point Four Youth Corps," *Commonweal* (May 6, 1960), p. 146.

4. Ibid. p. 148.

5. John F. Kennedy, "Staffing a Foreign Policy for Peace," speech given in San Francisco, November 2, 1960. *Freedom of Communications; The Speeches, Remarks, Press Conferences, and Statements of Senator John F. Kennedy.* August 1 through November 7, 1960. Part One. pp. 1238, 1240.

6. Ibid. p. 1240.

7. John F. Kennedy, "Inaugural Address," January 20, 1961. Public Papers of the President, Vol. 1.

8. Sargent Shriver, Report to the President on the Peace Corps, February 28, 1961. Peace Corps Library, Washington, D.C.

9. From a speech by Sargent Shriver delivered at the International Conference on Middle-Level Manpower, October 1962. Quoted in Sargent Shriver, *The Point of the Lance* (New York: Harper & Row, 1964), p. 55.

10. Public Law 87-293, Title 1, "Declaration of Purpose," September 22, 1961.

11. Ibid. Section 4(c) (2)–(3).

12. Quoted in *Washington Post*, April 27, 1990.

13. Quoted in Congressional Record, Senate, April 5, 1990.

14. From a paper by the Committee of Returned Volunteers, presented at the Fifteenth Conference of Organizers of International Voluntary Service, Geneva, Switzerland, December 1968.

15. Memorandum, Sargent Shriver to John F. Kennedy, June 20, 1961. National Security Files, John F. Kennedy Memorial Library, Boston. (Hereafter referred to as JFK Library.)

16. Letter, Sargent Shriver to John F. Kennedy, Presidential Office Files, Box 85, JFK Library.

17. *Atlanta Journal Constitution*, February 2, 1987.

18. Quoted in Steven Donziger, "Peace Corps Follies," *The Progressive* (March 1987), p. 28.

19. Sargent Shriver, "The Challenge to the Peace Corps," speech given at twenty-fifth anniversary conference, Washington, D.C., September 20, 1986.

## Part One: The Kennedy Years, 1961–63

### Chapter 1: Modern Miracles

1. Quoted in Coates Redmon, *Come As You Are: The Peace Corps Story* (San Diego: Harcourt Brace Jovanovich, 1986), p. 4.

2. Quoted in Alan Guskin, "Passing the Torch," in Milton Viorst, ed., *Making a Difference: The Peace Corps at Twenty-five* (New York: Weidenfeld & Nicolson, 1986), p. 14.

3. "It's a Puzzlement," *Wall Street Journal* (March 6, 1961), p. 10.

4. Text of White House press release appears in Harris Wofford, *Of Kennedys and Kings: Making Sense of the Sixties* (New York: Farrar, Straus & Giroux, 1980), p. 251.

5. Sargent Shriver, Report to the President on the Peace Corps, February 28, 1961; quoted in *Peace Corps Fact Book* (Washington, D.C.: Peace Corps, 1961) p. 21.

6. Warren Wiggins and William Josephson, "A Towering Task: The National Peace Corps." Unpublished, Peace Corps Library, Washington, D.C., pp. 10–11.

7. Oral History Interview: Mike Mansfield. John F. Kennedy Memorial Library, Boston, p. 5.

8. Quoted in *New York Times*, March 3, 1961.

9. Quoted in *New York Times*, March 24, 1961.

10. Quoted in Gerard T. Rice, *The Bold Experiment: JFK's Peace Corps* (South Bend, Ind.: University of Notre Dame Press, 1987), p. 240.

11. *Washington Post*, August 29, 1961.

12. Peace Corps Evaluation Report on the Philippines, 1963. Peace Corps Library, Washington, D.C.

13. Quoted in "Peace Corps Boot Camps," *Time* (August 11, 1961), p. 30.

14. Public Law 87-293, Title 1, Section 8(c).

15. *Peace Corps Handbook* (Washington, D.C.: Peace Corps, 1964), p. 12.

16. John F. Kennedy, Special Message on the Peace Corps (Office of the White House Press Secretary, March 1, 1961). Peace Corps Library, Washington, D.C., p. 4.

17. Quoted in John Griffin and Paul Jacobs, "Overseas Evaluation: Philippines, November 18 to December 10, 1963," National Archives, Washington, D.C. pp. 4, 8.

18. Peace Corps Evaluation Report, Peru, 1967. Peace Corps Library, Washington, D.C.

19. Volunteer quoted in Brent K. Ashabranner, *A Moment in History: The First Ten Years of the Peace Corps* (Garden City, N.Y.: Doubleday, 1971), p. 156.

20. "On the Job with the Peace Corps in Africa and South America," *U.S. News and World Report* (December 4, 1961). p. 68.

## Part Two: The Johnson Years, 1963–69

1. Kirby Jones, Letters, *The Nation* (March 18, 1968).

2. Quoted in Andrew Kopkind, "Peace Corps' Daring New Look" *The New Republic* (February 5, 1966), p. 15.

3. Quoted in *Washington Post*, October 22, 1965.

4. Brent K. Ashabranner, *A Moment in History: The First Ten Years of the Peace Corps* (Garden City, N.Y.: Doubleday, 1971), p. 229.

5. Jack Vaughn, "The Cause of the Rebels," speech printed in *Volunteer* magazine (Washington, D.C., Peace Corps Library), November, 1968, p. 12.

6. Memo, D. W. Ropa to McGeorge Bundy, January 3, 1966. NSF-Agency File, Box 42, Lyndon Baines Johnson Library, Austin, Texas (hereafter referred to as LBJ Library).

7. Letter, Chester Bowles to Bill Moyers, October 1, 1965. File: PC-2, White House Central Files, Box 75, LBJ Library.

8. Quoted in Harris Wofford, *Of Kennedy and Kings: Making Sense of the Sixties* (New York: Farrar, Straus & Giroux, 1980), p. 329.

9. *Washington Post*, April 2, 1966.

10. Ashabranner, *A Moment in History*, p. 222.

11. Ibid. p. 224.

12. Ibid.

## Chapter 2: Realism Versus Idealism: Views from the Field

1. "Jack Vaughn Reflects on his Peace Corps Experience," *Volunteer*, May 1969 (Washington, D.C., Peace Corps Library), p. 5.

2. Frank Mankiewicz, *The Peace Corps: A Revolutionary Force* (Washington, D.C.: Peace Corps, n.d.), p. 4.

## Chapter 3: Micronesia: The Peace Corps Goes to Paradise

1. Donald F. McHenry, *Micronesia: A Trust Betrayed* (New York: Carnegie Endowment for International Peace, 1975), p. 14.

2. Memo, Ross Pritchard to Jack Vaughn, November 9, 1966. FG 105–106, White House Central Files, LBJ Library.

3. Memo, Jack Vaughn to Robert E. Kintner, April 12, 1967. FG 105–106, White House Central Files, LBJ Library.

4. *Washington Post*, March 7, 1968.

5. "They Want to Go Back to Bikini," *Time*, June 7, 1968, p. 30.

6. Letter, Theodore Kupferman to John Pincetich, March 7, 1968. Private papers of John Pincetich.

7. Letter, Office of the Secretary [signature illegible], U.S. Department of the Interior, to Senator Quentin N. Burdick, March 12, 1968. Private papers of John Pincetich.

8. Letter, John Pincetich to Todd Jenkins, March 18, 1968. Private papers of Todd and Hope Jenkins.

9. Letter, Dirk Ballendorf to Todd and Hope Jenkins, March 27, 1968. Private papers of Todd and Hope Jenkins.

10. Quoted in *New York Times*, April 10, 1988.

### Chapter 4: The Dominican Republic, 1965: The Peace Corps Versus the War Corps

1. "Dominican Republic: The Work Goes On," *Volunteer*, May 1966 (Washington, D.C., Peace Corps Library), p. 4.

2. Quoted in *Washington Post*, May 6, 1965.

3. *Washington Post*, May 15, 1965.

4. Ibid.

5. Tad Szulc, *Dominican Diary* (New York: Delacorte Press, 1965), p. 152.

6. Oral History Interview: Frank Mankiewicz. JFK Library, p. 44.

### Chapter 5: Exporting the American Revolution: The Peace Corps and the Nigerian-Biafran War

1. "And Away They Go," *Time* (September 8, 1961), p. 22.

2. Letter, Harris Wofford to Sargent Shriver, December 24, 1963. LBJ Library.

3. Quoted in *Washington Post*, September 8, 1961.

### Part Three: The Vietnam Era

1. "Peace Corps?" *QCUP: Underground Press at Queens College*, December 7, 1966 (Washington, D.C., Peace Corps Library), pp. 1, 3.

2. Speech delivered at College Theology Society convention in San Francisco, April 14, 1968. Quoted in *New York Times*, April 15, 1968.

3. Memo, Joseph Blatchford to House Foreign Affairs Committee, April 14, 1970. Quoted in Brent K. Ashabranner, *A Moment in History: The First Ten Years of the Peace Corps* (Garden City, N.Y.: Doubleday, 1971), pp. 295–99.

4. "Who Wants the Peace Corps?" *Newsweek* (June 29, 1970), p. 42.

### Chapter 6: Volunteer Protest: "Peace Is a Silent Passion"

1. Letter, Jack Vaughn to volunteers in Chile, June 7, 1967. FG 105-106, White House Central Files, Box 147, LBJ Library.

2. Quoted in *Seattle Times*, November 18, 1969.

3. Quoted in *New York Times*, June 4, 1970.

4. Beth Whithouse, "Marching to Different Drummers: The Vietnam War and the Peace Corps," *World View*, Summer 1989 (Washington, D.C., National Council of Returned Peace Corps Volunteers), p. 8.

5. Jack Vaughn, "Now We Are Seven," *Saturday Review* (January 6, 1968), p. 91.

6. Letter, Jack Vaughn to volunteers in Chile, op. cit.

7. *New York Times*, July 9, 1967.

8. Transcript of House Foreign Affairs Committee hearing on the Peace Corps budget, September 1969.

9. *Washington Post*, September 25, 1969.

10. Transcript of House Foreign Affairs Committee Hearing, op. cit.

11. Brent K. Ashabranner, *A Moment in History: The First Ten Years of the Peace Corps* (Garden City, N.Y.: Doubleday, 1971), p. 280.

12. Francis Pollack, "Peace Corps Returnees: The New World They See," *The Nation* (July 3, 1967), p. 15.

13. Letters to the Editor, *Washington Post*, July 17, 1967.

14. Memo, Thomas S. Page, Peace Corps Office of Public Information, to Robert McCloskey, State Department, June 29, 1967. FG 105–106, White House Central Files, Box 147, LBJ Library.

15. Letter, Jack Vaughn to volunteers in Chile, op. cit.

16. Quoted in *Providence Journal*, September 17, 1969.

17. Quoted in *New York Times*, December 25, 1969.

## Chapter 7: A Haven for Draft Dodgers

1. Quoted in A. Chambers, "Ex-Marine Bill Broyles Befriends his Enemy in Vietnam," *People* (September 1, 1986), p. 69.

2. "Draft Changes: Troubles Ahead for Peace Corps, VISTA?" *U.S. News and World Report* (July 27, 1970), p. 69.

3. Quoted in *Washington Post*, November 20, 1967.

4. "The Peace Corps and the Draft," press release by Peace Corps Public Information, November 14, 1966. Peace Corps Library.

5. *Washington Post*, February 2, 1973.

## Chapter 8: The Committee of Returned Volunteers: "Confessions of an Imperialist Lackey"

1. Tom Newman, "Confessions of an Imperialist Lackey," in *Volunteer?* unpublished anthology, Committee of Returned Volunteers (CRV), Private papers of Alice Hageman.

2. CRV, Statement of Purpose, December 1966. Private Papers of Alice Hageman.

3. Quoted in *Ramparts*, (August 1967), p. 60.

4. Harris Wofford, *Of Kennedys and Kings: Making Sense of the Sixties* (New York: Farrar, Straus & Giroux, 1980), p. 437.

5. CRV Newsletter, February 1969. Private Papers of Elaine Fuller.

6. CRV, Position Paper on the Peace Corps, September 15, 1969, Published in CRV Newsletter, October 1969. Private Papers of Elaine Fuller.

7. Ibid.

8. Tom Newman, "Confessions of an Imperialist Lackey," op. cit.

9. Handwritten notes of H. R. Haldeman, May 9, 1970. White House Special Files, Box 41, Nixon Presidential Materials, National Archives, Alexandria, Va. (hereafter referred to as Nixon Materials).

10. Quoted in *Washington Post*, May 10, 1970.

11. CRV Newsletter, December 1969. Private papers of Elaine Fuller.

## Part Four: The Nixon-Ford Years, 1969-77

1. "Will the Peace Corps Open Its Doors to All Qualified and Dedicated Americans?" memo, David S. Burgess to Sargent Shriver, June 28, 1965. Peace Corps Library.

2. Ibid. p. 10.

3. Memo, Alexander Butterfield to Henry Kissinger, June 2, 1969. Nixon Materials.

4. *New York Times*, July 6, 1969.

5. Caroline Ramsey, "The Peace Corps Revisited," unpublished monograph, p. 112. Private Papers of Caroline Ramsey.

6. Memo, Patrick J. Buchanan to the President, February 20, 1970. White House Special Files, Box 33, Nixon Materials.

7. Ibid.

8. Memo, Patrick J. Buchanan to the President, March 7, 1970. Presidential Handwriting: March 1 to March 15, 1970, White House Special Files, Box 5, Nixon Materials.

9. Ibid.

10. Ibid.

11. David C. Anderson, "After Peace Corps, Some Turn Radical," *Wall Street Journal*, March 18, 1970.

12. Memo, John R. Brown, III, to John Ehrlichman and Henry Kissinger, Nixon Materials. Published in Bruce Oudes, *From the President: Richard Nixon's Secret Files* (New York: Harper & Row, 1989), p. 109.

13. Quoted in *Washington Post*, March 25, 1971.

14. *Washington Post*, May 15, 1971.

15. Quoted in *New York Times*, January 10, 1974.

16. Quoted in *Washington Post*, August 22, 1975.

17. Letter, Michael Balzano to Congressman Michael J. Harrington, Chairman, House Subcommittee on International Development, March 6, 1978.

## Chapter 9: The Peace Corps Meets the Brady Bunch: Skilled Volunteers and Families

1. Johnette B. Clark and Stanley Lichtenstein, "A Study of Married Peace Corps Volunteers with Families: Final Report," November 15, 1971 (Washington, D.C., American Institute for Research). Peace Corps Library, p. 3.

2. Gail Garland, "Peace Corps Volunteer Family Policy," October 1981 (Washington, D.C., Peace Corps Library), pp. 1-2.

## Part Five: The Carter Years, 1977-81

### Chapter 10: "The Hardest, Dirtiest Work There Is"

1. Quoted in Joseph Nocera, "Sam Brown and the Peace Corps: All Talk, No ACTION," *Washington Monthly* (September 1978), p. 8.

2. Quoted in *Wall Street Journal*, December 12, 1977.

3. Sam Brown, "The Peace Corps; A Beloved Institution at a Critical Crossroads," speech, p. 8. Private papers of Sam Brown.

4. Gerard T. Rice, *Twenty Years of the Peace Corps* (Washington, D.C.: Peace Corps, 1981), p. 42.

5. Sam Brown, "Peace Corps Overview," speech delivered at Peace Corps Latin American Regional Conference, Berkeley Springs, W.Va., December 1978, p. 5. Private papers of Sam Brown.

6. Brown, "The Peace Corps," op. cit. p. 14.

7. Dr. Roger Landrum, "The Peace Corps in Africa: The First 25 Years." Survey prepared for the University of Michigan International Symposium: America's Role in African Development: Past, Present, and Future, 1979. Private papers of Roger Landrum.

8. Sam Brown, speech delivered at the Secretary's Open Forum, State Department, August 30, 1977, p. 5. Private papers of Sam Brown.

9. Quoted in *Wall Street Journal*, January 16, 1979.

10. Committee on International Relations, U.S. House of Representatives, "The Peace Corps in West Africa, 1976" (Washington, D.C.: U.S. Government Printing Office, February 23, 1976). pp. 1–5.

11. General Accounting Office, "Changes Needed for a Better Peace Corps" (Washington, D.C.: General Accounting Office, February 6, 1978), p. 1.

12. Transcript of Senate Foreign Assistance Subcommittee Hearings, July 1975.

13. Brown, Secretary's Open Forum, op. cit. p. 11.

14. "Why Critics Lambast Sam Brown's Agency," *U.S. News and World Report* (January 15, 1979), p. 37.

15. Brown, "The Peace Corps," op. cit. p. 19.

16. Quoted in *Washington Post*, April 24, 1977.

17. *Washington Post*, May 17, 1979.

18. S. Dillon Ripley, "The View from the Castle," *Smithsonian* (December 1978), p. 8.

19. Quoted in Jeff Drumtra, "How Sports Builds Nations," *World View*, Fall 1988 (Washington, D.C., National Council of Returned Peace Corps Volunteers), p. 22.

## Part Six: The Reagan Years, 1981–89

1. "Peace Corps Opportunity—A New Beginning," memo from Richard F. Celeste to Ronald Reagan, January 19, 1981. Private papers of Richard F. Celeste.

2. David A. Stockman, *The Triumph of Politics: How the Reagan Revolution Failed* (New York: Harper & Row, 1986) p. 116.

3. Testimony before the President's National Bipartisan Commission on Central America, September 1983 (Washington, D.C., U.S. Government Printing Office), appendix, p. 777.

4. Quoted in Rich Goul, "Peace Corps Head Tells of Option for the Poor," *Tidings*, March 20, 1987.

5. Peace Corps Advisory Council Report to the President, December 1982, pp. 2, 5, 7; App. C, pp. 5–6. Peace Corps Library.

6. *Washington Times*, February 27, 1984.

7. Quoted in Daniel Barry, "Brainwashing the Peace Corps," *The Nation* (May 7, 1983), p. 572.

8. Mark Huber, "The Peace Corps: Out of Step with Reagan," position paper (Washington, D.C.: Heritage Foundation, December 5, 1984), p. 1.

9. "Leadership for Peace: A Challenge from the Peace Corps" (Washington, D.C.: Peace Corps, 1988), p. 2.

10. "Peace Corps Conference: Anti-Reagan Forum," *Human Events*, (July 11, 1981), p. 4.

11. Bill Moyers, "Words of Welcome," speech, Memorial Service, Arlington Cemetery Memorial Amphitheater (Arlington, Va.), September 21, 1986.

12. Theodore Hesburgh, "Dedication to the Future," speech, Memorial Service, op. cit.

13. Paul Wood, quoted in *Twenty-fifth Anniversary Conference and Annual Report of the National Council of Returned Peace Corps Volunteers* (Washington, D.C.: National Council of Returned Peace Corps Volunteers, 1987), p. 10.

14. Loret Miller Ruppe, "Continuing to Meet the Challenge," speech, *Twenty-fifth Anniversary Conference.* Washington, D.C., September 19, 1986.

15. Thomas J. McGrew, testimony at hearings before the House Appropriations Subcommittee on Foreign Operations and Related Agencies, 1983.

### Chapter 11: The Caribbean Basin Initiative: "What Does a Sociologist Know About Business?"

1. Loret Miller Ruppe, "Letters to the Editor," *Wall Street Journal*, February 2, 1985.

2. Gerard T. Rice, *Peace Corps in the 80's* (Washington, D.C.: Peace Corps Office of Public Affairs, December 15, 1985), p. 13.

### Chapter 13: Honduras: The Peace Corps as Smile Button

1. Lisa Swenarski, "The Peace Corps in Honduras," *Honduras Update*, November–December 1987 (Somerville, Mass., Honduras Information Center), p. 3.

2. Bruce Nussbaum, "Did Christ Wear a Crew Cut?" in *Volunteer?* unpublished anthology, CRV. Private papers of Alice Hageman.

3. Testimony before the President's National Bipartisan Commission on Central America, September 1983 (Washington, D.C., U.S. Government Printing Office), appendix, pp. 774–75.

4. "Recommendations of the National Bipartisan Commission on Central America" (Washington, D.C., U.S. Government Printing Office: 1984) p. 68.

5. Quoted in *New York Times*, September 24, 1984.

6. Desiree Loeb, "The Increasing Visibility of the International Presence in Honduras," *Returned Peace Corps Volunteers Committee on Central America Newsletter*, September 9, 1986.

7. Testimony before the President's National Bipartisan Commission on Central America, op. cit., pp. 782–83.

### Chapter 14: The African Food System Initiative: "They Used to Do a Thousand Hectares of Rice Here."

1. "Review of the African Food System Initiative: Peace Corps-Mali," Peace Corps internal report, February–March 1988, p. 1.

## Part Seven: The Bush Years, 1989–92

1. General Accounting Office, *The Peace Corps: Meeting the Challenges of the 1990s* (Washington, D.C.: General Accounting Office, May 1990), pp. 3–4, 32.

2. Committee on Government Operations, *The Peace Corps: Entering its Fourth Decade of Service* (Washington, D.C.: U.S. Government Printing Office, 1990), pp. 12, 18.

3. Memo, Jerry W. Leach to Paul Coverdell, May 29, 1990. Office files of Paul Coverdell, Peace Corps, Washington, D.C.

## Chapter 15: China: "Road to Nowhere"

1. Associated Press, May 30, 1989.

2. TVT Associates, "Week Three Report: June 16, 1989," Final Report: Pre-service Training for China Peace Corps Volunteers (Washington, D.C.: TVT Associates, September 1989).

3. TVT Associates, "Week Five Report: July 1, 1989," op. cit.

4. Quoted in *Washington Times*, June 1, 1989.

5. Quoted in letter from Jon Keeton to Ge Shouqin, Secretary General-Chinese Education Association for International Exchange, July 6, 1989. Office files of Jon Keeton, Peace Corps, Washington, D.C.

## Chapter 16: Eastern Europe: 121 Points of Light"

1. Quoted in Michael Ryan, "Should the Peace Corps Survive?" *Parade* (April 4, 1990), p. 4.

2. *Washington Post*, May 29, 1990.

3. Quoted in Charlotte Crystal, "Hungary for a Change," *World View*, Fall 1989 (Washington, D.C., National Council of Returned Peace Corps Volunteers), pp. 17–18.

4. Helena M. Tavares, "A Legislative History of the Peace Corps, 1961–1982," unpublished report. Peace Corps Library.

5. Quoted in "Giving and Getting: Sargent Shriver on the Peace Corps," *GAO Journal* (Winter/Spring 1990), p. 27.

6. "United States Peace Corps in the Republic of Poland: First Program Assessment Report," Peace Corps internal report, 1990, p. 1.

7. Ibid. p. 3.

## Conclusion

1. Quoted in *New York Times*, December 4, 1988.

2. Summary of Report to the President on the Peace Corps, from Sargent Shriver, February 28, 1961, quoted in *Peace Corps Fact Book* (Washington, D.C.: Peace Corps, 1961), p. 22.

3. Paul Coverdell, "Beyond 1989: The Dawn of a Global Renaissance?" speech delivered at meeting of Balboa Life and Casualty, Los Angeles, January 23, 1990.

4. Robert J. Berg and Phillip A. Hesser, "Partnership for Peace," unpublished report (Washington, D.C.: Overseas Development Council, 1989), p. 1.

5. Ibid, p. III-3.

6. Ibid, p. I-3.

7. "A Vision for the Peace Corps: A Summary of Findings and Recommendations of the National Seminar on Future Directions for the Peace Corps," July 8–12, 1986, Fort Collins, Colorado (Washington, D.C.: Peace Corps, 1986), p. 15.

# Index

volunteerism in, 287
United States Information Agency, 176
University of California at Berkeley, 31, 49, 50, 97
UPI, 105
Upper Volta, 51
U.S.-China Friendship volunteers, 265, 266
*U.S. News and World Report,* 36
Uzbekistan, 294

vaccinations, 220–221
van der Vlught, Theresa H., 219, 220
Vaughn, Jack:
  antiwar protests opposed by, 101, 103, 104, 105–106, 107
  draft deferments supported by, 114, 115
  Murray's expulsion and, 105–106, 107
  Peace Corps as viewed by, 50, 55, 97–98, 157
  as Peace Corps director, 50–54, 65, 104, 127
  Vietnam War as viewed by, 97–98
Vaughan, Lexie, 234
venereal disease, 218, 220, 223
Venezuela, 102
Versel, Malcolm, 184–185, 246, 247
Vespa, Hazel, 75, 76, 79, 83–84
Vietnam War:
  draft deferments during, 24, 97, 98, 99, 109–111, 112–123
  moratoriums against, 160
  Peace Corps during, 16, 24, 49, 52, 66, 97–137, 159, 160, 231
  student demonstrations against, 49–50, 97, 179
  volunteers' opposition to, 97, 98, 99, 101–111
VISTA (Volunteers in Service to America), 49, 120, 161, 186
*Volunteer,* 73
*Volunteer?,* 133
volunteers, Peace Corps:
  acclimatization by, 24
  anti-Americanism and, 60, 232–233
  application procedure for, 31
  assignment of, 22, 24, 33–36, 50–51, 113, 114, 119, 159, 204, 234, 247, 258, 259
  associate-, 292
  attrition rate for, 16, 159, 182, 258, 286

  children of, 165, 166, 170, 171, 174, 175, 176
  college graduates of, 16, 22, 32, 34, 49–50, 98, 158, 163, 183
  couples as, 44–45, 66–71, 168–176, 237–239
  dedication of, 15
  disillusionment of, 56
  draft deferments for, 24, 97, 98, 99, 109–111, 112–123
  dress habits of, 159
  early termination (ET) by, 16, 159, 185, 258, 286
  embassy personnel and, 19
  with families, 22, 165–176
  First Amendment rights of, 43, 69–72, 102, 105–111, 231, 241–242
  "grass roots" work by, 19
  health of, 113–114, 116, 218
  historical sense of, 39, 43
  homologs for, 249–250
  idealism of, 16, 24, 32, 37, 42, 90, 112, 133, 158, 161, 203, 229*n*, 285
  induction notices for, 110, 114, 115–116, 120, 121
  language instruction for, 24, 31–32, 51, 157, 190, 191, 237–238, 292
  lifestyle of, 16, 19, 35–36, 39–46, 71, 116, 117–118
  limited experiences of, 125
  loyalty oaths taken by, 32–33
  marijuana used by, 157
  married, 44–45, 66–71, 168–176, 237–239
  monitoring of, 245, 247–248
  motorbikes owned by, 188, 189
  number of, 30, 34–35, 51, 53, 97, 179–180, 198, 204–205, 259–260
  officials vs., 103–104
  older, 32, 168, 170, 284, 285
  "parachuted," 51, 291
  petitions signed by, 101, 102, 104, 109, 111
  political awareness of, 24, 32, 43, 46, 49–50, 55, 60, 65–66, 71–72, 74, 75, 78, 81–84, 98, 101–104, 105–109, 120, 124–127, 157–158, 160, 201, 209, 210, 214, 219, 236, 237–241, 263–265, 268–271, 274, 276, 285